Join the Recommended Country Inns® Travelers' Club and Save!

The Recommended Country Inns® guides are the preeminent guidebooks to the finest country inns in the United States. Authors personally visit and recommend each establishment described in the guides, and **no fees are solicited or accepted for recommendation in the books.**

Now the Recommended Country Inns® guides offer a special new way for travelers to enjoy extra savings: through the Recommended Country Inns® Travelers' Club. Member benefits include savings such as:

- Discounts on accommodations
- Discounts on food
- Discounts on local attractions

How to Save: Read the profile for each inn to see if it offers an incentive to members. For participating establishments, look for information at the end of the inn's profile or in the index at the end of the book. Simply mention that you are a member of the Recommended Country Inns® Travelers' Club when making reservations, and show your membership card when you check in. All offers are subject to availability.

How to Join: If you wish to become a member of the Recommended Country Inns® Travelers' Club, simply fill out the attached form and send it by mail to:

Recommended Country Inns® Travelers' Club
c/o The Globe Pequot Press
PO Box 833
Old Saybrook, CT 06475
Or fax to: 860–395–2855

A membership card will be mailed to you upon receipt of the form. Please allow four to six weeks for delivery.

Sign up today and start saving as a Recommended Country Inns® Travelers' Club member!

(All offers from participating inns expire May 31, 2001, unless otherwise mentioned.)

Recommended Country Inns®
Travelers' Club Membership Form

Name: _____

Address: _____

City _____ , State _____ Zip _____

Phone _____ Fax _____ E-mail _____

Age: 18–35 _____;   36–50 _____;   over 50 _____

Sex: Male _____   Female _____

Marital Status: Single _____   Married _____

Annual Household Income:

    under $35,000 _____; $35,000–$75,0000 _____;   over $75,000 _____

Credit cards:

    Mastercard _____;   Visa _____;   Amex _____;

    Discover _____;   Other _____

Book purchased at: Store Name: _____ ;

City _____ , State _____

Mail completed form to:

Recommended Country Inns® Travelers' Club
c/o The Globe Pequot Press
PO Box 833
Old Saybrook, CT 06475
Or fax to: 860–395–2855

RO

RECOMMENDED COUNTRY INNS® SERIES

Recommended ROMANTIC INNS™

OF AMERICA

Fourth Edition

by

Julianne Belote, Suzi Forbes Chase, Doris Kennedy,
Eleanor S. Morris, Bob Puhala, Elizabeth Squier,
Carol and Dan Thalimer

(The Authors of the *Recommended Country Inns®* Series)

The
Globe
Pequot
Press

OLD SAYBROOK, CONNECTICUT

Cover photo: Masaaki Kazana/Photonica
Text and cover design: Nancy Freeborn/Freeborn Design

Recommended Romantic Inns is a trademark of The Globe Pequot Press.
Recommended Country Inns is a registered trademark of The Globe Pequot Press.

ISBN 0-7627-0302-4
ISSN 1078-554X

Manufactured in the United States of America
Fourth Edition/First Printing

Contents

Indexes

Help Us Keep This Guide Up to Date

Every effort has been made by the authors and the editors to make this guide as accurate and useful as possible. However, many things can change after a guide is published—establishments close, phone numbers change, facilities come under new management, etc.

We would love to hear from you concerning your experiences with this guide and how you feel it could be made better and be kept up to date. While we may not be able to respond to all comments and suggestions, we'll take them to heart and we'll also make certain to share them with the authors. Please send your comments and suggestions to the following address:

> The Globe Pequot Press
> Reader Response/Editorial Department
> P.O. Box 833
> Old Saybrook, CT 06475

Or you may e-mail us at:

> editorial@globe-pequot.com

Thanks for your input, and happy travels.

Romantic Inn-Sights

When the mind and body have been kept too long to the tasks and worries of the workplace and, yes, even to those of the old homestead, the spirit rebels and begs for attention. "Ah, but for a little romance," your inner voice may sigh. This book is for you.

Describe romance in any terms you like, and you're likely to find an inn in these pages to satisfy your yearnings. Take your partner's hand and prepare to soak up delight after delicious delight at one of these most soul-soothing hostelries.

Researched and selected by eight incurable romantics, the inns profiled here define romance. If you are looking for starlight and moonglow, soft rain and sea breezes, shimmering sunsets and breathtaking vistas, Mother Nature will provide them. If you need candlelight, bubble baths, champagne, porch swings, fabulous food, breakfast in bed, carriage rides, secluded picnics, and turret bedchambers, the inns will provide them. And if you need whispered promises, urgent kisses, and passion of any sort these inns inspire you to kindle, *you* will provide them. True romance, after all, is what you bring with you.

Among these romantic establishments are inns at the seashore and inns in the mountains; inns miles (but not too many miles) from nowhere and inns close to hubs of culture and entertainment; inns with room for scores of travelers and inns with room for just a few (or even only two). The authors have chosen island inns, city inns, inns that provide gourmet meals and inns that will guide you to fine restaurants. Many of the inns are in historic structures; some are new or nearly new; but all share the ambience that harkens back to quieter times.

As in other volumes of the Recommended Country Inns® series, every inn in this book has been personally visited. Their inclusion depends on meeting the highest standards of atmosphere, service, comfort, hospitality, history, and location: the elements that make inn travel unique. Where but at an inn can you relax near a crackling fire, sipping wine or feeding each other strawberries? Where else can you stroll through glorious gardens to secluded benches and arbors specially placed so that none but the roses will hear your murmurs?

These innkeepers have endeavored to ensure your pleasure, delight your senses, renew your spirit, and relight your passion. Our authors have endeavored to share their experience so that, for any excuse at all, you can rendezvous most romantically at each and every one of these memorable inns.

How to Use this Inn Guide

This inn guide contains descriptions of 154 inns in seven regions of the United States. These inns were selected by the authors of The Globe Pequot Press's seven regional *Recommended Country Inns®* guides as the most romantic inns in their regions. *All inns were personally visited by the authors. There is no charge of any kind for an inn to be recommended in this or any other Globe Pequot Press inn guide.*

The guide is arranged geographically by region, beginning along the Atlantic Ocean. These regions, in order, are: New England; Mid-Atlantic and Chesapeake Region; the South; the Midwest; the Southwest; Rocky Mountain Region; and the West Coast. Within each region, the states are listed alphabetically; within each state, the towns are arranged alphabetically.

Preceding each region's listings is a regional map and a numbered legend of the twenty-two romantic inns found in that region. The map is marked with corresponding numbers to show where the inns are located.

Indexes: Special-category indexes at the back of the book will help you find inns located on a lake or at the seashore, inns with golf or tennis, inns with skiing, inns with swimming pools, and more. There is also an alphabetical index of all the inns in this book.

Rates: The guidebook quotes current low and high rates to give you an indication of the price ranges you can expect. They are more than likely to change slightly with time. Be sure to call ahead and inquire about the rates as well as the taxes and service charges. The following abbreviations are used throughout the book to let you know exactly what, if any, meals are included in the room price.

EP: European Plan. Room without meals.

EPB: Room with full breakfast. (No abbreviation is used when continental breakfast is included.)

MAP: Modified American Plan. Room with breakfast and dinner.

AP: American Plan. Room with breakfast, lunch, and dinner.

Credit cards: MasterCard and Visa are accepted unless the description says "No credit cards." Many inns also accept additional credit cards.

Reservations and deposits: These are so often required that they are not mentioned in any description. Assume that you'll generally have to pay a deposit to reserve a room, using a personal check or a credit card. Be sure to inquire about refund policies.

Pets: No pets are allowed unless otherwise stated in the description. Always let innkeepers know in advance if you are planning to bring a pet.

Wheelchair access: Some descriptions mention wheelchair access, but other inns may be feasible for the handicapped. If you're interested in a particular inn, call to check if there is a room suitable for a handicapped person.

Air-conditioning: The description will indicate if an inn has rooms with air-conditioning. Keep in mind, however, that there are areas of the country where air-conditioning is totally unnecessary. For example, in the Rocky Mountain region, where the inn is at a high elevation (stated in the description), you will be comfortable without air-conditioning.

Television: Some inns offer televisions and VCRs in guest rooms; the room description will mention if the rooms are so equipped. Sometimes there's a television or VCR in a common room. Note: Most innkeepers say there is so much to do at the inn or in the area that guests generally don't watch television. In addition, most inns inspire true romantics to engage in pleasures the television can't enhance.

Telephone: Assuming that when you yearn for romance you want to get away from it all, the descriptions generally do not state if you will find a telephone in your room.

Smoking: More than 60 percent of these inns forbid or restrict smoking. See the "Rooms" entry of each profile for specific information.

BYOB: It is often acceptable to bring your own bottle, especially if an inn has no bar service. If you see no mention of BYOB or a bar in the description, you may want to check in advance.

Meals: Most of the inns profiled offer dinner as well as breakfast. Those that do not are more than happy to make reservations for you at fine nearby restaurants. Some inns also offer brunches, lunches, hors d'oeuvres, or afternoon tea. The authors often indicate some favorite foods they enjoyed at an inn, but you should not expect the menu to remain the same forever. Menus usually change seasonally or monthly. The description of the inn's food should give you a general idea of the meals served; with notice, innkeepers and chefs are happy to fill special dietary requests or create celebration cakes and the like.

Recommended Country Inns® Travelers' Club: Please observe the discount, free night's stay, or other value offered by inns welcoming club members. Note that all discounts listed refer to room rates only, not to meals, and that most offers are subject to availability.

A final word: The authors have convinced the editors that these innkeepers are themselves the soul of romance. Drink deeply of their sweet ministerings and renew the promises romance makes so easy to whisper.

New England

by Elizabeth Squier

New England is a very special place, and you the visitor are in for a special treat whatever season you decide to come. Spring is so romantic; the trees bud and flowers poke up from sometimes-lingering snow. The birds do their mating dances; beautiful swans sit on their nests. Oh, yes—romance is all around. Country inns are a special part of the romance of New England—after all, this is the region where they started.

For this book I have selected some of the most romantic country inns I have visited. Each has been chosen for one romantic reason or another—a quiet corner, wonderful dinners, breakfast in bed, a walk in the snow. Just remember they are off the beaten track, and romance is everywhere. Winter brings its own magic—the snow, the glow of a fire. I know of nothing more romantic than sitting by a fire, a glass of wine and someone very special by your side.

Many of the inns have common areas with magazines and newspapers for guests to read—even whole libraries to browse in. There are puzzles to put together, games to play, televisions, and VCRs for movies. Special touches in the rooms are also important criteria for romance—fluffy pillows, good mattresses, extra blankets, good lighting, and chairs for reading. For bed readers like me, good bed lamps are a must.

In the fall, when the leaves are turning glorious colors, what a romantic feeling it is to turn up the driveway of a beautiful inn, meet a welcoming innkeeper, relax near a crackling fire, and enjoy a lovely, romantic interlude.

I can remember a few occasions when my husband and I were caught in one of these lovely inns either by rain or snow. We sat by the fire, played some gin rummy, and sipped some fine concoction to warm the tummy. Oh, what romantic times we had.

Well, by now you know it—I am a romantic, and I love my inns and their innkeepers. All inns in their own way are romantic. Come on up to New England and enjoy.

New England

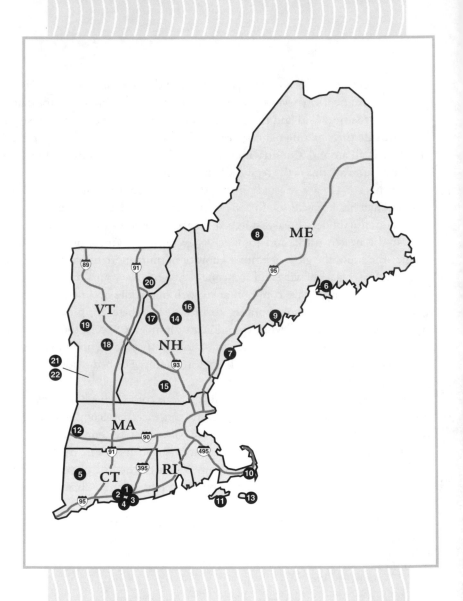

New England

Numbers on map refer to towns numbered below.

The Inn at Chester
Chester, Connecticut 06412

INNKEEPER: Deborah Lieberman Moore

ADDRESS/TELEPHONE: 318 West Main Street; (860) 526–9541 or
(800) 949–7829

WEB SITE: www.innatchester.com

ROOMS: 42, plus 2 suites; all with private bath and air conditioning,
some specially equipped for handicapped.

RATES: $105 to $185, double occupancy; $215 to $425, suites; continental breakfast.

OPEN: All year.

FACILITIES AND ACTIVITIES: Lunch, dinner, Sunday brunch. Bar and
tavern, elevator, sauna, exercise room, tennis court, conference room,
art gallery.

RECOMMENDED COUNTRY INNS® TRAVELERS' CLUB BENEFIT: 10 percent discount.

*J*ohn D. Parmelee, the original owner of this inn built from 1776 to
1778, would not know the place today, but he'd probably enjoy it.
The old house now serves as a private dining room and has a private
suite, and an L-shaped bar now graces the tavern, called Dunks Landing (after
the boat landing of the same name in the yesteryear shipbuilding heyday of
the town of Chester on the Connecticut River). The tavern serves light dinners
and daily specials, plus lunch. Try the spareribs grilled with an Oriental barbecue sauce, chicken wings Cajun-style, or crabcakes and more, while you listen to live music and enjoy your favorite cocktail. The tavern also makes stone
pies—a fancy name for pizza. When I was there, they offered a chicken pie with
roasted garlic, mozzarella, basil, and pomodoro sauce—so good.

There is much to do in the inn. Downstairs is the Billiard Room, where
you can play billiards, backgammon, or cards. The library is filled with
books—a nice place to have nearby. There is an exercise room with weights,
stationary bikes, a treadmill, and a Nordic ski machine. Get a massage here
or use the sauna. On the grounds are tennis, bocce, and croquet courts, and
bicycles for your riding pleasure.

Each of the inn's rooms is individually appointed with Eldred Wheeler
reproductions. The rooms really are lovely and include telephone, television,
and air-conditioning.

The chef of the inn's Post and Beam restaurant is very talented. Try Mediterranean fish soup, warm duck salad, or entrees like filet of beef, pork loin, lamb stew (so nice to have this on the menu), and lots of other wonderful dishes. The breast of duck sautéed in port wine with peaches, blueberries, and nutty wild rice sounds scrumptious.

This is a lovely inn in a beautiful part of Connecticut. Schedar is the inn cat—do ask about her beginnings. Bacchus means "little dog"—the inn dog is a golden retriever and what a beauty. Well-behaved pets are welcome here.

HOW TO GET THERE: Take exit 6 off Route 9 and turn west on Route 148. Go 3²/₁₀ miles to the inn. By private plane, fly to the Chester Airport.

Copper Beech Inn
Ivoryton, Town of Essex, Connecticut 06442

INNKEEPERS: Eldon and Sally Senner

ADDRESS/TELEPHONE: 46 Main Street; (860) 767–0330 or (888) 809–2056

WEB SITE: www.copperbeechinn.com

ROOMS: 4 in inn, 9 in carriage house; all with private bath, carriage house rooms with whirlpool tub, deck, phone, and TV.

RATES: $110 to $180, double occupancy; continental breakfast.

OPEN: All year.

FACILITIES AND ACTIVITIES: Restaurant closed on Mondays; Tuesdays in winter; Christmas Eve, Christmas Day, and the first week in January. Dinner, full license. Victorian-style conservatory.

One of the most beautiful copper beech trees in Connecticut shades the lawn of this lovely old inn and is the reason for the inn's name. The grounds are beautiful. Eldon, who really is a gardener, has done wonders with the property. There is an authentic English garden, many bulbs are in bloom at different times of the year, and everything is just breathtaking.

Sally is an interior designer, and her expertise really shows in this inn. There is a lovely parlor on the first floor, with bookcases and a table for playing cards or writing or whatever. Very warm and comfortable.

Accommodations at the Copper Beech are wonderful. There are four rooms in the inn itself, and they have unbelievable old-fashioned bathrooms. The towels are soft and fluffy. Nine more guest rooms are in the carriage house, and each one has a Jacuzzi tub, so delightful after a day of exploring the lovely towns of Essex, Mystic, and other area attractions. The carriage

house has an elegant country atmosphere. The halls have very nice early nineteenth-century botanical prints. In fact, there is nineteenth-century art all over the inn, as well as a wonderful collection of fine Oriental porcelain. The facilities are not well suited for children under ten years of age.

The four dining rooms have comfortable Chippendale and Queen Anne chairs. The Garden Porch, which is a favorite place for me, features white wicker and nice Audubon prints on the walls. The spacious tables are set far apart for gracious dining. Fresh flowers are everywhere, and the waiters are friendly and courteous.

The hors d'oeuvres menu is a beauty. One is made of layers of delicate puff pastry, with smoked salmon and mousse of smoked salmon, garnished with crème fraîche, diced onions, and capers. Another is a salad of chilled poached lobster and fresh orange with an orange-truffle vinaigrette. The lobster bisque is always spectacular, and there are about eight more appetizers to choose from. Choose from such treats as a salad of chilled, poached lobster, fresh mango and diced red onion, dressed with a mango vinaigrette;

fresh cultivated mussels steamed with white wine and served with a lavender-scented butter sauce; or sliced artichoke bottom, spinach, and goat cheese wrapped in a crisp, thin pastry and served with a warm spiced tomato and mushroom cream.

Good fresh fish is used for entrees. The lobster is always easy to eat; no struggling with it here. I had it on my last trip, and on another evening I had one of the veal dishes. The veal was so tender I didn't need to use a knife. Beef Wellington and roast rack of lamb are always winners here, and so are the fresh sweetbreads and a very different grilled breast of free-range chicken—a little French and a little Oriental. Roasted boneless saddle of lamb is a real winner as is the fillet of salmon stuffed with fresh arugula and shiitake mushrooms. The inn has won the AAA four-diamond award—is there any wonder? The food and service are superb.

Desserts are super. I love chocolate and raspberries, so I had some in the form of a cake and mousse and berries. No matter what you order, it is good at the Copper Beech and always exquisitely presented. The menu changes seasonally.

The Victorian conservatory is a wonderful addition to this fine inn. It's so nice for an aperitif before dinner or for coffee and cognac after.

HOW TO GET THERE: The inn is located 1 mile west of Connecticut Route 9, from exit 3 or 4. Follow the signs to Ivoryton. The inn is on Ivoryton's Main Street, on the left side.

Bee and Thistle Inn
Old Lyme, Connecticut 06371

INNKEEPERS: Bob and Penny Nelson, Jeff and Lori Nelson

ADDRESS/TELEPHONE: 100 Lyme Street; (860) 434-1667 or (860) 622-4946; fax (860) 434-3402

ROOMS: 11, plus 1 cottage; all with private bath, and phone.

RATES: $75 to $155, double occupancy; $210, cottage; EP.

OPEN: All year except Christmas Eve, Christmas Day, New Year's Day, and first two weeks of January.

FACILITIES AND ACTIVITIES: Breakfast. Lunch and dinner every day except Tuesday. Sunday brunch. Afternoon tea, November 1 to May 1. Bar, lounge, library.

*T*his lovely old inn, built in 1756, sits on five and one-half acres bordering the Lieutenant River in historic Old Lyme, Connecticut. During summer the abundant flower gardens keep the inn filled to overflowing with color.

The guest rooms are all tastefully decorated. Your bed, maybe a four-poster or canopy, is covered with a lovely old quilt or afghan. The bath towels are big and thirsty—how I love them! The cottage is air-conditioned and has a reading room, a bedroom with queen-sized bed, a kitchen, a bath, and a large television room. A deck goes around the outside. There are also a fireplace and a private dock on the river.

There are six fireplaces in the inn. The one in the parlor is most inviting—a nice place for a cocktail or just good conversation. On weekends there is music by A Wrinkle in Time, a wonderful husband-and-wife duo who make magic with their music. There is also a harpist on Saturday nights.

The innkeepers are very romantic-minded, and they will help in any way they can—even as far as proposing. Ask them for details; it's pretty funny.

Be sure to say hello to Callebaut (Bo), the Nelsons' large chocolate lab, and to Jack, a real inn dog.

Breakfast in bed is an especially nice feature of the inn. Freshly squeezed orange juice is a refreshing way to start any day. Muffins made fresh each day, buttery crepes folded with strawberry or raspberry preserves, and much more. Lunch is interesting and inventive. Try the  wild mushroom lasagne, Maryland-style crabcakes, or the Bee and Thistle shepherd's pie. Sunday brunch is really gourmet. Fresh rainbow trout, chicken hash, three different omelettes—I could eat the menu. And, of course, dinners here are magnificent, with candlelit dining rooms, a good selection of appetizers and soups, and entrees such as spiced breast of chicken, pork medallions, shrimp, scallops, veal, and rack of lamb. The list goes on and on. Desserts are wonderful. The menu changes seasonally, each time bringing new delights.

Afternoon tea is served from November 1 to May 1 on Monday, Wednesday, and Thursday from 3:30 to 5:00 P.M. The tea service is beautiful; coffee and aperitifs are also available.

The inn just keeps winning awards. *Connecticut* magazine voted the inn Best Overall Restaurant, Best Dessert, and Most Romantic Place to Dine in Connecticut. Wow! Let me tell you, the inn does deserve it.

This is a fine inn in a most interesting part of New England. You are in the heart of art, antiques, gourmet restaurants, and endless activities. Plan to spend a few days when you come.

HOW TO GET THERE: Traveling north on I-95, take exit 70 immediately on the east side of the Baldwin Bridge. At the bottom of the ramp, turn left. Take the first right at the traffic light, and turn left at the end of the road. The inn is the third house on your left. Traveling south on I-95, take exit 70; turn right at the bottom of the ramp. The inn is the third house on your left.

Saybrook Point Inn
Old Saybrook, Connecticut 06475

INNKEEPER: Stephen Tagliatela; Peter Scotella, restaurant manager; Lewis Kiesler, general manager

ADDRESS/TELEPHONE: 2 Bridge Street; (860) 395-2000 or (800) 243-0212 (outside Connecticut); fax (860) 388-1504

E-MAIL: saybrook@snet.net

WEB SITE: www.saybrook.com

ROOMS: 63, including 6 suites and 1 lighthouse apartment; all with private bath, phone, TV, air-conditioning, and refrigerator, 44 with working fireplace. Some smoke-free rooms and suites.

RATES: $149 to $295, double occupancy; $295 to $495, suites; EP. Package plans available.

OPEN: All year.

FACILITIES AND ACTIVITIES: Breakfast, lunch, dinner, Sunday brunch. Smoking in bar only. Banquet and meeting facilities; health club with whirlpool, sauna, and steam; spa; indoor and outdoor pools; marina with 120 slips and floating docks. Nearby: charter boats, theater.

"*E*xperience the magic at Saybrook Point Inn." These are the inn's words, and they're so true. The panoramic views of the Connecticut River and Long Island Sound are magnificent. From the moment you walk into the lobby, the Italian marble floors, beautiful furniture, and glorious fabrics let you know this is a special inn. Even the carpet is hand-loomed.

All the guest rooms and suites have a water view, and most have a balcony. They are lavishly decorated with eighteenth-century–style furniture, and Italian marble is used in the bathroom with whirlpool bath. Also in the rooms are a miniature wet bar and refrigerator; an unbelievable telephone that turns on lights; double-, queen-, or king-sized bed; and hair dryer. The suites feature VCR and data ports for personal computers. Secretarial services are also available, as is an exercise room with life bikes.

This is a full spa, with indoor and outdoor pools, steamroom, sauna, and whirlpool. The licensed staff will pamper you with a therapeutic massage, European facial, manicure, pedicure, even a quality makeup application.

Planning a wedding? No problem. The inn has banquet facilities for all occasions. The ballroom seats 240 people.

Breakfast, lunch, and dinner are served in an exquisite room that overlooks the inn's marina, the river, and Long Island Sound. There was a full moon the evening I dined here. What a beautiful sight to enhance the memorable food! Appetizers like smoked Norwegian salmon, escargots, smoked pheasant, and beluga caviar are an elegant way to begin your dinner. Pastas are cannelloni, linguine, or wild mushroom. I had one of the best racks of lamb I have ever had. There is always a fresh seafood special. My friend had shrimp Provençale—shrimp sautéed with garlic, shallots, and scallions. A flower may be a garnish on your plate; you can eat it.

Do try to save room for dessert. I had chocolate–chocolate chip cake, which was dark and beautiful and delicious. The service is also superb.

Sunday brunch is a winner. Too much to list, but believe me, you will not go away hungry. I was here for Easter, and the food was glorious.

The inn's fact sheet says, "Situated where the Connecticut River flows into Long Island Sound in the historic town of Old Saybrook." The unmatched views capture the essence of coastal Connecticut.

HOW TO GET THERE: From I–95 northbound take exit 67 (southbound, take exit 68) and follow Route 154 and signs to Saybrook Point.

The Mayflower Inn
Washington, Connecticut 06793

INNKEEPERS: John Trevenen; Adriana and Robert Mnuchin, owners

ADDRESS/TELEPHONE: 118 Woodbury Road (mailing address: P.O. Box 1288); (860) 868–9466; fax (860) 868–1497

ROOMS: 18, plus 7 suites; all with private bath, some with balcony, some with fireplace.

RATES: $260 to $420, double occupancy; $460 to $670, suites; EP.

OPEN: All year.

FACILITIES AND ACTIVITIES: Breakfast, lunch, dinner. Bar and lounge, gift shop, spa, heated pool, tennis.

*T*he Mayflower Inn is glorious. The entrance hall is huge and well-appointed with antiques, Persian rugs, and many works of art. Much of it has been collected by the Mnuchins over the years during their travels. There is a cherry-paneled library off this, and the other side has a large gameroom full of beautiful things.

The Shop at Mayflower has unusual vintage jewelry, cashmere gloves, sweaters, and silks; it is just grand.

There are rooms in three buildings: the Mayflower, the Standish, and the Speedwell. Facilities are sumptuous, with feather beds and down comforters and pillows. Frette linens grace the beds, which are either queens, kings, or a pair of twins. Some rooms have a balcony, and others have a fireplace. There is also nightly turndown service.

You can dine in one of three dining rooms or, if the weather is nice, outside on the dining terrace that overlooks the grounds and woods. The English pub–style lounge, which has a piano, leads out to the porch, where in summer there is wicker furniture. It is called the "drinking porch."

The teahouse is an executive retreat and a wonderful place for conferences. The spa, with a very strong emphasis on massage, is a plus—I had a massage, and Louise was wonderful. There are special classes down here, too; yoga is one.

Dining here is grand. I had a nice thick veal chop and salad. The inn has special Mayflower mashed potatoes, and boy, are they good! The menu changes not only seasonally but frequently. Foods from the local farms are used. There is not enough room to elaborate on breakfast, the luncheon specials, or even dinner. But wow, save room for the desserts!

Everyone who works here has a smile, and all are more than willing to make your stay a pleasant one.

Orchids are everywhere, the *New York Times* is brought to your door, and a minibar is in your room. One night was not enough for this inn creeper, so I stayed for two.

HOW TO GET THERE: From Hartford, take I-84 west to exit 15, Southbury. Follow Route 6 north through Southbury to Woodbury. It is exactly 5 miles from I-84 to "Canfield Corners" (an 1890s building on your right). Go left here on Route 47 to Washington. It is 8²/₁₀ miles to the inn.

Inn at Canoe Point
Bar Harbor, Maine 04609

INNKEEPERS: Tom and Nancy Cervelli

ADDRESS/TELEPHONE: Eden Street, Route 3, Box 216; (207) 288-9511; fax (207) 288-2870

E-MAIL: canoe.point@juno.com

WEB SITE: www.innatcanoepoint.com

ROOMS: 5, all with private bath.

RATES: $80 to $245, double occupancy, EPB.

OPEN: All year.

FACILITIES AND ACTIVITIES: Breakfast is only meal served. Afternoon cheese and crackers. BYOB. Hiking, all winter sports, whale watching, swimming, boating.

When you turn off the highway at the inn's sign, you may think you're driving into the ocean. Take a left turn, however, and there is this fabulous inn right at the edge of the ocean. It was built in 1889 and has not fallen into the sea so far.

It sits on two acres tucked into a quiet cove. You can walk beneath the trees, sit on the rocks, and watch boats sail by. Or, as their brochure says, relax in front of the granite fireplace in the ocean room where you can enjoy the 180-degree view of the sea and mountains beyond. From the surrounding deck you can look out over the ocean while listening to the rolling surf. Breakfast is served on the deck during warm summer mornings.

Accommodations are grand. The Garret Suite takes up the whole third floor, overlooking the water, has a king-sized bed, and separate sitting room.

The Master Suite, also overlooking the water, has a queen-sized canopy bed, nice bath, a sitting area with a gas fireplace, and French doors that lead to a shared deck. All of the other rooms have queen-sized beds and much comfort.

The view is of Frenchman Bay and the islands of Bean, Preble, and Bald Rock. Bar Harbor itself is 2 miles away, and the terminal for the ferry to Nova Scotia is 1 mile away. When I passed the entrance on my way to the inn, I was remembering taking the *Bluenose* from here many years ago. Acadia National Park is only a quarter-mile away.

Breakfast, the only meal served here, consists of fresh breads or muffins, a fruit course, and one of their daily specialties such as eggs Benedict, blueberry pancakes, lemon French toast, quiche, or omelettes. It is served in the ocean room by the fire or on the deck overlooking the sea. Wow, what a place!

HOW TO GET THERE: From Ellsworth, take Route 3 approximately 15 miles toward Bar Harbor. Just beyond the village of Hulls Cove, you'll pass the Acadia National Park entrance to your right. Continue ¼ mile on the left, you'll see the CANOE POINT sign and the drive that takes you to the ocean and the Inn at Canoe Point.

White Barn Inn
Kennebunkport, Maine 04046

INNKEEPERS: Laurie J. Bongiorno

ADDRESS/TELEPHONE: Beach Street (mailing address: P.O. Box 560-C); (207) 967–2321; fax (207) 967–1100

WEB SITE: www.whitebarninn.com

ROOMS: 16, plus 9 suites; all with private bath, some with phone, TV, and Jacuzzi, 11 with fireplace.

RATES: $180 to $450, double occupancy, continental breakfast and tea. Packages available.

OPEN: All year.

FACILITIES AND ACTIVITIES: Dinner, full license. Meeting room, bicycles. Nearby: beach, shops, galleries, golf, tennis.

A pre–Civil War farmhouse and its signature white barn have been transformed into this lovely inn, which is just a short walk from the beach and the charming village of Kennebunkport, with its colorful shops, galleries, and boutiques. When you consider the inn's exquisite food and its warmth and graciousness, it comes as no surprise that it is the only Maine member inn of *Relais et Châteaux* and one of just twenty in the United States.

Hospitality is evident throughout the inn. When you enter your room, you find a basket of fruit, flowers, luxurious toiletries, and a robe for you to wear. At night your bed is turned down and a pillow treat is left.

The rooms in the inn itself are attractively decorated with antiques, armoires, and brass and iron beds in a variety of sizes. The Gate House's rooms are large, with cathedral ceilings, ceiling fans, dressing areas, queen-sized beds, and wing chairs. May's Annex has six suites with king-sized four-poster beds and large sitting areas with fireplaces. There are oversized marble baths with whirlpool baths and separate showers. The towels are large and lush.

The sunroom is also the boardroom, seating up to fourteen people; it's a perfect, sunny spot for small retreats and reunions. The breakfast room is large and cheerfully decorated with flower arrangements. The main dining room is the barn; a lovely lounge and piano bar are here, too. Candlelight, linen, and soft music are nice touches. The menu changes weekly.

When I think about the food, I want to go back for more. The restaurant has received five diamonds and an AAA listing; these are prestigious awards

and well deserved. The menu changes weekly in order to offer the freshest and finest of ingredients. I know the greens are fresh—I watched them being picked. Soups are amazing: A light cream soup of potato, leek, and watercress is scented with thyme; lobster minestrone comes with black beans, roasted tomatoes, olive oil croutons, and a bacon pistou.

The appetizer of homemade ravioli is glorious. Dinner choices the week I was here included pan-seared striped bass with sautéed eggplant, Niçoise olives, and basil oil in a roasted tomato broth. The veal rib chop came grilled with glazed baby turnips, Swiss chard, garlic-roasted Parisienne potatoes, and an herb sauce. You can guess there are more seafood offerings from this Maine inn—lobster, halibut, and salmon were also on the menu.

No matter what size your party—two or eight— when your dinner is ready, that number of waiters arrives to stand behind each diner's chair and on cue serves everyone simultaneously. What a sight.

The little bar is copper, with eight upholstered chairs. The piano bar has a huge flower arrangement in its center.

After dinner, go relax in the living room with a glass of port or brandy, a book from the inn's well-filled bookshelves, or one of the many current magazines. Or you could be ambitious and go for a ride along the beach on one of the inn's bicycles. I took one and sure did enjoy it.

There's a new wine room, and it's a beauty for large parties or small. There's a new pool, and the area around it is grand. Sodas and lunch are served to guests out here. Also new is the fly-fishing school, offered in conjunction with Orvis—wonderful packages for anglers.

HOW TO GET THERE: From the Maine Turnpike, take exit 3 to Kennebunk. Follow Route 35 south 6 miles to Kennebunkport, then continue through the fourth traffic light onto Beach Street. The inn is in ¼ mile, on the right.

The Inn on Winter's Hill
Kingfield, Maine 04947

INNKEEPERS: Richard and Diane Winnick and Carolyn Rainaud

ADDRESS/TELEPHONE: RR 1, Box 1272; (207) 265-5421 or
(800) 233-9687; fax (207) 265-5424

WEB SITE: www.sugarloaf.com/IWH

ROOMS: 20, in 2 buildings; all with private bath, phone, coffee
machines, and cable TV, 1 specially equipped for handicapped.

RATES: $75 to $150, double occupancy, EP. Golf, skiing, and fly-fishing
packages available.

OPEN: All year.

FACILITIES AND ACTIVITIES: Dinner for public daily, by reservation.
Wheelchair access to dining room. Bar, lounge, meeting and banquet
facilities. Hot tub, indoor and outdoor swimming pools, croquet court,
tennis, cross-country skiing, ice skating. Snowmobiles are available.
Nearby: downhill skiing, hunting, fishing, hiking, golf, canoeing, Stanley
Steamer Museum, dogsled rides.

The Inn on Winter's Hill, located in the midst of western Maine's
Bigelow, Sugarloaf, and Saddleback Mountains, sits on top of a
six-acre hill on the edge of town. This Neo-Georgian manor house
was designed by the Stanley (steam car) brothers and built at the turn of the
century for Amos Greene Winter as a present for his wife, Julia. It is listed on
the National Register of Historic Places. Today it is owned by a brother and
sister who are doing a great job
as innkeepers, following a
longtime tradition of casual
elegance and warm hospitality.

Accommodations are var-
ied and range from the turn-
of-the-century luxury rooms in
the inn to the modern rooms
in the restored barn. Every one
is very comfortable, with nice
bathrooms, wonderful views, cable television, and telephone.

Julia's Restaurant is elegant, and the food served here is excellent. The
night I was here, for appetizers I had crackers and garlic cheese spread and
pineapple wrapped in bacon. My garden salad with house dressing was fol-

lowed by a light sorbet and then Sole Baskets, which were superb. The other entrees were Drunken Duck, chicken cordon bleu, and beef Wellington. Salmon in phyllo, Atlantic salmon fillet baked in phyllo with a Parmesan-cheese cream sauce, is superb; I had this on my last trip. Desserts are grand. Oh, it's all so good, it's hard to choose!

In the lounge area is an old piano; it came by oxcart from Boston for Julia Winter. It took two and a half months to arrive.

Spring, summer, fall, or winter, there is so much to do up here. Winter brings cross-country skiing from the door, and downhill skiing at Sugarloaf is minutes away. Hunting, fishing, canoeing, and hiking along the Appalachian Trail welcome outdoors people in the other seasons. If those do not appeal to you, try the pool table in the bar area. Television is here, too. All is watched over by Chee Sai and Kismet, the Shih Tzu inn dogs.

HOW TO GET THERE: Kingfield is halfway between Boston and Quebec City, and the Great Lakes area and the Canadian Maritimes. Take the Maine Turnpike to the Belgrade Lakes exit in Augusta. Follow Highway 27 through Farmington to Kingfield. The inn is on a small hill near the center of town.

The Bradley Inn at Pemaquid Point
New Harbor, Maine 04554

INNKEEPERS: Beth and Warren Busteed

ADDRESS/TELEPHONE: 361 Pemaquid Point (mailing address: Route 130 HC 61); (207) 677-2105 or (800) 942-5560; fax (207) 677-3367

ROOMS: 12, plus 1 cottage, 1 carriage house, all with private bath. Rooms with phone and TV, 5 with gas fireplace.

RATES: $125 to $185 in season, double occupancy, EPB. Off-season $95 to $150 double occupancy, EPB. Special packages available.

OPEN: All year except Christmas Eve and Christmas Day.

FACILITIES AND ACTIVITIES: Dinner. Bicycles and helmets. Wedding facilities. Nearby: ocean, tennis, golf.

*P*emaquid, an Indian word meaning "long finger," is an appropriate name for the point of land that extends farther into the Atlantic Ocean than any other on the rugged Maine coast. This information is from the inn's brochure. What a wonderful ride it is out here!

And once you arrive, the terrain is breathtaking. You're just a short walk from the Pemaquid Lighthouse or the beach with its lovely white sand. In the nearby seaside village of New Harbor, you can watch the working boats. Fort William Henry is close by. I drove around the point, parked my car, and watched the surf beating on the rocks below. It was quite a sight.

On this visit I scrambled down to the water's edge and back up. It was a bit scary but well worth it.

The inn is more than eighty years old. There's an attractive living room with a fireplace and a baby grand piano. On Fridays and Saturdays, the piano is played by John Mantica, who has entertained here for years. A folk singer also performs on Friday nights. The taproom has a long, custom-made bar of Portland granite with a mahogany rail.

The Bradley Inn Restaurant is decorated with some beautiful ship models and a huge ship's wheel. Some of the appetizers are chilled Spiney Creek oysters and smoked salmon terrine. Entrees may be filet mignon, Maine lobster, and sea scallops. The menu changes monthly. The wine list is impressive, and the dessert that won my vote was Chocolate Decadence cake.

The rooms are charming and very comfortable. The view from some of the second- and third-floor rooms is of Johns Bay or the gardens. The cottage has heat and a wood fireplace, a limited kitchen, a bedroom, and bath, living room, screened-in porch, and a TV. Chloe, a love of a yellow Lab, is the inn dog.

The carriage house has three lodging options. On the second floor is a large apartment with a kitchen, bedroom, bath, and a loft—a great place for children. On the first level is a bedroom with a private bath and another bedroom with a private bath and sitting room. The carriage house is available in summer only.

On a slate around the fireplace in the common room with a lovely piano is this saying by Harry Emerson Fosdick: *Bestow upon us, Eternal God, the fine gift of friendliness, forgive us our angers, hatreds, grudges and vindictiveness. Below all our varieties teach us the common goal. Amen.*

There's also a nice yard with lounge chairs. There's much to do and see out here, so come on up.

HOW TO GET THERE: Take the Maine Turnpike to exit 9, Falmouth—Route 1 interchange. Take I–95 21 miles to Brunswick. Continue on Route 1 to Damariscotta, 27 miles, and from there follow Route 130, 14 miles to the inn.

Wequasset Inn
Chatham, Massachusetts 02633

INNKEEPER: Mark Novata

ADDRESS/TELEPHONE: Route 28, Pleasant Bay, Cape Cod;
(508) 432–5400, (800) 352–7169 (in Massachusetts), or (800) 225–7125;
fax (508) 432–5032

ROOMS: 104, including 7 suites; all with private bath, some with private patio or deck.

RATES: $170 to $480, single or double occupancy, EP.

OPEN: April to late November.

FACILITIES AND ACTIVITIES: Breakfast, lunch, dinner. Croquet court, five all-weather PlexiPave tennis courts plus pro shop and lessons, fitness center, conference center, heated swimming pool, fishing, eighteen-hole golf course.

Taking its name from the American Indian word meaning "Crescent on the Water," Wequasset is a country inn resort that includes eighteen separate buildings and is worth a trip from anywhere. Tucked between a secluded ocean cove and a twenty-two-acre pine forest, the lands around Wequasset were once used by native peoples as a summer campground.

A nineteenth-century sea captain's home now houses the inn's main dining room, the Square Top, named for the building's unusual roof line. There is a spectacular view of Pleasant Bay from here, a nice complement to the inn's glorious food, which has been awarded Mobil Travel Guide's four-star rating and AAA's four-diamond rating. The breakfast menu offers so many choices that you could eat all day. At lunch there are six different salads, great burgers, and a deli board. One sandwich I liked was the Yorkshire—thinly sliced roast beef, creamy horseradish, and lettuce and tomato piled high on a kaiser roll. Way to go, Elizabeth—right to the fat farm. Of course, they do have a fitness platter. Well, maybe next time. There's also a lovely selection of really different drinks on the lunch menu.

The dinners? Well, you can imagine—four cold appetizers and six hot. I can taste the lump-meat crabcakes now. Soups, salads, and fresh pastas—one I tasted was spicy pepper fettucine and blackened shrimp. Oh my! The seafood is wonderful, as are the meat and poultry. It's nice to have half a rack of lamb on the menu. Desserts—are you ready? Wequasset Inn's chocolate truffle cake. I do not know where I put it, but it was all gone. There are eleven specialty coffees along with the regular ones.

The accommodations are unique. Each room has its own bath and entrance, simply styled pine furniture, traditional fabrics, and lots of charm. There are heating and cooling units, color television, and patios and decks. Suites feature fresh flowers, minibar, and VCR.

It would be hard to beat the serenity of sitting on the porch overlooking the bay at any time of the day, but oh, the early-morning calm!

HOW TO GET THERE: Wequasset Inn is on Pleasant Bay midway between Chatham and Orleans on Route 28. If you are driving from the north, take Route 6 east to exit 11. Turn left at end of exit ramp; go 25 yards to Pleasant Bay Road (your first left). Go straight through the first stop sign, and when you reach the second stop sign, you have arrived at Wequasset Inn.

The Charlotte Inn
Edgartown, Massachusetts 02539

INNKEEPERS: Gery and Paula Conover

ADDRESS/TELEPHONE: South Summer Street; (508) 627–4751

ROOMS: 23, plus 2 suites; all with private bath, some with fireplace, air conditioning, and phone. TVs in most rooms.

RATES: In-season, $250 to $650; interim-season, $165 to $550; off-season, $145 to $395; suites, $495 to $650; double occupancy, continental breakfast.

OPEN: All year.

FACILITIES AND ACTIVITIES: In-season, dinner. Off-season, dinner on weekends. Reservations a must. Gift shop and gallery. Nearby: sailing, swimming, fishing, golf, tennis.

*T*he start of your vacation is a forty-five-minute ferry ride to Martha's Vineyard. It's wise to make early reservations for your automobile on the ferry. Cabs are available if you prefer not to take your car.

When you open the door to the inn, you are in the Edgartown Art Gallery, with interesting artifacts and paintings, both watercolor and oil. This is a well-appointed gallery featuring such artists as Ray Ellis, who has a fine talent in both media. The inn also has an unusual gift shop, now located next to the Garden House.

On one of my visits here, four of us had dinner in the inn's lovely French restaurant, L'Etoile. The food was exquisite. Capon breast stuffed with duxelles, spinach, and sundried tomatoes with coriander mayonnaise was the best I have had. I tasted everyone's food—nice occupation I have. Rack of lamb, served rare, with red wine—rosemary sauce and accompanied by potato and yam gratin was excellent. During my last visit I had grilled Angus filet mignon—it was glorious. My friend Audrey had a halibut fillet. They also have a special or two, but then everything is so special, the word really does not fit. The menu changes weekly; desserts the week I was there included blackberry and lemon curd napoleon and rhubarb and raspberry tart—oh my! For breakfast I had a strawberry crepe that I can still remember vividly. Freshly squeezed juices and fruit muffins . . . heaven!

The rooms are authentic. There are fireplaces and Early American four-poster beds, and the carriage house is sumptuous. The second-floor suite has a fireplace I could live in. Paula has a touch with rooms—comfortable furniture, down pillows, down comforters, and all the amenities. As an example, the shower curtains are of eyelet and so pretty. As a finishing touch, there are plenty of large towels.

Across the street is the Garden House, and it is Edgartown at its best. The living room is unique and beautifully furnished, and its fireplace is always set for you. The rooms over here are just so handsome. The Coach House is magnificent, furnished with fine old English antiques, a marble fireplace, and a pair of exquisite chaise lounges in the bedroom. It is air-conditioned.

Paula, by the way, has green hands, and all about are gardens that just outdo one another.

Gery and Paula are special innkeepers, but they do need the help of Ozzie and Jezebel, a pair of golden reteiever's.

HOW TO GET THERE: Reservations are a must if you take your car on the ferry from Woods Hole, Massachusetts. Forty-five minutes later you are in Vineyard Haven. After a fifteen-minute ride, you are in Edgartown, and on South Summer Street is the inn.

Wheatleigh
Lenox, Massachusetts 01240

INNKEEPERS: Susan and Linfield Simon; Francois Thomas, general manager

ADDRESS/TELEPHONE: West Hawthorne; (413) 637-0610; fax (413) 637-4507

WEB SITE: www.wheatleigh.com

ROOMS: 17; all with private bath, air conditioning, and phone; 9 with working fireplace.

RATES: $175 to $625, double occupancy, EP.

OPEN: All year.

FACILITIES AND ACTIVITIES: Lunch for houseguests, dinner, Sunday brunch. Grill room, lounge. Swimming, tennis, cross-country skiing.

RECOMMENDED COUNTRY INNS® TRAVELERS' CLUB BENEFIT: Stay two nights, get third night free, subject to availability.

*I*n the heart of the picturesque Berkshires, overlooking a lake, amid lawns and gardens on twenty-two self-contained acres stands the estate of Wheatleigh, former home of the Countess de Heredia. The centerpiece of this property is an elegant private palace fashioned after an Italian palazzo. The cream-colored manse re-creates the architecture of six-

teenth-century Florence. You must read the brochure of Wheatleigh, for it says it all so well.

Patios, pergolas, porticos, and terraces surround this lovely old mansion. The carvings over the fireplaces, cupids entwined in garlands, are exquisite. In charming contrast, the inn also has the largest collection of contemporary ceramics in the New England area. There are many lovely porcelain pieces on the walls. In the dining room are tile paintings weighing more than 500 pounds. They are Doultons from 1830; this was before it became Royal Doulton. They are just beautiful.

The portico is a prime dining room—all glass with glorious views. And the food—wow! The grill room, which is open in-season, provides an a la carte menu of light fare prepared to the same high standards of the dining room. Its casual ambience features an elegant black-and-white color scheme—the plates are beautiful.

There is a service bar in a lovely lounge, and boy, you sure can relax in the furniture in here! It has a wonderful fireplace, and the views from here are glorious. And imagine a great hall with a grand staircase right out of a castle in Europe. There are also exquisite stained-glass windows in pale pastels, plus gorgeous, comfortable furniture. From the great hall you can hear the tinkle of the fountain out in the garden.

The whole inn was done over very recently, and wow, the rooms are smashing! Do you long for your own balcony overlooking a lovely lake? No problem. Reserve one here. The facilities are not well suited to children under eight.

At the entrance to the dining room, the homemade desserts are beautifully displayed, along with French champagne in six sizes, from a jeroboam to a small bottle for one. This is very nice indeed. I chose grilled quail on young lettuce leaves and raspberries for a dinner appetizer; it was superb. Tartare of fresh tuna was strikingly presented, just like a Japanese picture, and delicious. I also had chilled fresh pea soup with curry and sorrel, followed by monkfish coated with pistachios, sautéed, with red wine sauce.

Homemade sorbets are very good, but then so is everything else here. The executive chef is Peter Platt. He has been here for years, and he offers cooking classes on Sunday through Thursday—a French immersion course!

Susan's description of the inn is "elegance without arrogance," and Lin's is "the ultimate urban amenity." Mine is "a perfect country inn."

There are very special weekend pacakges; do call and ask. Two that come to mind are a Burgundy Weekend with Louis Jadot and a Chocolate Lover's Weekend. Wow—wish I lived closer!

HOW TO GET THERE: From Stockbridge at the Red Lion Inn where Route 7 turns right, go straight on Prospect Hill Road, bearing left. Travel about 4 ½ miles, past the Stockbridge Bowl and up a hill to Wheatleigh.

From the Massachusetts Turnpike, take exit 2, and follow signs to Lenox. In the center of Lenox, take Route 183, pass the main gate of Tanglewood, and then take the first left on West Hawthorne. Go 1 mile to Wheatleigh.

The Woodbox Inn
Nantucket, Massachusetts 02554

INNKEEPER: Dexter Tutein

ADDRESS/TELEPHONE: 29 Fair Street; (508) 228–0587

ROOMS: 3 queens, plus 6 suites in two buildings; all with private bath.

RATES: $150 to $260, double occupancy, EP. No credit cards.

OPEN: Memorial Day to Columbus Day. Weekends only from Columbus Day to January 1.

FACILITIES AND ACTIVITIES: Full breakfast, dinner, beer and wine license. Wheelchair access to sunrooms, dining rooms. Nearby: swimming, boating, biking, tennis.

RECOMMENDED COUNTRY INNS® TRAVELERS' CLUB BENEFIT: Stay two nights, get third night free, Monday–Thursday, from late October to end of May, excluding holidays.

For forty-five years there has been a Tutein running this inn. Built in 1709, it is the oldest inn on Nantucket Island. What a treat to be here!

The suites are unique. In an old building like this, you cannot change the structure to modernize it, so the bathrooms have been very inventively fit in.

Very pretty and comfortable. The suite I was in had a fireplace in the living room, two bedrooms, one with a huge canopy bed, and a lovely little private patio. It was hard to leave.

There are three dining rooms in the inn. I'm sure I had dinner in what must be the oldest public dining room in New England. The room has two "king's boards" on the wall of the immense, almost walk-in fireplace. Today the fireplace holds an old cradle with dried flowers. The china is old, and there are nice touches on the tables, like your own pepper mill. Tall candlesticks add to the charm of this inn.

The inn is famous for its popovers, and I can understand why, having devoured quite a few. The food is truly gourmet. Naturally, the entrees include the catch of the day; I had fresh sea bass that was delicious. My dinner companion had the veal chop, saffron rice, and glazed pear chutney. The house salad dressing is excellent. And for dessert, well, the best crème brûlée I have ever had.

The inn's breakfast is a great way to start the day—choose Belgian waffles or pancakes or the eggs Benedict—an inn tradition. The pancakes and waffles come with pure maple syrup, blueberries, strawberries, peaches, or apples. Those wonderful popovers come with any egg dish. The chef has cooked several times at the James Beard Foundation in New York City. One night during our stay, Dexter took us to a real Nantucket hot spot for a very unusual dinner at Black Eye Susan's (508-325-0308) at 10 India Street—do go try this one.

The powder room must be seen. There are no words to describe it.

HOW TO GET THERE: Take the ferry to Nantucket or fly from Hyannis. The inn is at 29 Fair Street. You can walk to it from the ferry.

The Notchland Inn
Bartlett, New Hampshire 03812

INNKEEPERS: Les School and Ed Butler

ADDRESS/TELEPHONE: Route 302; (603) 374–6131 or (800) 866–6131; fax (603) 374–6168

WEB SITE: www.notchland.com

ROOMS: 7, plus 5 suites; all with private bath and fireplace, 1 specially equipped for handicapped.

RATES: $185 to $275, double occupancy, MAP. B&B is available.

OPEN: All year.

FACILITIES AND ACTIVITIES: Full liquor license. Dinner is not served on Mondays. Hot tub. Hiking, canoeing, swimming, fishing, bicycling, cross-country skiing, sleigh rides, snowshoeing, and ice skating. Nearby: downhill skiing.

The inn was built in 1862 by a wealthy Boston dentist, Samuel Bemis. He used native granite and timber, and you can bet that the construction of this building was some job. Seventeen fireplaces are in the inn, and all the rooms have a working fireplace. Some of the suites have a two-person spa bath. One suite has an exquisite Japanese wedding kimono posted on a wall, and a few suites are in the carriage house and schoolhouse. The Carter Suite is grand; it has a deck, a wood-burning fireplace, a Jacuzzi tub in a large bathroom, a queen-sized bed, and a nice living room.

There are high ceilings and beautiful mountain views. The front parlor was designed by Gustav Stickley, a founder of the Arts and Crafts movement. The music room is inviting with its piano and stereo, and the sunroom has

a fountain and is full of beautiful plants. The dining room dates back to 1795, has a raised hearth fireplace, and looks out onto the pond and gazebo.

Every evening dinner is served at 7:00, and patrons are offered a choice of two soups, two appetizers, three entrees, and three desserts. To give you an idea of the varied menu, soup might be lightly curried sweet potato and butternut squash, orange-scented tomato with a fresh herbed yogurt, or Szechwan carrot. Appetizers might be crabcakes or three-tier vegetable pâté with a red pepper coulis. Entrees might be filet mignon with béarnaise sauce, chicken champagne, poached catfish, or poached salmon stuffed with scallops and herbs. And dessert might be very lemon pie, apricot cheescake, or chocolate walnut tart. If you can even think about breakfast after such a dinner, you'll delight in the full country breakfast that will start your next day right.

There's so much to do in this area that you may have a hard time deciding where to start. Hiking is by far the nicest you'll find almost anywhere. There are beautiful waterfalls and granite cliffs to scale. The Saco River is the place for swimming, fishing, or canoeing, and two swimming holes are on the inn's property. Whitewater Class III and IV are here in the spring, so come on up with your canoe. Or bring your bicycle, as biking is fun here. Skiing of all kinds is very close by (there are 45 miles of ski trails)—or do you want to try snowshoeing? This is the place for it, or you can go ice skating on the inn's pond. If more sedentary activities suit your fancy, rocking chairs on the porch are ideal for reading and needlework.

The innkeepers love animals as much as I do. Mork and Mindy are the miniature horses, and Dolly is a Belgian draft horse. DC and Sid are the llamas. Coco, their Bernese mountain dog, is a love and even has "Coco Loco" cookies to give to guests—boy, are those good! Coco's Corner is in the Inn's newsletter, and what a wag he is! He reports on all of the animals that visit—ducks, bears, and birds. Keeps him busy.

While you are here, do read the history of the Inn; it's a fascinating story. When you come in the door of the inn and turn left, there is a living room with a puzzle going at all times; it's always fun to work on it. By the fireplace is a slate marker about Nancy Barton—be sure to read it—it's a riot.

Romance is in the air you breathe up here. At any time of year, the area's activities will keep couples discovering new adventures together. Even the scenic roads are lively—there's no better place to take a drive and enjoy the magic in the air.

HOW TO GET THERE: Follow Route 302 from North Conway. 20 miles north to the inn.

The Hancock Inn
Hancock, New Hampshire 03449

INNKEEPERS: Joe and Linda Johnston

ADDRESS/TELEPHONE: Main Street; (603) 525-3318 or (800) 525-1789
(outside New Hampshire); fax (603) 525-9301

E-MAIL: innkeeper@hancockinn.mv.com

WEB SITE: www.hancockinn.com

ROOMS: 11; all with private bath, air conditioning, cable TV, and
phone. 1 suite for handicapped. No smoking inn.

RATES: $98 to $150, double occupancy, EPB. Special package rates.

OPEN: All year.

FACILITIES AND ACTIVITIES: Dinner, lounge. Wheelchair ramp into
the inn. Parking. Nearby: swimming, hiking, antiquing, summer
theater, skiing, tennis.

Operated as an inn since 1789—George Washington's first year in office—The Hancock Inn is now in the competent hands of old friends and good innkeepers, Joe and Linda Johnston.

This is a nice old inn. Carefully preserved is The Mural Room, believed to date back to the early years of the inn. The recently remodeled Carriage Lounge is a comfortable and very unusual common room and bar. The name of the inn stems from the fact that founding father John Hancock, once owned most of the land that composes the present town of Hancock. Set among twisting hills and featuring a weathered clapboard facade, graceful white pillars, and a warm red door, the inn represents all that is good about old inns.

At the end of the day, you will retire to the comfort of a four-poster bed, where the sound of the Paul Revere bell from a nearby steeple will gently lull you to sleep. This is a town that hasn't changed much in the past two centuries.

The dining rooms are lovely, and the food is superb. The inn has been awarded the best of the best award: four diamonds, designating this to be one of the top one hundred restaurants in the country in the category of American food. Appetizers like cranberry shrub, Maryland crabcake, and baked brie are followed by good soups and an excellent house salad. The famous Shaker cranberry pot roast is alone worth the trip, but perhaps you'd like to try the roasted maple duck, rainbow lake trout, or summer garden linguine.

Swim in summer in Norway Pond, within walking distance of the inn. Climb mountains, or just sit and listen to the church chimes during foliage time. Alpine and cross-country skiing are nearby in winter. Or browse in the antiques shops on a cool spring morn.

The governor, Stephen Merrill, has given a commendation to the inn for its 200-plus years as a country inn.

The inn dogs are Duffy, a springer spaniel, and Maggie, his niece.

The TVs are under cozies, and on top of each one is a saying: "Caution! Do not remove unless you wish to return to the twentieth century."

HOW TO GET THERE: From Boston take I–93 north to I–293, then Route 101 to Peterborough. Take a right onto Route 202, then a left onto Route 123. Turn left at the stop sign.

The Inn at Thorn Hill
Jackson, New Hampshire 03846

INNKEEPERS: Jim and Ibby Cooper

ADDRESS/TELEPHONE: Thorn Hill Road; (603) 383-4242 or (800) 289-8990; fax (603) 383-8062

WEB SITE: www.innatthornhill.com

ROOMS: 19, in 2 buildings, plus 3 cottage suites, all with private bath and phones; 7 Jacuzzis and 1 soaking tub. No smoking inn.

RATES: $150 to $250, double occupancy, MAP. Higher in peak season.

OPEN: All year.

FACILITIES AND ACTIVITIES: Bar, swimming pool, hot tub, cross-country skiing. Nearby: downhill skiing, golf club, tennis, horseback riding, canoeing, ice skating, sleigh rides.

Over the Honeymoon Bridge to The Inn at Thorn Hill you go, and when you get there you will find a Victorian beauty. Mountains are everywhere you look from this inn. Relax on the porch in a New England rocking chair and enjoy the view. Even on a bad day, it is spectacular.

I loved the Victorian parlor, with a baby grand piano, and the spacious drawing room, with a wood stove and an unbelievable view. There are board games, cards, and books for you to enjoy. A cozy pub with a fireplace and five bar stools has lots of cheer.

Elegant country dining by candlelight is what you get, and the food is good. The menu changes nightly, offering the freshest and most innovative ingredients the season has to offer. Casually elegant service, an extensive wine list, and a full-service pub are to be found here.

Sautéed almond- and Parmesan-crusted shrimp served with a grilled pineapple, radish, and caper salad with fresh tarragon dressing is just an example of the appetizers—there are more.

The soups and salads are interesting. And the entrees are grand. Lobster Pie Thorn Hill, served with brandy Newburg sauce in a puff pastry shell. Crisp roast duckling, served with Cointreau sauce and sautéed orange slices. Lamb chops stuffed with tomato, feta cheese, and fresh mint. The list goes on. The desserts that follow are excellent.

All the inn rooms have a Victorian flair. A variety of beds are available—canopies, singles, doubles, kings, and queens—and all rooms have wonderful views of the mountains. The carriage house next door has a 20-by-40-foot

great room with a fireplace and seven guest rooms, so bring several couples. This is the place to be. The cottages are very nice and just great for those who want more privacy. The three cottages have just been beautifully refurbished, each with a Jacuzzi, front porch, wet bar, television, gas fireplace, and air-conditioning. Some have a deck and view. I stayed in one of the cottages, and, believe me, you could move right in and be very comfortable.

There is much to do here. The inn has its own swimming pool; hiking and downhill skiing are close at hand. Cross-country skiing begins at the doorstep and joins the 146-kilometer Jackson touring network. Say hello to Gizmo, the inn cat, and Snuggles, the inn dog.

No wonder the inn was one of ten winners of Uncle Ben's Best Country Inn awards! I was one of the judges.

HOW TO GET THERE: Go north from Portsmouth, New Hampshire, on the Spaulding Turnpike (Route 16) all the way to Jackson, which is just above North Conway. At Jackson is a covered bridge on your right. Take the bridge, and two roads up from the bridge on the right is Thorn Hill Road, which you take up the hill. The inn is on your right.

Foxglove
Sugar Hill, New Hampshire 03585

INNKEEPERS: Janet and Walter Boyd

ADDRESS/TELEPHONE: Route 117 at Lovers Lane, Sugar Hill; (603) 823–8840; fax (603) 823–5755

ROOMS: 6, all with private bath.

RATES: $85 to $165, double occupancy, EPB. MAP available in foliage season.

OPEN: All year.

FACILITIES AND ACTIVITIES: Breakfast, dinner, BYOB. Conference room for small executive retreats. Nearby: tennis, swimming, hiking, cross-country and downhill skiing, snowshoeing, and much, much more.

*S*ugar Hill is a wonder. When the lupine is in bloom, it's one of the most beautiful sights I've seen—the fields are a blaze of color. This is a village you must see to believe it's real. The meeting house was built in 1831, and the post office has one room.

Foxglove, at Lovers Lane, is made for all ages of lovers. I just spoke to Walter, and he reported a lot of snow had fallen. To be up here with it all white has to be just beautiful. There are local cross-country trails nearby. Also not too far away are four major ski areas. Anyone for ice skating? There are ponds for this. There's a glass porch that's really a picture window looking out at wildlife and sheer beauty—apple trees and maybe a deer. The fireplaces are warm and so inviting. So is dinner; some unusual choices for seating are

offered in a sitting room for two, in the innkeepers' library with a stone fireplace, on the porch, or, how about the dining room? Try the good soups—black bean, cream of cauliflower, Belgian carrot, and more. There are good salads. Entrees might be grilled corncob smoked ham steak with apple cream sauce and fresh chives served with whipped sweet potatoes and corn bread, tenderloin of beef, shrimp, or poached salmon. The desserts are awesome: home-baked fruit pie or tart, strawberry rhubarb or maybe bittersweet chocolate torte. Way to go, Elizabeth! Eating my way through New England. What a life.

Accommodations are grand. Rooms are named so you won't get lost, laughed Walter. The Garden Room has a deck, indoor and outdoor shower, hot tub, king-sized bed, and sitting area, all looking at the forest. Oh my. The Paisley Room is lovely; the artwork in the inn is glorious. The Gingham Room is on a corner; Mrs. Harmes is a turret with magnificent views; the Blue Room is a favorite for honeymooners; and Serengheti speaks for itself. A small sitting room with a TV is between Gingham and Blue.

Breakfasts are well served. Extra-thick orange French toast is a winner, but there are also steamed eggs, pancakes, and more.

Do ask to see their beautiful cat.

HOW TO GET THERE: Take I–93 to exit 38. Go right on Route 18 for ½ mile. Go left on Route 117 to inn, 2³/10 miles on right. From I–91, take Exit 17. Follow Route 302 east 16 miles. Turn right onto Route 117 to inn, 5⁶/10 miles on the left.

Twin Farms
Barnard, Vermont 05031

INNKEEPERS: Shaun and Beverly Matthews; Thurston Twigg-Smith, owner

ADDRESS/TELEPHONE: Stage Road (mailing address: P.O. Box 115); (802) 234–9999 or (800) 894–6327; fax (802) 234–9990

ROOMS: 4 suites, 8 cottages, 2 suites in lodge; all with private bath, phone, TV, air-conditioning, minirefrigerator, and CD player.

RATES: $800 to $1,500, double occupancy; all inclusive. $14,500 per day for the whole property.

OPEN: All year except April.

FACILITIES AND ACTIVITIES: Full license, spa, all winter sports, mountain bikes, tennis, croquet, swimming, canoeing, fitness center.

*T*win Farms is a 235-acre hideaway estate that was owned by novelist Sinclair Lewis and given to his wife, Dorothy Thompson, as a wedding present. During the 1930s and '40s, they came here to rest and entertain many literary figures of the time.

You arrive at the entry gate and dial a number indicating who you are. Then you enter an unbelievably unique property. Drive down the lane and along a circular drive to the main house.

The gameroom, with a beautiful fireplace, has many games and Stave wood puzzles. Off this is the Washington Suite, where my friend Audrey and I stayed. It has beautiful quilts and down-filled beds, two televisions, a CD player, and a bathroom with a large skirted antique tub and a huge shower. The sitting room has a bay window with a nice view, good couches, and a beautiful fireplace. There's a fireplace in the bedroom, too.

Dorothy's Room, on the second floor, is where she preferred to read and write. Red's Room, the original master suite, is glorious, with a view of Mount Ascutney. Red was Sinclair's nickname.

The guest room's walls and curtains are covered in toile de Jouy, a green-and-ivory French linen that tells a story. It's just beautiful.

The cottages have fireplaces, sumptuous baths, very private screened porches, and lots of comfort. They all have names. The Studio is splendid and has a huge copper soaking tub and front and back porches; a porch overlooks a stream, and a lot of fish-related items decorate the interior. The Treehouse is a wow, with Chinese fretwork in the bedroom. Orchard Cottage is set amid the old apple orchard and features two handcarved granite fireplaces. The two-story Barn Cottage offers grand views, and the Meadow, with its Moroccan interior reminiscent of a desert king's traveling palace, is stunning; the tent ceiling is something you'll just have to see. Wood Cottage has an Italian oak writing table and much charm. And the Log Cabin is an authentic old Tennessee log cabin refurbished the Twin Farms way. It's very hard to choose here, so come a lot of times—you won't be disappointed.

A covered bridge takes you to the pub. Here are a self-service bar, pool table, fireplace, and television. Below this is a fully equipped fitness center. In-room massages are available. Up the road is a Japanese *furo*. There are separate tubs for men and women, separated by fragrant pine walls, and one larger one for both men and women.

The main dining room is rustic; however, you can dine wherever you choose. We were in the original dining room, and both the food and the service were incredible. Cocktails are at 7:00 P.M. There are two bars for you to help yourself from any time of the day or night. Lunch may take any form, and you can have it anywhere. Tea is glorious.

There is much to do here, whatever the season. Tennis and croquet; a lake for swimming, canoeing, or fishing; walking; biking. (You can use the inn's mountain bikes.) The inn also has its own ski slopes, ski trails, snowshoes, toboggans, and ice skating.

This is an experience few may be able to afford, but what a wonderful trip. The inn was awarded five stars by the *Mobil Travel Guide*. Say hello to Maple, the golden inn dog.

HOW TO GET THERE: Take I–91 north to I–89 north. Take exit 1 off I–89. Turn left onto Route 4 to Woodstock, then Route 12 to Barnard. At the general store, go right and follow this road for about 1½ miles. As the road changes from blacktop to dirt, you will see two stone pillars and a wrought-iron gate on your right, marking the driveway entrance.

The Lilac Inn
Brandon, Vermont 05733–1121

INNKEEPERS: Melanie and Michael Shane

ADDRESS/TELEPHONE: 53 Park Street; (802) 247–5463 or (800) 221–0720; fax (802) 247–5499

E-MAIL: lilacinn@sover.net

WEB SITE: www.lilacinn.com

ROOMS: 9; all with private bath, 1 with whirlpool tub, 3 with fireplace. Phone available.

RATES: $100 to $250, double occupancy, EPB. MAP rates available.

OPEN: All year. Restaurant closed to public between Easter and Mother's Day.

FACILITIES AND ACTIVITIES: Sunday brunch, dinner Wednesday through Saturday. Catering and room service. Winter Arts Festival on

Friday and Saturday nights in February and March. Jazz and classical concerts in summer.

*W*ow! This is a beauty. It's a 10,000-square-foot Georgian Revival mansion that was built in 1909 as a summer cottage. Adorned with yellow and white paint, it is a lovely country inn today. Michael and Melanie have recaptured the charm of the era in which it was built.

To the left of the coach entrance is the library, which has a nice fireplace, books galore, chess, and a ton of comfort and charm. On the right, a stupendous butler's pantry hall leads to the tavern. Here is a beautiful copper-topped bar with six leather chairs with backs. Boy, are they comfortable!

The tavern has its own menu, full of glorious food. How about a Loaf of Soup—a freshly baked miniboule filled with the soup of the day?

The dining room menu changes weekly. Usually there are four appetizers and soup du jour. A few of the choices when I visited were grilled Angus sirloin, baked cheddar scrod, raspberry lamb, and baked stuffed salmon. Two of the desserts take thirty minutes to prepare. I won't tell you what they are. Come up and find out; they are wonderful.

The staircase is grand. In 1991 a time capsule was inserted into its newel post. At the top of the stairs is an ornate Chinese chest from the 1850s.

The rooms are spacious and well-appointed. The bridal suite has a two-person whirlpool tub and wedding dolls on the fireplace mantel. Melanie makes the dolls. There is one of her in her wedding dress when you first enter the inn. Televisions are in armoires, and there also are VCRs.

What a talented pair of innkeepers we have here! They're assisted by three inn cats—Brown Nose, White, and Sebastian, a wonderful Himalayan. The inn dogs are pugs called Dr. Watson, Winston, Carmel, and Bella.

HOW TO GET THERE: Follow Route 7 to Brandon. Turn right on Route 73 east (Park Street). The inn is about the fourth building on the right.

Rabbit Hill Inn
Lower Waterford, Vermont 05848

INNKEEPERS: Brian and Leslie Mulcahy

ADDRESS/TELEPHONE: Lower Waterford Road; (802) 748–5168 or
(800) 76–BUNNY; fax (802) 748–8342

E-MAIL: info@rabbithillinn.com

WEB SITE: www.rabbithillinn.com

ROOMS: 21: 8 luxury (fireplace and whirlpool tub for two), 4 fireplaced
rooms and suites, and 9 classic rooms; all with private bath, radio/
cassette player, hair dryer, robes, coffeemaker; 1 room specially equipped
for handicapped (wheelchair access to dining rooms). No smoking inn.

RATES: $235 to $370, double occupancy; MAP, includes all gratuities.
Midweek and winter rates available.

OPEN: All year, except first two weeks of April and first two weeks of
November.

FACILITIES AND ACTIVITIES: Breakfast and dinner served. Bar, gameroom, library, video den. Snowshoeing, sledding, cross-country and
downhill skiing, hiking, biking, swimming, and canoeing. Nearby: ice
skating, golf. Two quaint towns are within a ten-minute drive in either
direction.

R abbit Hill Inn is one of the lovingly restored crisp white buildings
that make up Vermont's "White Village." This Historic District is
one of the state's prettiest and most photographed places.

The inn was built by Samuel Hodby in 1795 as a tavern, general store, and
lodging for those traveling between Canada and the ports of Boston and
Portland. In 1825 Jonathan Cummings built his home and workshop here (it
is now part of the foyer and front dining room). The two properties have
operated as one since the 1830s. In the 1930s the inn was renamed the Rabbit Hill Inn for the many rabbit warrens then found on the property. The
inn's present owners have preserved the charm of this lovely old inn. And
what a job they've done!

Accommodations are grand. Every room or suite has its own enchanting
theme. Some of them are the Toy Chamber (inspired by *The Velveteen Rabbit)*,
the Music Chamber (with a 1857 pump organ and antique victrola), and Top
of the Tavern (a real beauty with a grand four-poster bed, fireplace, and Victorian dressing room). I was in Victoria's Chamber, a lovely room with a
king-sized 1850s reproduction bed, empire sofa, and glorious mountain
view. A diary is in each room for people to write in during their stay. What

fun they are to read! In every room you'll find pretty things, wonderful touches, and a stuffed rabbit sitting on the bed.

The first and second floor porches face the Presidential Mountain Range. It is a special place to just sit and rock with Zeke, the inn cat.

Do spend some time in the inviting common rooms. Afternoon tea and pastries are served in the Federal Parlor. The old crane in the fireplace here is still used in the winter for hearth cooking on Saturday afternoons. The Snooty Fox Pub is modeled after Irish pubs of the eighteenth century. Oh, boy, what a place! There's also a comfortable library full of books and games to enjoy.

Everything is very nice indeed at the award-winning restaurant. The intimate candlelit dining rooms feature Windsor chairs and polished tables set with crystal and fine china.

Five-course gourmet dinners here are a true joy. It takes two hours to dine; it is all done right. The menu changes seasonally and frequently, each time bringing new delights. Everything is prepared from scratch. Try the seared Nantucket scallops or venison and pork pâté to start. Then sample the grilled tenderloin of beef with a maple molasses sauce; roasted chicken breast stuffed with shrimp, basil, and pine nuts; or sautéed monkfish. Heart-healthy and vegetarian options are always available. Be sure to savor the homemade sauces, mustards, and salsas prepared with herbs and edible flowers from the inn's garden. Save room for dessert. Chocolate hazelnut cheesecake and espresso crème caramel are a sampling of the goodies you might find.

In the evening while you're dining, your bed is turned down, your radio is tuned to soft music, and your candle is lit. A handcrafted fabric heart is placed on your doorknob. You are invited to use it as your DO NOT DISTURB sign and then keep it as a memento of your visit.

You'll wake in the morning to a full candlelit breakfast of homemade granola (not to be missed), fruits, yogurts, juices, and hot entrees. Delicious!

The inn is splendid. So is the pretty little village. You will not be disappointed.

HOW TO GET THERE: From I–91 (north or south), take exit 19 to I–93 south. Take exit 1 onto Route 18 south and follow 7 miles to inn. From I–93 north, take exit 44 onto Route 18 north; follow 2 miles to inn.

The Inn at Ormsby Hill
Manchester Center, Vermont 05255

INNKEEPERS: Chris and Ted Sprague

ADDRESS/TELEPHONE: Historic Route 7A (mailing address: 1842 Main Street); (802) 362–1163 or (800) 670–2841; fax (802) 362–5176

ROOMS: 10; all with private bath, air conditioning, double whirlpool tub, fireplace, phones, and robes.

RATES: $160 to $290, double occupancy, EPB.

OPEN: All year.

FACILITIES AND ACTIVITIES: Friday-night supper, Saturday dinner by reservation only, BYOB. Hammock, porch. Nearby: golf, bicycling, antiquing, fishing, tennis, hiking, downhill and cross-country skiing.

RECOMMENDED COUNTRY INNS® TRAVELERS' CLUB BENEFIT: Stay three or more nights in one of the fireplace and Jacuzzi rooms and receive a $50 gift certificate for dinner at a local restaurant, which may be redeemed Sunday–Thursday, excluding foliage season and holiday weeks.

*I*t's nice to have good innkeepers back in business. Chris and Ted Sprague had a beauty in Maine, but this inn far surpasses that one. When you enter the inn, the first room on the left is a beautifully furnished formal living room. Go on into the gathering room, which has a huge fireplace, games, and books. Continue into the conservatory–dining room. It's a wow. When the inn is full, three tables are in use. There's a really different-looking fireplace in here. The mantel came from either Europe or Newport. It's a beauty. The glass windows at the end of the room remind me of a ship, and Chris has nice plants all around.

The view of the mountains is awesome. There's an apple checkerboard at the ready.

The inn was built around 1760 and added onto in the 1800s. The new wing was constructed in 1996. You cannot tell where the old and new meet. The rooms are just beautiful. Almost all have two-person whirlpool baths—now that's romantic—and fireplaces, either gas or wood. The beds are kings and queens and so comfortable. There are four-posters and canopies. Everything is restful, and the colors are muted. The towels are big and fluffy. The inn reminds me of a gracious manor house in the English countryside and it has a full sprinkler system and alarms.

The tower room is the latest addition, and it's a dream. There are some steps, so be prepared (but it's worth every step). Up seven steps from the second floor to a queen-sized canopy bed, a gas fireplace, and lots of windows. Up a few more to an unbelievable bathroom with a Jacuzzi for two as well as a two-person shower/steam shower and more windows. Wow.

Breakfast is the main meal here, but Chris serves supper on Friday nights and a four-course dinner on Saturdays. I was lucky enough to be here then, and we had risotto with asparagus, porcini, and basil for the first course. This was followed by a garden salad with champagne vinaigrette and cream biscuits. The next course was peppered fresh tuna on top of garlic spinach with a shallot sauce. Dessert was a bittersweet chocolate soufflé with white chocolate and rum sauce. This is just a sample of Chris's spectacular food.

At breakfast time Chris makes breakfast desserts. Honest. I had one. Try the espresso coffee cake, cantaloupe with honey sauce, individual baked pancakes, and much more.

HOW TO GET THERE: From Route 30 go north to Historic Route 7A in Manchester. Turn left. Go south about 3 miles to the inn.

The Village Country Inn
Manchester Village, Vermont 05254

INNKEEPERS: Jay and Anne Degen

ADDRESS/TELEPHONE: Route 7A (mailing address: P.O. Box 408, Manchester); (802) 362–1792 or (800) 370–0300; fax (802) 362–7238

E-MAIL: vci@vermontel.com

WEB SITE: www.villagecountryinn.com

ROOMS: 12 standard rooms, plus 21 luxury rooms and suites; all with private bath, phone, and air conditioning; some with TV; 4 with fireplaces. No smoking inn.

RATES: $160 to $300, per room, double occupancy, MAP. Special packages available.

OPEN: All year.

*M*anchester's favorite front porch beckons you as you arrive at The Village Country Inn, located in the heart of town. The porch is 100 feet long, with wicker furniture and rockers covered with rose chintz and full of pink flowers all summer long. It's the icing on this beautiful inn.

This is a French country inn, done in shades of mauve, celery, and ecru and stunning inside and out. Anne was a professional interior decorator, and the inn reflects her expertise. Mauve is a color I adore. The boutique is The French Rabbit, with well-dressed rabbits to greet you. Anne has wonderful taste, and the boutique is full of very nice things.

Tavern in the Green, the bar and lounge, has an upright piano and nice people who play and sing. One night when I stayed here, a playwright was in this room with a marvelous selection of music and songs. What an unexpected treat! A door from here leads out to the swimming pool and gardens. During the winter the large patio is flooded for ice skating. The inn has a large collection of skates for guests to use, and twinkling lights are hung in the trees all around the patio. In the summertime breakfast and dinner may be served out here.

There is a large fieldstone fireplace dating back to 1889 in the living room, with comfortable couches and chairs around it. Tables are provided for all sorts of games.

The rooms are magnificent, and each one is different, done in ice cream colors. Lots of canopied beds, lace, plush carpets, down pillows, and nice things on dressers and tables give the rooms an elegant atmosphere. Good towels are such an important feature to inn guests and, needless to say, they are here.

There's a new suite called Chantel's Boudoir, and I stayed in it. Done in soft greens, the king-sized bed is a beauty. There's also a fireplace, television, phone, chaise lounge, and couch. I could live in here.

Victoria's Room has a queen-sized bed with a lovely spread, a gas fireplace, a chaise lounge, air-conditioning, a television, phone, and a two-person soaking tub in a lovely large bathroom. It all overlooks the pool area.

Dining is a joy in the lovely dining room. The bishop-sleeve lace curtains and trellis alcoves create a cozy and romantic atmosphere for the glorious

food. Chilled tomato bisque with dill is excellent. Salads aren't run-of-the-mill, and entrees are creative. Grilled loin of lamb with rosemary and juniper sauce, and medallions of veal with wild mushrooms, shallots, and Madeira in a natural veal sauce are just two of the selections. Vermont lamb chops with black currant cassis and almonds are a house favorite. I chose crème brûlée for dessert. It was grand. Freshly made bread pudding with apples and hazelnuts captivated my dinner companion. Very good indeed. Breakfast is a full one, with many choices.

Affairs of the heart are wonderful up here. Rekindle the romance by having an "Enchanted Evening," an affair for the "too busy" and "too stressed." As the inn literature notes, this "intimate dinner affair is perfect for those of you who: go out to dinner a lot, cook at home a lot, need a break, are looking for a good time and romance." Also offered is the "Blooming Affair," a romantic champagne picnic lunch in the lovely gazebo and formal gardens. These affairs are offered spring, summer, and winter. Christmas, as you can imagine, is very special up here.

HOW TO GET THERE: Coming north on historic Route 7A, you will find the inn on your left in Manchester Village.

Mid-Atlantic & Chesapeake Region

by Suzi Forbes Chase

I have a friend whose husband plans their annual Valentine's Day idyll all year long. He reads literature, searches the Internet, and then presents her with a beautifully wrapped basket under the tree at Christmas that includes bubble bath, a bottle of champagne, and perhaps some new lingerie—and hints about where they will go for their retreat. But he merely heightens the anticipation by not revealing the exact location. He's a hard-charging professional coach by day, who few would suspect of harboring this romantic streak. But because his wife anticipates their time alone as much as he does, he knows his efforts will be appreciated.

For many of us romance is heightened by illusion and anticipation—the joy in a loved one's face when presented with a delightful surprise, the wonderment of sharing a sky full of brilliant stars on a crystal-clear night, the intimacy of snuggling before a crackling fire while sharing a bottle of wine. Joy, beauty, playfulness, intimacy, and delicious privacy all heighten our romantic senses.

In selecting twenty-two country inns that I consider to be most conducive to romance in the Mid-Atlantic states, I was drawn to those that encourage privacy and intimacy. My husband and I have shared some wonderfully romantic evenings at the inns I have selected. Some are sophisticated and offer elegant dining and double whirlpool tubs in the bath, while others are more remote and rustic.

Each of these inns will offer an ideal environment for romance, but we must be ready to seize the opportunity. I believe our most cherished memories begin with the simplest things—a tender look, a thoughtful gesture, a heart-felt kiss—and the rest will follow.

Agnes de Mille once said, "Then I did the simplest thing in the world. I leaned down and kissed him. And the world cracked open." I sincerely hope that as you experience the pleasures of these inns that your world will crack open with love and romance as well.

Mid-Atlantic & Chesapeake Region

Mid-Atlantic & Chesapeake Region

Numbers on map refer to towns numbered below.

The Inn at Montchanin Village
Montchanin, Delaware 19710

INNKEEPER: Brooke Johnson White; Daniel and Missy Lickle, proprietors

ADDRESS/TELEPHONE: Route 100 and Kirk Road (mailing address: P.O. Box 130); (302) 888-2133 or (800) COWBIRD; fax (302) 888-0389

E-MAIL: montchan@gte.net

WEB SITE: www.montchanin.com

ROOMS: 33, including 25 suites; all with private bath, air-conditioning, telephone, television, minirefrigerator, coffeemaker, hair dryer, porch, dataport, robe, iron, ironing board, and wet bar; 9 with fireplace, 2 with whirlpool. No smoking inn. Wheelchair accessible.

RATES: $170 to $450, double occupancy; includes full breakfast. Two-night minimum some weekends, holidays, and special events.

OPEN: All year.

FACILITIES AND ACTIVITIES: Krazy Kat's Restaurant open for dinner daily 5:30 to 10:00 P.M. (entrees $21 to $28). Nearby: museums and gardens.

*M*ontchanin is a tiny hamlet named for Anne Alexandrine de Montchanin. She was the grandmother of Eleuthère Irénée duPont, founder of the DuPont Gunpowder Company. The inn is located in a cluster of buildings built in the early 1800s to house laborers from the nearby DuPont powder mills. The complex includes several houses, a cluster of cottages, a former blacksmith shop, a schoolhouse, and a massive stone and post-and-beam barn.

The restoration is the ambitious undertaking of local preservationists Missy and Daniel Lickle. When they acquired the property, they sought an adaptive use that would preserve the quaint buildings in their original setting. They achieved this goal admirably. The entire six acres are on the National Register of Historic Places. Work continues on the inn, where the next project is to restore the massive fieldstone barn, which will eventually house the inn's guest reception room and a library where a fieldstone fireplace will offer cozy warmth.

The restoration is so true to the village's origins that even the original tiny concrete outhouses remain as garden curiosities. Privy Lane leads guests to the restaurant in the former blacksmith shop, where an elegant full breakfast is served every morning to inn guests—and it's complimentary.

The guest rooms are luxuriously furnished with antique four-poster and canopy beds, armoires, and painted blanket chests. There are chain-stitched rugs on hardwood floors, graceful moldings, and sponged walls. Nine of the units have fireplaces, and almost all have either a private garden, porch, balcony, or terrace. The beds are swathed in pretty fabrics and dressed in Frette sheets, and the marble baths have every possible luxury, including oversized whirlpool tubs in some. Look carefully and you'll see whimsical displays of Dan and Missy's cow and bird collection—in the bathroom tiles, on the bath mats, and peeking out of unexpected places throughout the rooms.

The blacksmith shop now houses Krazy Kat's Restaurant, which is setting records of its own for fine dining. One of the area's top chefs is at its helm; he designed the kitchen as well as the menu. The fanciful paintings of costumed dogs and cats that decorate the walls will delight and amuse you. You'll find such dishes as pan-roasted pork porterhouse crusted with brandy pepper and laced with caramelized pearl onions and rosemary demicream, or grilled Atlantic salmon and shrimp bouillabaisse. The restaurant is open for breakfast, lunch, and dinner.

The inn is in the Brandywine Valley, where the Wyeth family has been painting for years. It's close to Winterthur Museum and Gardens, Longwood Gardens, Brandywine River Museum, and Wilmington. Although there are no sports facilities on the premises, a golf course is located 2 miles away, and this is a terrific area for bicycling.

HOW TO GET THERE: From I–95 take the Concord Pike/Route 202 exit. Travel north on Route 202 to Route 141. Turn left onto Route 141, continuing to the Rockland Road intersection. Turn right onto Rockland Road, passing the DuPont Country Club. Continue on Rockland Road over the Brandywine River and bear left at the fork, just past the river. At the corner of Rockland Road and Route 100, turn right onto Route 100 north. Travel approximately 500 feet and turn into the entrance at Kirk Road and Route 100.

Ashby 1663 Bed and Breakfast
Easton, Maryland 21601

INNKEEPERS: Cliff Meredith and Jeanine Wagner

ADDRESS/TELEPHONE: 27448 Ashby Drive (mailing address: P.O. Box 45); (410) 822–4235 or (800) 458–3622; fax (410) 822–9288

E-MAIL: info@ashby1663.com

WEB SITE: www.ashby1663.com

ROOMS: 12 suites; all with private bath, air-conditioning, telephone, and TV; 9 with whirlpool tub, 7 with fireplace, 6 with patio or deck. No smoking inn. Children over the age of 12 welcome.

RATES: $215 to $595, double occupancy; includes full breakfast and complimentary cocktails. Two-night minimum when stay includes Saturday night from April to November.

OPEN: All year.

FACILITIES AND ACTIVITIES: On twenty-three acres; waterfront views, pool, lighted tennis court, exercise room, billiards room, dock for private boats, paddleboat, canoe. Nearby: golf courses, restaurants, antiques shops, boating, fishing, hunting, the Talbot County Historical Society, the Historic Avalon Theatre, annual waterfowl festival.

The gracious Greek Revival mansion on the banks of the Miles River was abandoned and crumbling when it was purchased by Cliff Meredith and Jeanine Wagner in 1985. The team was undaunted, however, and immediately began a restoration that virtually rebuilt the house from top to bottom. Palladian-style windows now open the living room to views of the pool, terrace, and spa with the Miles River beyond, and a graceful stairway sweeps up from the mellow heart-pine floors of the entrance hall to the second and third levels of the house.

Elegant antiques grace all the rooms, and the chairs and sofas are covered with sophisticated English prints and stripes. In the dining room an antique Waterford crystal chandelier illuminates the handsome fireplace and mahogany dining room table. The library has a marble fireplace and a bay window overlooking the garden. The screened porch has iron and wicker furniture and offers views of the formal gardens.

The guest rooms are gracious and refined. The Robert Goldsborough Suite on the second floor contains a canopy bed that's lushly skirted, flounced, and covered with a rich peach-and-green fabric. There's a fireplace and a wall of windows that overlook the pool and the bay. The marble bath,

however, is the pièce de résistance. It has a raised double whirlpool tub with a view of the bay from the floor-to-ceiling windows, as well as a fireplace, which casts a seductive glow across the room. There are five rooms in the manor house and two more in the George Goldsborough House. The inn is located on an undulating point of land that juts into the Miles River and provides a half mile of waterfront. Miles River Cottage, a new building directly on the banks of the Miles River, was completed in 1996. It contains five additional guest rooms with terrific views of the river, fireplaces, canopy beds, and whirlpool tubs. Several of the rooms have private decks.

Service at Ashby 1663 is as gracious as the decor. Every evening guests gather in the library for complimentary cocktails—an opportunity to become acquainted with one another as well as their hosts. On sunny days and warm evenings they enjoy the use of the pool and the lighted tennis court, or they may play a game of billiards, ride one of the inn's bicycles along the quiet country roads, or exorcise all hint of stress by indulging in a stint on the tanning bed, the massage machine, or the sauna machine. On the other hand, they may decide to retain the fitness regime they enjoy at home by using the treadmill, stair master, bicycles, or rowing machine in the inn's exercise room.

Breakfast is served every morning in the formal dining room or on the sunporch. In addition to fresh fruits and juices and freshly baked muffins and breads, guests may enjoy an entree of asparagus in crepes with hollandaise sauce or baked French toast with bananas and walnuts topped with maple syrup.

HOW TO GET THERE: From Washington, D.C., take Route 50 across the Chesapeake Bay Bridge and follow it to Easton. At Airport Road turn right and travel to the stop sign. Turn right again onto Goldsborough Neck Road and bear left at the fork, traveling past the NO OUTLET sign. Turn left again at the sign that reads ASHBY 1663. Continue on the paved road for ¾ mile to the B&B.

Combsberry
Oxford, Maryland 21654

INNKEEPER: Catherine Magrogan; Dr. Mahmood and Ann Shariff, proprietors

ADDRESS/TELEPHONE: 4837 Evergreen Road; (410) 226–5353; fax (410) 228–1453

WEB SITE: www.combsberry.com

ROOMS: 7, including 2 suites and 2 cottages; all with private bath, air-conditioning, and hair dryer; 5 with fireplace, 4 with whirlpool tub and/or porch or patio. No smoking inn. Children over the age of 12 welcome.

RATES: $250 to $395, double occupancy; includes full breakfast and cocktail/tea hour. Two-night minimum weekends preferred.

OPEN: All year except Thanksgiving, Christmas, and Easter.

FACILITIES AND ACTIVITIES: On nine acres; formal English garden, private dock, swimming, fishing, crabbing, paddleboat, canoe. Nearby: historic Oxford-Bellevue Ferry across Tred Avon River, Oxford Museum, Oxford Customs House, Tilghman Island Seafood Festival.

*S*ometimes, my most important bed-and-breakfast discoveries are the result of recommendations by other innkeepers. This was certainly the case with Combsberry. I was on a B&B inspection trip on the Del-MarVa Peninsula, and an innkeeper insisted that I *must* see the new inn that had just opened in Oxford. I love to be the first to report a new discovery, so I couldn't resist.

Combsberry is one of those gentle brick plantation homes tucked away off the road where the unsuspecting cannot see them. Construction of the manor house began in 1738, meaning that parts of it are 260 years old. Set among arching weeping willows and towering magnolia trees on the banks of Island Creek, the sense of tranquility is almost palpable.

Combsberry's common rooms are inviting and gracious. The living room, which still has the original wide-plank pine floors, includes elegant antiques, Oriental rugs, and English chintz fabric draped across the windows. A green-paneled library with a fireplace is reached through a wide archway painted with flowers. In front there's a tile-floored sunroom with magnificent views of the water. French doors lead to a formal garden enclosed by a tall brick wall.

The guest rooms, which are spacious, refined, and lovely, are also quite different. Were I to chose a favorite, it might be the Victoria Garden Room, which is entirely decorated in blue and white. There's blue-and-white-checked wallpaper and a blue and white rug. The wrought iron bed has a floral spread, and there are pretty English chintz curtains on the windows. Chairs and tables are in white wicker, and there are glorious views of the water from both the bedroom and the bath. A pretty door leads to the formal garden. But I also love Oxford Cottage, a private two-story cottage that has a brick terrace. In the first-floor living room, there's a fireplace; in the upstairs bedroom, there's a brass and white iron bed. A Carriage House was completed in 1997 to house a living room with a fireplace as well as two additional guest rooms. These have hand-painted furniture, whirlpool tubs in the baths, and glorious water views. Both rooms have a fireplace.

For breakfast guests have the option of dining formally in the dining room or informally in the bright country kitchen. Personally, I can't resist one of the kitchen cafe tables, set along the bay window-wall that offers views of the water. I love the omelette that Catherine prepares with crab caught at the B&B's pier. Or perhaps she'll fix her Combsberry casserole that includes hash browns, cheese, ham, and onions baked in an egg and milk sauce. In addition there will be fresh fruit and juice and sweet breads and muffins.

HOW TO GET THERE: From Washington, D.C., and Baltimore take Route 50 across the Chesapeake Bay Bridge. Stay on Route 50 to Route 322 south, the Easton Parkway. Then take Route 333 south toward Oxford and continue for 6 8/10 miles. Turn left onto Evergreen Road. Turn left again at the second driveway through the brick pillars. Drive down a long driveway to the inn.

Antrim 1844 Country Inn
Taneytown, Maryland 21787

INNKEEPERS: Richard and Dorothy Mollett

ADDRESS/TELEPHONE: 30 Trevanion Road; (410) 756–6812 or
(800) 858–1844; fax (410) 756–2744

E-MAIL: azmz94a@prodigy.com

ROOMS: 23, including 8 suites and 6 cottages; all with private bath,
air-conditioning, radio, hair dryer, desk, robes, and CD player; 18 with
whirlpool tub and fireplace; 1 with TV and VCR. Children over the age
of 12 welcome. Wheelchair accessible. No smoking, except in tavern.

RATES: $200 to $350, double occupancy; includes full breakfast, afternoon snacks, and evening hors d'oeuvres. Special packages available on
holidays. Two-night minimum if stay includes Saturday night and some
holidays.

OPEN: All year, except Christmas Eve.

FACILITIES AND ACTIVITIES: Tavern, twenty-three acres, swimming
pool, 2 Nova grass tennis courts, croquet lawn, bowling green, golf-
chipping green, volleyball, badminton, horseshoes, formal gardens.
Dinner by reservation Wednesday to Sunday (fixed price $55, higher
on holidays). Nearby: 12 miles to Gettysburg. Golf courses: Wakefield
Valley, Carroll Valley, Bear Creek.

*Y*our day unfolds gently. You might begin with a cup of fresh coffee
presented at your door by a wooden butler along with the morning
paper. It's one of those lazy days with no particular place to be or
time to be there. Perhaps you'll enjoy a game of tennis before breakfast, or a
stroll in the gardens.

You may have slumbered in the third-floor Brandon Room with its raspberry walls and green-and-raspberry canopy over the bed. You would have
admired the antique dresser and drop-leaf table, and you certainly would
have reposed in the raspberry-colored whirlpool tub while admiring the view
of the gardens and cottages on the twenty-three-acre estate grounds below—
perhaps you would have turned out the lights and basked in the glow of the
fat candles on the rim of the tub.

Other guest room options include the Boucher Suite, which has a canopy
bed facing a fireplace and two balconies, the Lamberton Room, with its
1790s canopy bed with turned posts; and the Clabaugh Room, which has a
half-tester Empire-style rosewood bed. Additional rooms with whirlpool

tubs and fireplaces are found in the Ice House, the Cottage, the Smith House, the Barn, and (opened in 1998) the Carriage House.

Eventually you go down to breakfast, which is served in a room with lacquered green walls and red drapes. You'll have fruit and juice, sweet breads and muffins, and, maybe, Belgian waffles or an omelette. Later you'll browse through the books in the library or spend an hour or two reading in one of the elegant twin parlors with their matching marble fireplace mantels or, perhaps, out on the veranda.

As the day warms you'll decide whether to take a swim in the pool; engage in a game of badminton, horseshoes, croquet, or lawn bowling; or, maybe, practice your putting on the inn's putting green. This, of course, is all merely a prelude to dinner.

Chef Sharon Ashburn has created a distinctive Antrim cuisine that marries the local regional flavors and ingredients with the delicacy of French cuisine. Even if you are unable to stay here, you should come for dinner. The setting is romantic, charming, and elegant. You might be seated in the original brick-floored smokehouse, the summer kitchen, the slave kitchen, or the

new room that also has a brick herringbone floor and looks as old as the rest. The silver and crystal will sparkle, and fresh flowers will brighten the crisp white cloths. You will appreciate the oil portraits on the walls that glow in the light of the candlestick lamps.

You will start the event at 6:30 P.M. in the inn's common rooms. You might chat quietly together or with other guests as staff persons pass hors d'oeuvres and glasses of wine. At 7:30 you will be seated. Your dinner may start with an *amusée*—on one recent visit, a squab egg served in phyllo. The next course might be a sweet potato vichyssoise with crispy caramelized pecans in the center, followed by a spinach salad with chicken livers and bacon bits and a pansy on top. Next comes a sherbet intermezzo. You may have chosen a beef filet for your entree. If so, it is tender and juicy and accompanied by a red-wine sauce, roasted potatoes, carrots, zucchini, beans, and okra. Dessert will be positively decadent. A plate of five selections is shared by two people. Among the offerings you may find a cinnamon crème brûlée, a white chocolate cheese cake, a bourbon-pecan pie, a cylinder of spun sugar filled with fresh berries, and chocolate chip ice cream.

HOW TO GET THERE: From Baltimore Beltway I–695 take exit 19 onto I–795 north. Exit onto Route 140 west to Taneytown. In town turn left onto Trevanion Road and go 150 feet to inn on right. From Frederick take I–94 north to Taneytown. Turn right at light on Route 140, proceed ½ mile, turn right at fork onto Trevanion Road. Go 150 feet to inn on right. Signs indicate where to park.

The Mainstay Inn
Cape May, New Jersey 08204

INNKEEPERS: Tom and Sue Carroll; Kathy Moore, manager

ADDRESS/TELEPHONE: 635 Columbia Avenue; (609) 884–8690

WEB SITE: www.mainstayinn.com

ROOMS: 16, including 7 suites; all with private bath; 4 suites with fireplace, whirlpool, television, telephone, snack kitchen, and VCR. One room wheelchair accessible. No smoking inn. Children 6 and older welcome in Officers' Quarters; children 12 and older welcome in main inn and cottage.

RATES: $110 to $295, double occupancy; $10 less for single; includes full breakfast, afternoon tea, and beach passes. Additional person, $20. Three-night minimum in season; two-night minimum spring and fall weekends.

OPEN: All year; reduced number of rooms mid-December to mid-March.

FACILITIES AND ACTIVITIES: Nearby: restaurants, beach, historic Cape May mansions, bicycling, bird-watching, sailing, trolley rides, state park, lighthouse museum, carriage rides.

RECOMMENDED COUNTRY INNS® TRAVELERS' CLUB BENEFIT: Stay one night, get second night free, Sunday to Thursday, end of October to end of April, excluding Thanksgiving, Christmas, and Presidents' Day week, subject to availability.

I never return to The Mainstay Inn without remembering my first visit in the 1970s. The entire B&B movement was in its infancy, but Tom and Sue Carroll had the foresight to recognize that the grand Victorian mansions of Cape May would make lovely B&Bs. They opened their first in the late 1960s, and then sold that to buy their dream "cottage" in 1971. In the almost thirty years they have owned The Mainstay, they have continuously expanded and improved the property. Along the way they added a neighboring house that they call The Cottage and a building across the street that they converted into four elegant suites called The Officers' Quarters. Their fledgling business was eventually copied by others, and there are now more than one hundred B&Bs in Cape May.

Tom and Sue are the kind of hands-on innkeepers that innkeeping used to be all about, and their B&B is a reflection of their love of history and architecture. The original inn was built as a gambling club in 1872, and much of the paneling, stained glass, and woodwork remain. Tom and Sue have added elaborate Bradbury and Bradbury wallpapers and borders to enhance the vintage feeling. I have spent many lazy afternoons in a rocking chair on the porch listening to the clip-clop of the horses hooves as they pull tourists through town. I have spent an equal amount of time up in the belvedere, where the salty sea breezes whisper through the sycamore trees.

The guest rooms are as refined and elegant as the common rooms—Bradbury and Bradbury wallpapers and borders are used, and all rooms are furnished with magnificent antiques that are true to the period. You will sleep in a Victorian walnut bed in Henry Clay, for example, and in a brass bed in the Grant Suite. In the newer Officers' Quarters, the suites are decorated with country Victorian or country pine furnishings. The living rooms contain gas fireplaces, there are private decks, and each suite has its own snack kitchen. The large, modern baths have whirlpool tubs, separate steam showers, and back-lighted stained-glass windows that cast a romantic glow throughout the room.

Except in summer, Sue prepares a sumptuous full breakfast for her guests. Generally it's served in the dining room, but we have sometimes taken our coffee out to the veranda. In summer a hearty continental breakfast is served on the veranda. Guests in the Officers' Quarters are given a continental breakfast that they can prepare themselves in their kitchen.

Don't miss afternoon tea at The Mainstay. If you are staying there, it's included in the price of your room, but if you weren't fortunate enough to book a room, you can pay a nominal fee and be taken on a tour of the inn and then enjoy tea on the veranda. You'll savor such delicacies as tea sandwiches, cheese daisies, and almond cake squares or lemon bars. Undoubtedly you'll want to leave with a copy of Sue's new cookbook, *Breakfast at Nine, Tea at Four.*

HOW TO GET THERE: From the Garden State Parkway merge onto Lafayette Street. Turn left onto Madison, right onto Columbia, to 635 on the right.

The Woolverton Inn
Stockton, New Jersey 08559

INNKEEPERS: Elizabeth and Michael Palmer

ADDRESS/TELEPHONE: 6 Woolverton Road; (609) 397–0802 or (888) AN–INN–4U; fax (609) 397–4936

E-MAIL: woolbandb@aol.com

WEB SITE: woolvertonbnb.com

ROOMS: 10, including 2 suites; all with private bath and air-conditioning; 3 with fireplace, 2 with Jacuzzi. No smoking inn. Wheelchair accessible. Children over the age of 12 welcome.

RATES: $90 to $210, double occupancy, includes full breakfast and afternoon refreshments. Two-night minimum weekends; three-night minimum holiday weekends.

OPEN: All year.

FACILITIES AND ACTIVITIES: Located on ten acres with croquet lawn, hiking trails, and horseshoes pit on property. Nearby: Delaware River towpath and park ½ mile, canoeing, rafting, historical sites, boutiques, antiques shops.

BUSINESS TRAVEL: Fax and telephone available, early breakfast and late check-in, meeting room and services.

RECOMMENDED COUNTRY INNS® TRAVELERS' CLUB BENEFIT: Stay two nights, get third night free, Monday to Thursday.

*I*n the 1980s The Woolverton Inn was my special secret retreat. I would come on summer afternoons, to sit either on the upstairs porch or on the flagstone veranda, and write. In the evening after dinner, I would play the piano or complete a jigsaw puzzle into the wee hours of the morning. But then the innkeeper moved away and it just wasn't the same.

Therefore, it was with a keen sense of hope that I visited The Woolverton Inn again in late 1994, when I learned that it had been purchased by Elizabeth and Michael Palmer, an enthusiastic couple who had great plans for the majestic, 1792 stone manor house. By early 1996 the renovations were complete, and I found that this magnificent manor house once again met—and exceeded—my expectations. Private baths have been added to every guest room, and two rooms even have two-person Jacuzzis. There are canopy beds,

olive Metcalf

lush fabrics, fireplaces in two rooms, and walls charmingly handpainted with flowers or pastoral scenes. The guest rooms are named for people who have had a connection to the house. My favorite is Amelia's Garden, which has a four-poster cherry bed with a fishnet canopy, a pretty sitting room, and an elegant bath with pink walls and a lovely walnut dresser outfitted with a sink.

Downstairs, in the living room, the piano remains in the corner, and the game table by the window is just waiting for a couple to put a jigsaw puzzle together. The antique furniture is elegantly upholstered, oil paintings embellish the walls, and a fire glows in the hearth in cool weather. On the wicker-filled side porch, guests relax with a book and enjoy the gardens, perhaps while enjoying tea, coffee, or lemonade with cookies, cheese, and fruit, which are offered every afternoon.

A full gourmet breakfast is served in the formal dining room. Elizabeth might prepare a baked apple or poached pear for the fruit course and perhaps an entree of blueberry johnnycakes or creamy scrambled eggs with asparagus and chives.

The inn is located on ten acres. Sheep graze in a meadow. There are a stone spring house, a picturesque barn that may one day be restored, and a carriage house with two guest rooms. Hiking trails meander about, and there's a croquet lawn and a horseshoes pit. For those of us who love country inns with a deep-felt passion, we can add another to our collection of favorites.

HOW TO GET THERE: From New York take the New Jersey Turnpike south to exit 14 and follow I–78 west to exit 29. Follow I–287 south to Route 202 south and take the second Lambertville exit onto Route 20, traveling north to Stockton. Travel through the village to the fork. Veer right onto Route 523 and go for $^2/_{10}$ mile. Turn left onto Woolverton Road. The inn is reached along the second driveway on the right.

Old Drovers Inn
Dover Plains, New York 12522

INNKEEPERS: Alice Pitcher and Kemper Peacock

ADDRESS/TELEPHONE: Old Route 22 (mailing address: P.O. Box 100); (914) 832-9311; fax (914) 832-6356

E-MAIL: Old-Drovers-Inn@juno.com

WEB SITE: www.olddroversinn.com

ROOMS: 4; all with private bath and air-conditioning; 3 with fireplace. Pets by prior approval. Children over the age of 12 welcome. Smoking permitted.

RATES: $350 to $450, weekends per couple, includes full breakfast and dinner; $175 to $250, double occupancy, midweek; continental breakfast. Two-night minimum if Saturday stay included.

OPEN: All year, except two weeks in January.

FACILITIES AND ACTIVITIES: On twelve acres. Dinner Thursday through Tuesday; Saturday, Sunday, and holidays served from noon (entrees: $17 to $35). Nearby: Hyde Park, golf courses, horseback riding, antiquing, country drives, fairs and festivals.

*E*lizabeth Taylor and Richard Burton reserved the entire inn and its discreet staff for some secluded and romantic private time when they finished filming *Cleopatra*. After opening night of *Phantom of the Opera*, Andrew Lloyd Weber and Sarah Brightman didn't reserve the entire inn, but they did retreat to the Meeting Room, with its vaulted ceiling and fireplace, probably with a bottle of champagne and a privately served dinner to celebrate. Recently Barbra Streisand received some much-needed rest and relaxation when she stayed in the Cherry Room. Another guest, the Marquis de Lafayette, was likely content with more humble accommodations at the inn.

Today as you enter the low-slung doorway from the street of this inn that's steeped with history and pass under the ancient beamed ceiling, dark with age and smoke, you might pull up a stool to the old oak bar and savor the warmth from the mammoth stone fireplace. Listen carefully. History is preserved so thoroughly at the Old Drovers Inn that you can almost hear the banter of the eighteenth-century drovers and their rough-tongued sidekicks. The more-gentlemanly drovers, or cattle owners, were accustomed to driving their cattle to market in New York along this road, timing their journey to stop here for drink, refreshment, gambling, and sleep. The anklebeaters, the dust-covered cowboys who urged the cattle onward, were lucky to receive a bed of straw in the stables.

Alice Pitcher and Kemper Peacock have so perfectly preserved the inn and its unique atmosphere that few places on the East Coast offer such elegant accommodations in such a thoroughly historic setting. Dinner guests enter the inn just as their rowdy predecessors did, on the ground floor, proceeding into the intimate dining room by passing the bar, where Charlie Wilbur will greet them by name and deliver their favorite drink to the table almost before they have time to sit down. Beware! Mixed drinks are served in double portions here. A waiter will bring a large blackboard menu to the table and hang it from a hook on a beam. You may wish to start with the hearty cheddar cheese soup, a specialty of the house. I must say that I love everything on the

menu, but the browned turkey hash with mustard sauce is a specialty, as is the double cut rack of lamb chops with Charlie's tomato chutney.

There are only four guest rooms, but they are all special—all but one has a working fireplace—and they are decorated with English chintz fabrics, canopy beds, and antique dressers, tables, and chests. They sometimes have quirky elements as well. The tiny bath in one requires that you peek around the corner to shave. The largest is the Meeting Room. It was originally the inn's ballroom and later became the village meeting hall.

Overnight guests park behind the inn and enter on the second floor, where the wide entry hall includes a sitting area before a fireplace. You will probably be greeted by one or all of Alice's adorable Yorkshire terriers: Gordon Bennett, Goodness Gracious, or Jeepers Creepers. A remarkable feature of this incredible inn is that those of us who love to travel with our pets are welcome to bring them here with us.

Other common rooms include a paneled parlor furnished with antique sofas and chairs and a cozy library decorated with bright English chintz and including a fireplace and a multitude of books. There's a lovely shell corner cabinet whose twin is now featured in the American Wing of the Metropolitan Museum of Art. Breakfast is served in the Federal Room, a room lined with historical murals of the area, painted in the style of the Hudson River School of painters by Edward Paine in 1942.

HOW TO GET THERE: From New York City take I–684 to Brewster, then take Route 22 north. On Route 22 a sign for the inn is 3 miles south of Dover Plains. Turn east and drive ½ mile. Inn is on the right. Dinner guests enter on the ground floor; overnight guests park in back and enter on the second floor.

J. Harper Poor Cottage
East Hampton, New York 11937

INNKEEPERS: Gary and Rita Reiswig

ADDRESS/TELEPHONE: 181 Main Street; (516) 324–4081; fax (516) 329–5931

E-MAIL: info@jharperpoor.com

WEB SITE: www.jharperpoor.com

ROOMS: 5; all with private bath, telephone, television, VCR, desk, and robes; 4 with fireplace, 3 with whirlpool tub, 1 with balcony. Radio, minirefrigerator, hair dryer, fax, CD player, iron, and ironing board available. No smoking inn.

RATES: $195 to $450, double occupancy; includes full breakfast. Three-night minimum in July and August, four-night minimum holiday weekends, two-night minimum weekends rest of year.

OPEN: All year.

FACILITIES AND ACTIVITIES: On one acre with beautiful sunken gardens; parking, beach passes, and towels provided; wine and a fully stocked bar. Nearby: Guild Hall and John Drew Theater, ocean beaches, tennis, golfing, fishing.

*T*he J. Harper Poor Cottage is one of the most unique buildings in East Hampton, although that fact is not readily apparent from the street, as it's hidden away behind a buff-colored stucco wall. The original section, a saltbox, dates to the early eighteenth century. You can still see its hand-hewn oak beams and cooking fireplace in the breakfast room. It began to take on its distinctive English manor house appearance in 1885 when it was enlarged and the mullioned windows and the carved lintel angels were added to the entrance. In 1900 the house was purchased by James Harper Poor, who hired English architect Joseph Greenleaf Thorp to give it an Arts and Crafts appearance. Current owners Gary and Rita Reiswig have impeccably restored the house to this period.

Comfortable, inviting, restful, and gracious, this inn has developed through its various incarnations from the time the Reiswigs first purchased it, and it is with tremendous pride that I highly recommend it now. You enter the spacious entry hall and feel as though you have been transported into an elegant early twentieth-century home. A library to the left holds an oak library table and chairs, and along the wall are several thousand volumes neatly arranged in oak book-cases. To the right is the break-fast room, which has French doors opening to a wisteria-covered loggia, raised-panel pine walls, and a woodstove. Beyond the library the massive living room has a plaster-relief ceiling, oak-paneled walls, an oak window seat in the bay window, and a huge fireplace with a floor-to-ceiling tile sur-round. William Morris–design

linen covers the chairs and is mirrored by a hand-blocked paper border.

The guest rooms are decorated with as much flair as the common rooms, and all are romantic—all but one have a working fireplace. I believe my favorite is Number 13, which has a little balcony overlooking the village green. It has hand-hewn oak beams and paneled walls. There's an iron bed with a matelassé spread, an antique oak secretary with books filling the shelves, and a fabulous bath. The largest room is Number 11, which has both a bedroom (with a wonderful Arts and Crafts bed) and a sitting area—decorated in a William Morris–inspired green floral pattern that seems to bring the lovely garden right inside the room. There's a window seat by the mullioned windows for viewing the gardens. The bathroom is positively romantic. It has a whirlpool tub-for-two, a separate shower, and pedestal sinks.

You may relax with a glass of wine in the living room or out on the courtyard while you admire the gardens after you arrive, allowing the pressures of the drive to melt away. You will certainly go to one of the fine local restaurants for dinner. If it's a balmy summer day, you will have breakfast the next morning on the courtyard. You will start with coffee, juices, and breakfast breads. For an entree, you might be served a frittata, an omelette, or, perhaps, pancakes.

HOW TO GET THERE: From New York City take I–495 (Long Island Expressway) east to exit 70 (Manorville). At the stop sign turn right (south) and follow County Road 111 to its end at Route 27 (Sunrise Highway). Follow Route 27 east about 30 miles to East Hampton. At the traffic light by the pond, turn left. You are now on Main Street. The inn is on the left.

Rose Inn
Ithaca, New York 14851

INNKEEPERS: Charles and Sherry Rosemann

ADDRESS/TELEPHONE: Route 34N (mailing address: P.O. Box 6576); (607) 533–7905; fax (607) 533–7908

E-MAIL: roseinn@clarityconnect.com

ROOMS: 15, including 5 suites; all with private bath, air-conditioning, telephone, radio, robes, and hair dryer; 10 with iron and ironing board, 6 with desk, 4 with whirlpool tub, 2 with fireplace. No smoking inn. Children over the age of 10 welcome.

RATES: $110 to $185 rooms, $185 to $275 suites, plus 15 percent gratuity and 11 percent tax, double occupancy; includes full breakfast. Extra person in room, $25. Two-night minimum April to November if stay includes Saturday.

OPEN: All year.

FACILITIES AND ACTIVITIES: Dinner Tuesday to Saturday (prix fixe $55, 4-course). Wine, gratuity and tax extra. Carriage House restaurant serving dinner Friday and Saturday nights (entrees $17 to $23) with live jazz entertainment. Seventeen acres with fishing pond, apple orchard, rose garden. Nearby: winery tours, ski Greek Peak, lake mailboat tours, bicycling, cultural events, Cornell University.

RECOMMENDED COUNTRY INNS® TRAVELERS' CLUB BENEFIT: 25 percent discount, Monday to Thursday.

When I think of romantic inns, the Rose Inn often comes to mind first. For one thing Charles and Sherry Rosemann are friendly and solicitous about their guests needs, but they are also absolutely serious and professional about their inn. Charles has managed hotels in Europe and the United States, and Sherry is a professional interior designer. Together they're an unbeatable team who know just what to do to make every guest's stay memorable.

I love to wake in the Honeymoon Suite (you can stay here even if you're re-creating the mood) to watch the sun rise across the fields—there were two deer one morning—and to hear the birds trilling as I gaze through the Palladian windows. It's a stunning room—all decorated by Sherry in beige; bold chocolate brown; rich, warm caramel; and gray. The bed has an ivory tapestry padded headboard, and the linens are positively luxurious in beige and brown with black-and-white tattersall sheets. You can sit in the two-person whirlpool tub in front of the Palladian windows late at night, with candles burning while you watch the flames from the fireplace. In the morning you can take a shower in the bath that is done all in gray marble. Each of the rooms is distinctive. There isn't a single one that you won't be happy with.

Don't even think of eating elsewhere. Dress in your finest, and plan for a leisurely and fabulous dinner, hopefully in the company of a loved one. The dining rooms occupy a series of parlors that are exquisitely restored to the elegance they knew when the mansion was first built. Pause to take it all in and you will be rewarded with views of wonderful antiques, such as a corner cabinet hand-painted with flowers and scrolls and filled with antique silver and china. Needlepoint carpets accent the polished parquet pine floors.

Dinner is served on gold-rimmed china, often with a rose motif. You place your order for the appetizer and entree when you make your reservation. Ken Atlas is a fabulous chef. One meal started with a "Bounty of Mushrooms," an artful mélange of mushrooms and herbs in a puff pastry topped with melted brie. The salad was as artistic as the appetizer—various vegetables were presented in cups of radicchio. I had ordered the honey almond duck for my entree, and it was moist and lovely.

You should definitely spend time meandering about the seventeen-acre property. Sit awhile in the 8,000-square-foot formal garden with its wedding chapel; pluck an apple from one of the trees in the orchard if the season is right, or pick berries from the raspberry patch. Sit in the rose garden to admire the varieties. Charles creates terrific jams and jellies from his bountiful gardens that can be purchased in the gift shop.

An 1850s carriage house across the drive serves as a conference room during the week. On weekends it becomes the Carriage House restaurant, where casual dining is accompanied by live jazz.

HOW TO GET THERE: From I–90 (New York State Thruway) take exit 40 to Route 34 south and continue for approximately 36 miles. The inn is on the left, about 10 miles north of Ithaca. From Ithaca head north on Route 34 and travel 6 miles to the intersection with a flashing red light. Turn right and continue for ½ mile. At the fork in the road go left (onto Route 34, *not* Route 34B). The inn is 3½ miles farther on the right.

Lake Placid Lodge
Lake Placid, New York 12940

INNKEEPERS: Christie and David Garrett; Kathryn Kincannon, managing director

ADDRESS/TELEPHONE: Whiteface Inn Road (mailing address P.O. Box 550); (518) 523–2700; fax (518) 523–1124

E-MAIL: info@lakeplacidlodge.com

WEB SITE: www.lakeplacidlodge.com

ROOMS: 37, including 5 suites and 15 cabins; all with private bath, air-conditioning, and telephone with dataport; 35 with private deck or patio, 17 with fireplace. Children welcome. Pets permitted in 2 rooms at $50 per day. Wheelchair access. No smoking inn.

RATES: $225 to $650, double occupancy; meals extra. Two-night minimum weekends; three-night minimum holidays.

OPEN: Year-round.

FACILITIES AND ACTIVITIES: Restaurant serving breakfast, lunch (entrees $14 to $19) and dinner (entrees $24 to $31); pub with lighter menu; room service. Championship 18-hole golf course, four tennis courts, hiking trails, sandy lakeside beach, marina, canoes, fishing boats, paddleboats, Sunfish, open-deck sightseeing barge, mountain bikes, cross-country ski touring center in winter. Nearby: downhill skiing, ice skating, hunting.

*I*t was a sunny October afternoon when we arrived. We immediately fetched a glass of wine from the cozy bar and retired to Hawkeye, our generous two-level retreat, to watch the sunset from our upper deck. As the sun slid behind Whiteface Mountain, it cast its dark reflection in the waters as we watched the streaking sky change from orange and fuschia to the palest pink. It was then that I realized I could happily stay right here and write for the rest of my life.

This former 1882 Adirondack camp was renovated and opened to guests in 1994. True to its origins, it has a log exterior, and its decks are framed by arching unpeeled birch branches. The guest rooms have beds made of twisted birch trees and walls made of logs, bark, and bead-board panels. There are twig furniture and sofas and chairs dressed in bright patterns.

Most rooms have stone fireplaces with log mantels, and several, including Hawkeye, have two fireplaces. Six buildings are scattered about the grounds, each containing several rooms or suites. Even the smallest rooms on the ground floor of the main lodge seem spacious, and they have their own private patios, with terrific views of the lake.

After we watched the evening spectacle, Managing Director Kathryn Kincannon, full of energy and enthusiasm, escorted me through the inn's common rooms, where some guests were playing billiards and others were completing a jigsaw puzzle, and then down to the marina to see the fleet of restored boats. She pointed out a nature trail that leads past trees labeled with identifying tags. We walked to the boat dock, where several couples were just returning from the sunset cocktail cruise on the inn's open-deck sightseeing barge.

It was warm enough at night to eat on the restaurant deck, romantically lighted by flickering candles. Following a dinner of confit of duck leg with sautéed potatoes and foie gras, and deliciously ending with a summer pudding with raspberries, we returned to our room to contemplate the difficult decision before us: Should we take a relaxing soak in the two-person tub; wrap ourselves against the evening chill and sit on the deck awhile longer, listening to the night sounds; or light the fire in one of the massive stone fireplaces? Reluctant to spoil the mood of this amorous place, we chose the latter and lingered with a port before snuggling into the luxurious featherbed, knowing we would be warm enough to leave the windows open all night as we listened to the loons call across the water.

Bright and early in the morning, as the sun was rising, and with the heavy scent of pine permeating the room, I arose to join Kathryn on the boat deck for tai chi, and my companion did his morning jog around the golf course. We left feeling relaxed, rested, and renewed.

HOW TO GET THERE: From I–87 take exit 30. Travel northwest on Route 73 for 30 miles to Lake Placid. In the village take Route 86 for 1½ miles toward Saranac Lake. At the top of the hill, turn right onto Whiteface Inn Road. Follow it for 1½ miles and turn right at the LAKE PLACID LODGE sign. Travel through the golf course to the lodge.

The Vagabond Inn
Naples, New York 14512

INNKEEPERS: Celeste Stanhope-Wiley and Mica Pierce

ADDRESS/TELEPHONE: 3300 Sliter Road; (716) 554–6271

ROOMS: 5, including 3 suites; all with private bath, television, VCR, minirefrigerator, and coffeemaker; 4 with fireplace and whirlpool tub, 3 with patio or deck. No smoking inn. Children over the age of 12 welcome.

RATES: $115 to $200, double occupancy; includes full breakfast.

OPEN: All year.

FACILITIES AND ACTIVITIES: On sixty-five acres with hiking and cross-country ski trails, a 9-hole golf course, swimming pool, and gardens. Nearby: numerous wineries, Bristol Valley Playhouse, fishing, and boating on Canandaigua Lake.

We wound up and up and up into the Bristol Mountains above Canandaigua Lake until we felt we could touch the sun. It was a hot, clear day, and as we climbed above the vineyards, the views got better and better. Lured by one of the most beautiful brochures I've seen and one that promised "serenity" on a mountaintop where "peace, elegance, and romance (will) stir the soul," I was on a mission.

I was not disappointed by all the grand statements, for this truly is a unique inn. The setting is spectacular, and when you walk into the gray contemporary board-and-batten house, the panoramic view from the 60-foot Great Room is of more mountains beyond the gardens, a nine-hole golf course, and a swimming pool. The Great Room is anchored at both ends by massive fieldstone fireplaces, and there are numerous selections of books to curl up with in the leather sofa. You will find the fabulous gift items that cover tables, counters, and windowsills irresistible. There's a vast array of blown glass dishes filled with potpourri, wind chimes, candles, hand-cast steel trays from Mexico, and a huge selection of fine-art jewelry. Celeste Stanhope-Wiley is a world traveler, and she brings back treasures for her shop wherever she goes.

There are five guest rooms, and each is beautifully designed with its occupant's ultimate comfort in mind. The Bristol includes a gas stove and a bed with a fishnet canopy. The fabulous bath has a raised redwood whirlpool tub with wonderful views of the mountains, a separate dining porch, and a sundeck. My favorite, however, is the grotto-like room named The Lodge. It has a stone floor, fieldstone walls, and a massive river-rock fireplace. The huge pine bed is stenciled with a tulip design, there are oversized boxed beams, and the "bathing chamber" includes a private hot tub. (Guests can also reserve an outside hot tub.)

Celeste prepares a full and delicious breakfast for her guests, and she arranges a flexible time. She has also thoughtfully provided a full kitchen. She has learned that once her guests return in the evening, they are so mesmerized by the setting that they often prefer to eat in. She suggests that they bring selections from the gourmet shops and wineries nearby; she provides everything else. She has more than 400 videos, and she finds that her guests often snuggle in before their VCR to watch a movie.

HOW TO GET THERE: From I–90 (New York State Thruway) take exit 42. Turn right and then right again onto Route 96 north. Watch for the Log Cabin Tavern on the right. Just beyond take County Road 6 (on the left) to Routes 5 and 20. Turn right (east) onto Routes 5 and 20 and then turn left (south) onto Route 14A. Stay on Route 14A until you reach Route 245. Bear right onto Route 245 and stay on this for about 20 miles to Middlesex. Turn left in Middlesex onto Route 364 and go uphill for $1/2$ mile to Shay Road. Turn right onto Shay Road and continue for $4^{2}/_{10}$ miles to Sliter Road, which will be on the left. Take Sliter Road to The Vagabond Inn (the last $3/_{10}$ mile will be on gravel).

Old Chatham Sheepherding Company Inn
Old Chatham, New York 12136

INNKEEPERS: George Shattuck III and Melissa Kelly; Nancy and Tom Clark, proprietors

ADDRESS/TELEPHONE: 99 Shaker Museum Road; (518) 794–9774; fax (518) 794–9779

E-MAIL: oldsheepinn@worldnet.att.net

WEB SITE: www.oldsheepinn.com

ROOMS: 14, including 9 suites; all with private bath, air-conditioning, telephone, hair dryer, and robes; 9 with private porch, 6 with fireplace, 2 with whirlpool tub. Children under 12 welcome with prior arrangements. No smoking inn.

RATES: $185 to $525, double occupancy; includes full breakfast every day except Sunday, when a continental breakfast is served. Two-night minimum weekends May to November; three-night minimum holiday weekends.

OPEN: All year except January.

FACILITIES AND ACTIVITIES: Restaurant serving dinner Wednesday to Monday (entrees $18 to $25) and Sunday brunch; patio dining in summer. Walking and hiking on 500 acres; seminars and events throughout the year, ranging from sheep-shearing demonstrations to cooking classes and wine dinners; tennis court, bicycles and cross-country skis available, fishing in Kinderhook Creek on property. Do not miss the Shaker Museum across the street from the inn. Nearby: Mac-Haydn Theater in Chatham features Broadway musicals in summer.

*I*s this heaven or am I merely dreaming? We are sitting in a wicker rocker on our private porch in the Suffolk Room looking beyond the sunken garden with its fountain to the lush green pastures brimming with sheep. The quiet is punctuated occasionally by a lamb bleating for its mother, but otherwise the air is still. This will always be my favorite memory of the Old Chatham Sheepherding Company Inn—this and the extraordinary cuisine, that is.

"I'm just a farmer at heart," owner Tom Clark laughed one night in the relaxed but sophisticated living room of the inn, as he tried to describe how he and his wife, Nancy, created their unique inn and its unusual by-products.

"From the time I raised and exhibited three sheep at the local Dutchess County Fair," he went on to say, "I've had an interest in sheep."

This interest in sheep has led the couple to create an entirely new American business. Not only does the inn offer overnight lodging and a fine-dining restaurant, but on their 500-acre farm, the Clarks also raise sheep that are producing milk used for cheese, yogurt, ice cream, and other products. One morning my companion and I rose early to walk down to the Shaker-style sheep barn to watch the 6:30 A.M. milking and to pet the lambs. The operation is as modern and as interesting as a large-scale dairy operation.

The inn is gracious and charming—but that's not surprising, since Nancy is an interior designer and also an artist. Her luminous watercolors decorate several guest rooms. Fine antiques are liberally combined with unusual new furnishings, and elegant fabrics cover chairs, love seats, and beds. There are carved four-poster beds padded with fluffy lamb's-wool cushions. A nearby cottage contains two suites that are perfect in every detail. The masculine Cotswold Suite has a high four-poster bed, a brick fireplace, and a private deck; the Hampshire Suite is charmingly done in shades of pink and yellow. There are two more suites in a new barn and one suite in the carriage house. The inn is a member of the prestigious Relais & Chateaux.

As elegant as the inn appears, however, innkeeper George Shattuck best described the casual atmosphere when he said, "We want guests to feel comfortable. We know we've achieved our goal when they come to breakfast in their terry robes," and he swears it's actually happened.

The dining room is presided over by Executive Chef Melissa Kelly, a graduate of the Culinary Institute of America and the protégée of such acclaimed chefs as Larry Forgione and Alice Waters. Her rack of lamb was exquisite, as was the grilled ahi tuna. There's a kitchen garden and greenhouse from which she collects her herbs and vegetables every day, but she is noted for her distinctive new cuisine using sheep's milk instead of cow's or goat's. She serves a sheep's-milk yogurt with breakfast every morning and often has a lovely ice cream on the dinner dessert menu. There's also a separate bakery and an impressive gift shop in the carriage house.

The manor house was originally the home of John S. Williams, Sr., whose interest in Shaker life was piqued by his home's proximity to several major

Shaker communities. He began collecting examples of Shaker artifacts and eventually opened a museum across the street from his home. The museum contains one of the finest collections of Shaker-made articles in the world.

HOW TO GET THERE: From New York City take the Taconic Parkway north to the exit for Route 295 (the last exit before the end of the parkway). Turn left at the end of the exit ramp and, at the following intersection, turn right onto Route 295 east. Follow Route 295 for 2½ miles into East Chatham. Turn left onto the Albany Turnpike at the sign for Old Chatham and follow this for 3 miles into the center of Old Chatham. After passing the general store turn left onto Route 13 and follow this for 1 mile. Bear right onto Shaker Museum Road and follow this for ½ mile to the inn, which is on the left.

Lakehouse Inn . . . On Golden Pond
Stanfordville, New York 12581

INNKEEPERS: Judy and Richard Kohler

ADDRESS/TELEPHONE: Shelly Hill Road; (914) 266–8093; fax (914) 266–4051

E-MAIL: judy@lakehouseinn.com

WEB SITE: www.lakehouseinn.com

ROOMS: 7; all with private bath, air-conditioning, telephone, television, VCR, stereo, CD player, minirefrigerator, wet bar, coffeemaker, balcony or deck, fireplace, and Jacuzzi. VCR and CD libraries in each room. No smoking inn. Children welcome in The Boathouse.

RATES: $350 to $550, double occupancy; includes full breakfast. Two-night minimum some weekends; three-night minimum holiday weekends.

OPEN: All year.

FACILITIES AND ACTIVITIES: On twenty-two acres; rowboats, paddleboats, hiking. Nearby: historic Hyde Park home of Franklin Roosevelt, Wilderstein, Montgomery Place.

RECOMMENDED COUNTRY INNS® TRAVELERS' CLUB BENEFIT: Stay two nights, get third night free; Monday to Thursday.

*J*udy and Richard Kohler owned a Victorian gingerbread house that they called the Village Victorian Inn in Rhinebeck for many years, but when they built this contemporary home overlooking tiny Golden Pond in 1991, they created a thoroughly sophisticated and elegant retreat, as different from the fussy Victorian as Jekyll is from Hyde.

At first sight the cedar-sided house appears modest and unremarkable; even when we walked along the flying-bridge entrance to the house, we were unprepared for the gracious and urbane interior. The house envelops its guests in country charm but also offers luxurious and spacious private retreats. For a total getaway from the fast-paced city, I can't imagine a more relaxing sanctuary.

The living room is decorated with flair in gentle earth tones. The vaulted, rough-sawn pine ceiling and the wall of view windows toward the lake give the room a warm, inviting glow. It's furnished with antiques, Oriental rugs on oak floors, twig furniture, comfortable sofas, piles of magazines and books, and an ornately carved oak English bar on which Victorian flow blue

china is displayed. It's surrounded by a wraparound deck overlooking the lake.

Lakehouse Inn is the ultimate romantic retreat. The Casablanca Suite, for example, has its own fireplace, laid with logs and ready to be lighted, and a private deck. There's a pink damask sofa on which to watch the flames with a loved one while sipping a glass of wine chilled in the refrigerator.

The canopy bed is swathed in lace. A television, VCR, and CD player hide in a pine armoire. In the bath a Jacuzzi for two has a serene view and is surrounded by a lip holding an array of fat candles.

The equally spacious Master Suite, located downstairs, has a private deck offering a view of the lake. Oriental rugs cover oak floors, another lace canopy decorates the bed, fat shutters shield the windows, and the pink-tile bath has another Jacuzzi. Each of the rooms is so large and so well equipped that it's possible to spend an entire weekend in the room and never feel claustrophobic. Two new rooms were added in 1997 in a building across the lake called The Boathouse.

Every possible amenity is provided. As Judy explained, "We just want our guests to be comfortable. We're too far from a town for them to run out for a soft drink, so we provide all of that in the room. We have soft drinks, wine, cookies, appetizers such as smoked salmon, truffles, and even Baby Watson cheesecakes in the refrigerator in case someone has a late-night sweet-tooth craving."

In the morning our breakfast was delivered to our room in a covered basket. One day it included an individual quiche with fresh fruit and breads. Another day we had cheese blintzes and chicken Chardonnay.

If guests do venture forth, they will find rowboats and paddleboats for use on the lake, hammocks, trails through the twenty-two-acre property, and a VCR library that includes almost 150 selections. Historic mansions, local wineries, and superb restaurants are located nearby.

HOW TO GET THERE: From New York City take the Henry Hudson Parkway north to the Saw Mill River Parkway, and then travel north on the Taconic Parkway to the Rhinebeck/Route 199 exit. Turn right onto Route 199 and go ½ mile. Take the first right onto Route 53 (South Road). Go 3½ miles. Turn right onto Shelly Hill Road and go exactly 9/10 mile. Turn into paved driveway. The Lakehouse Inn is at the end of the road.

Glendorn, A Lodge in the Country
Bradford, Pennsylvania 16701

PROPRIETORS: The Dorn Family; Linda and Gene Spinner, managers

ADDRESS/TELEPHONE: 1032 West Corydon Street; (814) 362–6511 or for reservations (800) 843–8568; fax (814) 368–9923

E-MAIL: glendorn@penn.com

WEB SITE: www.glendorn.com

ROOMS: 10, including 2 suites and 6 cabins; all with private bath, telephone with dataport, television, radio, hair dryer, CD player, robes, iron, and ironing board; 9 with desk, 8 with fireplace and/or patio or porch, 6 with minirefrigerator and coffeemaker, 3 with VCR (available for other rooms on request), 2 with air-conditioning. Children over the age of 12 welcome. Smoking permitted.

RATES: $475 to $645, double occupancy; includes all meals and recreational activities. Two-night minimum for cabins throughout the week and for all rooms on weekends. Three-night minimum some holidays.

OPEN: February to New Year's Day.

FACILITIES AND ACTIVITIES: Tennis, skeet and trap shooting, canoes, fishing, bicycling, swimming, hiking, cross-country skiing, snowshoeing, billiards and pool. Massages and facials arranged by appointment. Nearby: golf, downhill skiing, the Allegheny National Forest.

*I*magine yourself on the private porch of a secluded stone cabin tucked away among stands of hemlock and maple. In the hush of this misty morning, you've already watched several deer graze on the lawn, and you scarcely breathed when you saw a red fox dart from the woods to race across the clearing. A family of rabbits is still nibbling on the flowers in the beds. Just beyond a stone bridge crosses a gentle stream, and you believe you saw several trout hugging the shady waters under the overhanging bank. It's this seamless communication with nature that we experienced on our visit to Glendorn.

Once the family retreat of the Dorn family, founders of Forest Oil Corporation, the family converted their 1,280-acre estate into a country inn in 1995. Clayton Glenville Dorn began building the complex in 1929 with the construction of the Big House, a remarkable all-red-wood structure that contains a 27-by-45-foot great room with a 20-foot-high cathedral ceiling and a massive two-story sandstone fireplace. The dining room is now located at the end opposite the fireplace. Additional cabins with fireplaces (one even has three fireplaces) were added for family members over the years. These and the Big House now contain guest rooms.

The guest rooms at Glendorn are far from ordinary. Reminiscent of the style that the Dorns enjoyed in the 1930s and 1940s, they are spacious and elegant. They feature butternut- or chestnut-paneled walls; oil paintings; and beds, chairs, and sofas covered in floral prints and checks. The rich, warm woods give the rooms a soft glow, and even in the Big House, most have stone fireplaces. We loved the Dorn Suite in the Big House, which has a fireplace in both the living room and the bedroom as well as a private sunroom. We had both a tub and a shower in the bath.

All meals are included in the room price, as is the use of all the recreational facilities, which are extensive. Indeed, it would take weeks to sample them all. There are fishing streams, three stocked lakes for fishing, 20 miles of marked trails for hiking and cross-country skiing with promontories offering romantic picnic sites with views (the inn will pack a lunch), three tennis courts, skeet and trap shooting (guns, clay pigeons, and instruction provided), canoes, and bicycles; a gymnasium with a NordicTrack, vertical ascent climber, weights, a treadmill, and a half-basketball court; a 60-foot outdoor swimming pool, snowshoeing, and a game room with billiards and pool.

Few places in America offer an escape from the workaday pressures in such a serene setting. The Dorns have long known that their retreat offered a unique, environmentally sensitive sanctuary that had an ability to restore the spirit and renew the psyche. Now we are able to share it.

HOW TO GET THERE: From I–80 take exit 16 onto Route 219 at DuBois. Go north on Route 219 for 69 miles to Bradford. At South Avenue intersection, follow South Avenue to Corydon Street. Turn left onto Corydon. Travel for 4³⁄₁₀ miles to the Glendorn gate, which is just after a bright red barn. The complex is 1½ miles farther on a private paved road.

Whitewing Farm Bed & Breakfast
West Chester, Pennsylvania 19382

INNKEEPERS: Wanda and Ed DeSeta

ADDRESS/TELEPHONE: 370 Valley Road; (610) 388–2664; fax (610) 388–3650

ROOMS: 9, including 2 suites; all with private bath, air-conditioning, television, and radio; 2 with porch or patio and/or fireplace. Wheelchair accessible. No smoking inn.

RATES: $120 to $215, double occupancy, including full breakfast and afternoon tea. Two-night minimum weekends.

OPEN: All year except two weeks in February.

FACILITIES AND ACTIVITIES: On forty-three acres with extensive gardens including ponds, greenhouses, rose garden; tennis court, ten-hole chip-and-putt golf course, swimming pool, and Jacuzzi. Nearby: Longwood Gardens; Winterthur Museum, Gardens, and Library; Brandywine River Museum; Hagley Museum; Nemours.

"We'd never even stayed in a country inn ourselves when we decided to open one," laughed Wanda DeSeta. The gregarious couple must be possessed with an innate sense of hospitality then, because they obviously knew exactly what to do. This is one of the most gracious country inns I've ever stayed in. It's beautifully decorated, located in a quiet country setting in the Brandywine Valley with streams, ponds, gardens, and outbuildings, and yet it's utterly comfortable and unpretentious— just like the innkeepers.

We entered the spacious 1700s Pennsylvania farm house through the bright and welcoming kitchen. The aroma of a wonderful cake that was still warm from the oven wafted through the open door. It's obvious that the kitchen is where Wanda presides—unless she's in her greenhouse. All the gorgeous big orchids throughout the inn were grown by Wanda in the huge glass-enclosed building beside the former stables. You must pay the greenhouse a visit to see the pretty walls and cupboards that Wanda painted flowers and greenery on.

The house has three primary common rooms. The living room has a fireplace and an elegant reproduction of an eighteenth-century Rhode Island secretary, an original of which resides at Winterthur, as well as a huge collection of tin soldiers and papier-mâché santas. The cozy, pine-paneled den is filled with bookshelves laden with books. There's another fireplace here, and this is where the guest telephone is located. In the Pine Room, which serves as an informal living room, there are beamed ceilings, a wall of pine paneling, and an oak floor. It contains a pool table and a deep cooking fireplace, complete with the old wrought-iron ratchets and a handsome woodstove.

I'm not crazy about stuffed deer heads, but the taxidermy in the Pine Room is extraordinary— especially a leaping bobcat catching a quail. There's a television here, and the casual comfort of the room is a natural magnet. A sunroom has a flagstone floor and a wonderful view of a lily pond. Outside stone terraces oversee the sloping lawns and the ponds that are nourished by a stream that spills down the hillside, neatly contained in a stone trough.

The guest rooms are distributed throughout the property—in the carriage house, the stables, a gate house, and a cottage that overlooks the ponds. We stayed in the Paddock Room, which has green carpeting, yellow walls, a vaulted ceiling, and period reproduction furniture. A pretty blue-and-white chintz covered the bed and chairs. It was springtime and a bright bunch of daffodils sat on a table next to a dish of candy. The marble tile bath included a spacious shower for two and a counter that held another vase of fresh flowers. There were horsy prints on the walls and a beautiful leather statue of a horse—these one-of-a-kind artifacts are found in every guest room.

A formal breakfast is offered in the dining room every morning. Wanda loves to bake, and her lemon-poppyseed bread is the stuff legends are made of. We also munched on apple and blueberry breads while Ed told us about places to visit and things to do. Wanda fixed a wonderful version of stuffed French toast that she served with a blueberry sauce.

Frankly, I could describe much more, but then you really must stay here to see for yourself. Do take time to walk down to the pasture to feed a carrot to the pet cows, Mickey, Oreo, or Doublestuff. They'll come when you call. The farm is adjacent to Longwood Gardens and an easy drive to Winterthur.

HOW TO GET THERE: From I-95 in Wilmington, Delaware, take exit 7 and follow Route 52 north, crossing the state line into Pennsylvania. Continue on Route 52 for about 6 miles to Valley Road. Turn left onto Valley Road. The driveway to Whitewing Farm is on the right in ¾ mile.

Clifton: The Country Inn
Charlottesville, Virginia 22911

INNKEEPERS: Mitch and Emily Willey; Keith Halford, general manager

ADDRESS/TELEPHONE: 1296 Clifton Inn Drive; (804) 971–1800 or (888) 971–1800; fax (804) 971–7098

E-MAIL: reserve@cstone.net

WEB SITE: www.cliftoninn.com

ROOMS: 14, including 10 suites; all with private bath, air-conditioning, robes, and fireplace; 4 with porch or patio. Wheelchair accessible. Children welcome. No smoking inn.

RATES: $150 to $315, double occupancy; includes full breakfast and afternoon tea. Two-night minimum weekends.

OPEN: All year.

FACILITIES AND ACTIVITIES: Restaurant serving prix fixe dinner Friday and Saturday $58; Sunday to Thursday $48. On forty-eight acres with pool and waterfall, year-round heated spa, lake for fishing and tubing, croquet lawn, clay tennis court, gardens with gazebo. Nearby: Ash Lawn-

Highland (home of James Monroe), Monticello (home of Thomas Jefferson), Mitchie Tavern, Montpelier (home of James Madison), Museum of American Frontier Culture, Charlottesville Ice Park, wineries.

We came for a post-holiday weekend getaway with friends. A winter storm had passed and daytime temperatures hovered in the 50s, while at night they dipped to below freezing. The countryside surrounding Charlottesville is laced with historic estates, often hidden away along winding country roads that pass fields of grazing cattle and horses. Just outside the town proper, Clifton is announced by a discreet sign at the entrance to a tree-shrouded drive. The driveway leads through a historic forty-eight-acre estate where Thomas Jefferson and other American luminaries were frequent visitors.

The manor house, a combination of Federal and Colonial Revival styles with a series of boxed columns across the front, was built in 1799 by Thomas Mann Randolph, who married Martha Jefferson, Thomas Jefferson's daughter. Randolph eventually became Governor of Virginia, a member of the Virginia House of Delegates, and a member of the U.S. Congress.

His grand house has been enlarged and embellished numerous times throughout the years, yet it retains its colonial ambience. The polished pine floors and the simple Federal fireplace mantels date to the late 1700s, while the fan- and side-lights are more recent additions. For comfort and style, however, the inn is strictly twentieth century.

In the elegant entry the walls are sponge-painted an apricot color, and there's a massive floral display on a Federal sideboard. The drawing room has a grand piano and sofas and chairs grouped near a gracious fireplace. The library is furnished with green leather chairs, another fireplace, and numerous books in built-in cases. Games are available here also for the enjoyment of the guests. To the rear an enclosed stone terrace has an abundance of plants, iron tables and chairs, and a fireplace at one end. This is where breakfast is served, overlooking the formal gardens and gazebo, and dinner on occasion as well.

The guest rooms all have fireplaces and are furnished with antiques. Room 5 has a window seat overlooking the croquet lawn, a sofa in pink damask, and a pencil-post bed. The quaint rooms in the Old Livery Buildings overlook the lake. They have bead-board walls and cabbage rose fabric covering sofas and chairs in the sitting areas, which also have fireplaces. Beds are located on raised platforms; baths have old-fashioned tubs with bead-board surrounds, tiled showers, and built-in benches. On this visit we stayed in Blue Ridge, a funky room in the main house, with an entrance through a private sunporch that leads through the bathroom. As with all the rooms it's loaded with charm, but you must do some gymnastics to crawl into the deep soaking tub, and the commode is hidden behind a pair of louvered doors. The double-sized tiled shower, however, has wonderful multiple showerheads, and the antique bed, which sits next to the fireplace, is dressed with fine linens.

The estate was turned into an inn in 1987, and it's gained a wide following for its distinguished cuisine as well as its rooms. Dinner is an event. We dressed in our finest and gathered in the drawing room for wine. Chef Rachel Greenberg soon came in and described each of the items on tonight's menu. As we listened to the description of the luscious courses we were about to sample, we ate pheasant liver mousse on toast points. We were then escorted to our tables in the dining rooms.

We dined on the enclosed stone-floored terrace, which has paned windows, a shingled wall, and a stone fireplace. At our table an appetizer of thinly sliced smoked salmon with long threads of portobello mushrooms and little potato cakes waited. Our soup, a fabulous marriage of buttered squash and apple bisque, followed. A salad of organic greens with blue cheese and walnuts, lightly drizzled with a pungent dressing, was next, trailed by a tiny intermezzo of warm dried fruits macerated in cognac. Our entree was a thick fillet of mahi mahi in a tarragon-truffle butter sauce with Yukon gold potatoes, shoestring carrots, and *haricot verts*. The perfect finale to this perfect meal consisted of a white chocolate mousse with fresh berries and three sauces. It was served with a beautiful mint flower that perfumed the entire dish. Naturally, there's a fine wine list.

Were Thomas Jefferson still alive, I have no doubt this would be his favorite place to dine.

HOW TO GET THERE: From I-64 east of Charlottesville, take exit 25 onto Route 250 south. Go 2 miles and turn right onto Route 729. Travel for ¼ mile and turn left at the discreet sign into the inn's driveway.

The Oaks Victorian Inn
Christiansburg, Virginia 24073

INNKEEPERS: Margaret and Tom Ray

ADDRESS/TELEPHONE: 311 East Main Street; (540) 381–1500 or (800) 336–OAKS; fax (540) 381–3036

WEB SITE: www.bbhost.com/theoaksinn

ROOMS: 7; all with private bath, air-conditioning, private line telephones with dataport, television, desk, radio, minirefrigerator, and robes; 5 with fireplace, 3 with VCR, 2 with whirlpool tub. Children over the age of 12 welcome. No smoking inn.

RATES: $115 to $160, double occupancy; $85 single occupancy Sunday to Thursday; all include full breakfast. Additional person $15. Two-night minimum in October and special-event weekends.

OPEN: All year, except first two weeks in January.

FACILITIES AND ACTIVITIES: Parlor, patio, hot tub, bicycles available. Nearby: state-of-the-art fitness center, bicycle trails, 26 miles to Blue Ridge Parkway; Transportation Museum in Roanoke, antiquing, outlet shopping, Long Way Home Outdoor Drama; hiking, Mill Mountain Theatre, Virginia Tech University, Radford University.

*T*here had been a terrific snow storm several days earlier, and mounds of freshly plowed snow lined the streets of Christiansburg. Twilight had turned the evening into shades of black and white. And there, straight ahead at the fork in the road, stood a magical and welcoming scene. The Oaks Victorian Inn was brilliantly lighted from top to bottom, its lights twinkling in the reflection of the pristine white snow. This was my first sight of The Oaks—an unforgettable one.

Presided over by seven majestic white oak trees (one is 400 years old), the grand Victorian is a medley of porches and turrets and gables and bays. Tom and Margaret bought the house in 1989, and today it's hard to imagine the crumbling edifice they purchased, since the restoration is so perfect in every way. The house is now listed on the National Register of Historic Places.

From the grand wraparound porch, with its Kennedy rockers mingled with white wicker, you can admire the lovely gardens, and in the back there's a brick terrace with wrought-iron tables and chairs, a fish pond with a fountain, and a gazebo containing a hot tub.

The common rooms include a rust-colored study with an elegant antique walnut buffet and a fireplace. Family photos grace the mantel. A parlor is entered beneath fanciful Victorian fretwork. There are turret windows, another fireplace, and an oil painting of a beautiful young woman. There are wonderful examples of stained glass in the house, especially in the stair landing.

The guest rooms are equally impressive. Bonnie Victoria, on the second floor, is a favorite. It has a bow-top bed with a fishnet canopy and a gas fireplace and two baths—one for him and one for her. It's decorated in rich hues of burgundy, green, and cream. Both the Julia Pierce and the Major Pierce rooms have fabulous hand-painted slate fireplace mantels. Julia Pierce has an

elegant carved Victorian bed, wicker chairs, a polished cherry chest dating to 1820, and a romantic bath with a Jacuzzi for two. Major Pierce has an iron canopy bed and a diamond-patterned quilt. A stained-glass lamp and an oak chest of drawers complete the picture. I believe my favorite room, however, is the hideaway called Lady Melodie's Turret, located on the third floor. The blue-and-white motif is richly used on the half-canopy bed and the tiles of the bath. It's also carried out in a Victorian lamp with a deep blue stained-glass shade. A table and chair in the turret offer the ideal vantage for watching the sunset.

If you want to be totally pampered, I can't imagine a better place to come. The warmth and solicitousness of Tom and Margaret are incredible. I heard them ask one guest, "Can we turn on your VCR for you?" To another they said, "Your private refrigerator is already stocked with soft drinks, but since it was a special occasion, we thought we'd tuck in a bottle of our own wine." Special chocolates and a decanter of sherry await bedside in the evening.

Margaret turns breakfast into an event. It's served by candlelight in an oak-floored sunroom that has another fireplace. She uses her elegant sterling silver and antique Dresden china that once belonged to Tom's grandmother. She might feature shirred eggs in a spinach nest and whole-wheat-buttermilk pancakes topped by a praline syrup with toasted pecans and maple cream for entrees.

HOW TO GET THERE: From I–81 take exit 114. Turn left if approaching from the south and right if coming from the north, and you will be on Main

Street. Continue for approximately 2 miles to the fork at Park and Main Streets. Bear right onto Park, then turn left into The Oaks driveway.

The Ashby Inn
Paris, Virginia 20130

INNKEEPERS: John and Roma Sherman; Debby Cox, manager

ADDRESS/TELEPHONE: 692 Federal Street; (540) 592–3900; fax (540) 592–3781

E-MAIL: ashbyinn@mnsinc.com

ROOMS: 10, including 4 suites; 8 with private bath; all with air-conditioning, 8 with telephone, 5 with fireplace and balcony, 4 with steeping tub and television. Children over the age of 10 welcome. Smoking permitted in Tap Room and Library only.

RATES: $130 to $220, double occupancy; includes full breakfast; $30 charge each additional guest; additional $20 to $30 surcharge for Saturday-only stay.

OPEN: All year.

FACILITIES AND ACTIVITIES: Restaurant serving dinner Wednesday to Saturday (entrees $18 to $27) and brunch Sunday (prix fixe $19); Tap Room. On four and one-half acres with perennial, herb, and vegetable gardens; horseshoe pit. Nearby: hiking Sky Meadows State Park and Appalachian Trail, Bellgrove Mansion, antiquing, vineyard tours, horse shows, trail rides, Shenandoah River sports.

The tiny village of Paris (formerly known as Pun'kinville) was renamed to honor the Marquis de Lafayette, who paid the town a visit after the Revolutionary War—perhaps to stop at Ashby's Tavern, just across the street from the present Ashby Inn, with his friend George Washington.

Time has been kind to the town, which probably looks much the same as it did then. And travelers still visit primarily to partake of the fine food and spirit (both liquid and convivial) that are offered at the village inn. After a local hunt the Tap Room fills with exuberant laughter, and on Sundays a crowd in a more leisurely frame of mind arrive from the city for the buffet brunch. Dinner is my favorite time to visit, however, especially if I can merely walk upstairs or down the street to the old schoolhouse to my room.

You might sit in the lower dining room, as I have done, in one of the intimate booths, where you can watch the swirl of activity from a quiet outpost. Or you might sit in one of the more formal dining rooms. Regardless, you will probably spend a few minutes perusing the collection of books in the library, warmed by the fire in the fireplace if it's winter, before you go to dinner. And you will certainly spend time admiring the wonderful, vibrant oil paintings on the walls. Should one particularly suit your fancy, you can take it home; they are all for sale.

Maybe your meal will begin with the unique Ashby Caesar Salad that includes freshly grated Parmesan cheese and polenta croutons. I had a wonderful roasted Chilean sea bass one night with couscous, olives, and roasted red peppers. For dessert the chocolate torte with coconut ice cream and chocolate sauce was terrific.

The guest rooms are perfection. All are furnished in lovely period antiques, but they are not the pretentious sort. Instead they are the kind that make you feel comfortable and relaxed. Roma collects and repairs priceless antique quilts, and you will see one or several of these in most guest rooms. There are balloon shades in pretty floral patterns on the windows.

In the main inn the New England room, a medley of greens, has a beautiful star-patterned quilt on the hand-painted bed; the Victorian Room has a cannonball bed and a bath with a red iris pattern on the walls. The Fan Room, which has its own private entrance, has a beautiful Palladian window and its own balcony.

The nicest rooms, however, are in the converted schoolhouse just down the road. I love Lafayette. It has a fabulous porch that looks out over the fields below and to the Appalachian Mountains beyond. In the misty early morning light, you will see deer, Canada geese, and wild turkeys. The room has a cathedral ceiling, a fireplace, a canopied four-poster bed, and a window wall. A window seat stretches beneath the window, and it's overseen by wall sconces perfectly placed for reading a good book found on the shelves. I couldn't resist rereading several stories in *Great Short Stories of the Twentieth Century,* which included "The Man Who Would Be King" by Rudyard Kipling.

John and Roma are an engaging couple who had high-powered careers in Washington, D.C., before creating their sanctuary from the city. During the dinner hour especially, the inn is filled with their friends and longtime customers, who obviously appreciate their consummate professionalism.

HOW TO GET THERE: From Washington, D.C., take I–66 west to exit 23 (Delaplane/Paris). Follow Route 17 north for 7½ miles. Turn left onto Route 701, the little road that runs through the center of Paris. The inn is straight ahead.

The Inn at Vaucluse Spring
Stephens City, Virginia 22655

INNKEEPERS: Karen and Mike Caplanis; Neil and Barry Myers

ADDRESS/TELEPHONE: 140 Vaucluse Spring Lane; (540) 869–0200 or (800) 869–0525; fax (540) 869–9544

E-MAIL: mail@vauclusespring.com

WEB SITE: www.vauclusespring.com

ROOMS: 12, including 2 suites and 2 cottages; all with private bath, air-conditioning, fireplace (some suites have two fireplaces), and radio; telephone and dataport available for all rooms; 11 with whirlpool tub, 4 with porch or patio. Wheelchair accessible. Children over the age of 10 welcome. No smoking inn.

RATES: $145 to $250, double occupancy; includes full breakfast. Two-night minimum from mid-April through mid-June and from mid-September through mid-November, as well as holidays, if stay includes Saturday night.

OPEN: All year except Thanksgiving and Christmas.

FACILITIES AND ACTIVITIES: Four-course dinner Saturday night to house guests only (prix fixe $35 plus 15 percent gratuity); on 103 acres with swimming pool, spring, millpond, stream, gardens with perennial border, two herb gardens, and one hundred acres of pasture for small herd of Holstein cattle. Nearby: golfing, winery tours, hiking, antiquing, canoeing, visits to Route 11 potato chip plant, historic house tours at Belle Grove and Glen Burnie, Wayside Theatre.

hat a perfect little country inn! It has a secluded country setting, friendly innkeepers who have thought of everything to make a stay flawless, beautifully restored historic buildings, and exceptional decor. Oh, yes, also lovely romantic dinners on Saturday nights exclusively for their guests. I would like to move into the Mill House Studio for six months to write a novel. But instead I must content myself to stay here on occasion.

Karen and Mike, along with Neil and Barry, purchased their 103-acre enterprise in 1995. It had formerly been the studio and home of John Chumley, a well-known local artist. The picturesque tumble of buildings housed his studio, which overlooked a spring pond, an art gallery with a porch across the front, and a charming "home place" where he and his wife lived. A grand Federal brick manor house stood high on the hill, desperately in need of restoration.

The farm originally belonged to Gabriel Jones, known throughout the area as the "valley lawyer." In about 1785 Gabriel's son Strother built the magnificent manor house. Hard times brought on by the Civil War descended on the family, however, and they lost "Vaucluse." The manor house was abandoned for some fifty years, and only the brick chimney was left of Mr. Jones's original law office.

Those hard-luck days are well behind the estate now. The manor house has been fully restored, and this is where the reception area is now located. Massive triple-hung, 10-foot-high Jeffersonian windows and dramatic cherry and walnut doors rise almost to the 11-foot ceilings. The deep claret–red living room has an 1830s Greek Revival fireplace mantel, plus a chintz sofa and piles of books on the coffee table.

The inn's two dining rooms are located here also, where breakfast is served every morning and dinner is served to inn guests on Saturday nights. The menus are inventive, colorful, and yet uncomplicated. Dinner guests might start with a twin pepper soup (red and yellow pepper soups poured into the same bowl and topped with a disc of Boursin cheese), followed by a salad of baby greens dressed with a maple Balsamic vinaigrette. For an entree there might be a salmon fillet crusted with smoked salmon and topped with warm horseradish sauce. This could be served with southern creamed rice and broccoli sautéed with caramelized shallots. A dessert might be cinnamon apples in phyllo shells topped with ginger ice cream and caramel sauce.

For nights when they are not serving dinner at the inn, you might go to One Block West in Winchester, as I did one night. I had a delicious meal of grilled shrimp, followed by a salad of marinated Bermuda onions with a tomato marmalade and pesto sauce. A dish of grilled chicken came with garlicky mashed potatoes and spinach. For dessert I had a fabulous bread pudding with Jack Daniels sauce.

My favorite guest rooms are not in the manor house, where they are undeniably beautiful, but in the Chumley Home Place, where a common room called the Keeping Room has log walls, beamed ceilings, and a huge stone fireplace. There's a pretty stone-floored terrace room with wicker furniture and a wall of windows that look out to the perennial garden. The guest rooms here are quirky and wonderful, with low ceilings and lots of little nooks and crannies. My ultimate favorite accommodation, however, is the Mill House Studio. It has a living room on the main floor with a fireplace, and a terrace and it sits on the banks of the millpond. Upstairs there's a bedroom with a brass bed, Chumley prints on the wall, and a view of the water. You can hear the sound of the water rushing over a waterfall beside the studio and on into the stream.

HOW TO GET THERE: From I–66 westbound take exit 1B onto I–81 north. Go 1 mile and take exit 302 onto Route 627 toward Middletown. At the end of Route 627 turn right onto Route 11. Go 2 miles and turn left onto Route 638 (Vaucluse Road). Go ¾ mile and turn left at the sign for the inn.

The Inn at Little Washington
Washington, Virginia 22747

INNKEEPERS: Patrick O'Connell and Reinhardt Lynch; D. Scott Little, general manager

ADDRESS/TELEPHONE: Middle and Main Streets (mailing address: P.O. Box 300); (540) 675-3800; fax (540) 675-3100

ROOMS: 14, including 4 suites; all with private bath, air-conditioning, telephone, and robes; 9 with balconies or patios, 4 with Jacuzzis, 1 with a fireplace. Wheelchair accessible. Children welcome. Pets permitted, but they must stay in a separate building; guests bring their own cage. Smoking permitted except in dining rooms.

RATES: $275 to $575, double occupancy, Sunday to Thursday; $385 to $685, all Fridays and every day in October as well as selected holiday weekends; $440 to $730, all Saturdays and Valentine's Day; all include continental breakfast and afternoon tea.

OPEN: All year except Tuesdays and Christmas Day.

FACILITIES AND ACTIVITIES: Dinner Wednesday, Thursday, and Sunday, $88 per person; four-course, full-choice menu; Friday evening, $98; Saturday evening, $118 per person, seven-course, full-choice menu; beverages additional). Nearby: vineyard tours, antiquing, horse events, The Theatre at Washington Virginia, Skyline Drive, Shenandoah National Park.

he Inn at Little Washington is the mecca and nirvana for gourmets and oenophiles around the world. At least once in every food-lover's lifetime, a pilgrimage should be made to this hallowed spot. It has won every possible award, including five stars, five diamonds, and Restaurant of the Year from the James Beard Foundation, and *Zagats* readers made it the number-one restaurant in America for food, decor, and service. It is a member of the prestigious *Relais et Châteaux* organization. Expensive? Yes. Worth it? Yes! Yes! Yes! Every penny.

The restaurant and inn are located in the town the inn built. It has literally grown up with the restaurant. When Patrick O'Connell and Reinhardt Lynch opened their inn in 1978 in a little building that formerly housed a garage and then a general store, the town was a wide spot on a little country road that had been passed by. Not so today. There are now antiques shops, galleries, a theatre, and a multitude of bed-and-breakfast establishments.

If the decor and furnishings at The Inn at Little Washington seem a bit dramatic, it's no accident. They were designed by Joyce Conway-Evans, a London theatrical designer, whose charming sketches for each of the guest rooms are framed in the upstairs hallway. Unusual touches include walls papered with wallpaper and borders created by hand-cut paper flowers; the entryway ceiling is covered with a spectacular collage. Fabrics—used lavishly in window treatments, draping canopy beds, tenting the dining room, or creating a canopy for a sofa in a guest room—are exotic and lush. The baths are a medley of brass and marble. Lavish bouquets of fresh flowers sit by the bed, on the desk, and in the baths, and a bowl of fruit awaits guests' arrival. Museum-quality antiques and custom-made furniture are found through-out. Patrick and Reinhardt are inveterate collectors (how do they find time?), and some of their whimsical or elegant pieces in each of the rooms add to their charm.

As beautiful as the rooms are (and two new rooms were added in 1998), the dining room is the raison d'être for coming. Its decor is equally elegant, but it's the wonderful cuisine that we've come for. Patrick is the chef, and he completed a stunning new kitchen in 1998 that is absolutely fabulous. It has one wall of windows that look out onto the gardens and another wall fin-ished in blue-and-white tiles. Two chef tables right in the kitchen can be reserved for those who like to watch the behind-the-scene action.

A tiny sampling of the vast selections on the menu include an appetizer of a seared slab of goose foie gras served with pears poached in Sauternes and pickled cranberries; there's an intermezzo of lemon-rosemary sorbet with vermouth. One entree features a sandwich of veal and veal sweetbreads with oyster mushrooms, country ham, and onion-plum confiture. Desserts, of course, are fabulous—such as the warm Valrhona chocolate cake with molten center, with a side of roasted-banana ice cream. The menu changes every day, however, so you might have entirely different choices to make. Naturally there's an exceptional wine selection—some 13,000 bottles in the cellar, when I last asked.

If you can think about breakfast the next morning, you could have it brought to the room. It will include a basket of just-baked breads, juice, and a bowl of fresh fruit (we had perfect little raspberries one time) topped with crème fraîche, and coffee or tea.

HOW TO GET THERE: From Washington, D.C., take I–66 west 22 miles to exit 43A (Gainsville). Follow Route 29 south for 12 miles to Warrenton and turn right onto Route 211 west. Go 23 miles, turn right at sign for Washington Business district. Go ½ mile to stop sign; the inn is on the right.

The Glens Country Estate
Berkeley Springs, West Virginia 25411

INNKEEPER: C. G. Everhart

ADDRESS/TELEPHONE: New Hope Road (mailing address: P.O. Box 160); (304) 258–4536

WEB SITE: www.wvglens.com

ROOMS: 8; all with private bath, air-conditioning, telephone, private deck, television, and VCR; 3 with Jacuzzi. Not appropriate for children. Wheelchair accessible. No smoking inn.

RATES: Rates, which include full breakfast, dinner, and all taxes, are discussed when reservation made. Two-night minimum weekends.

OPEN: All year except closed Monday and Tuesday nights.

FACILITIES AND ACTIVITIES: Dinner served Wednesday to Sunday to inn guests (included in room rate); swimming pool, two outdoor hot tubs, video library, private massages arranged; limousine pickup arranged.

We needed time together—just the two of us—far from the pressures of our stress-filled jobs. Romance was definitely on our minds. We couldn't have chosen more wisely.

The Glens Country Estate is unique among country inns. It was conceived and built as a romantic adult retreat. Located on twenty serene acres that include two mountain streams and a duck pond and surrounded by several hundred acres of woods and meadows, it is peaceful, quiet, and lovely. There are seven acres of manicured lawns, bordered in places by flower beds.

We reveled in the calm. Shortly after our arrival we heard a soft knock on the door, and there was the masseuse we had inquired about. An hour later we were thoroughly relaxed and utter tranquility had set in.

The manor house, which is the centerpiece of the inn, was built in 1910 with plans purchased from the Sears and Roebuck catalog. After Chase Everhart bought the property in 1991, however, he completely transformed the cute farmhouse into an elegant manor. We entered a hallway with a 30-foot cathedral ceiling. Two oak staircases lead to the upper floors. There's a charming sitting room in burgundy and rose. A Victorian sofa is inviting, and wingback chairs sit before a large fireplace. An oak table for backgammon or cards awaits takers, and a 700-volume video library offers selections to please any taste.

The guest rooms are furnished with beautiful antique-reproduction oak beds with high carved headboards and carved dressers. Pretty floral fabrics cover down comforters and feather pillows, and the all-natural cotton sheets are freshly pressed. Most rooms have examples of the owner's fine collection of lithographs. Every room has a television and VCR as well as a private deck, and all the private baths have tile floors; three have Jacuzzis. There are luxurious robes in every room.

We were anticipating dinner and we were not disappointed. We dressed for the occasion because we were in the mood, but a jacket and tie are not required. The handsome dining room, with old-world moldings and door trim, is a medley of oak, and the oak tables are covered with crisp white table-

 cloths. Dinner is served on Lenox china with Gorham silverware and crystal stemware.

All breads, desserts, soups, stocks—literally everything—are made on the premises, and there are raised beds of herbs and vegetables from which the chef can choose her ingredients. The five-course meal will start with, perhaps, an herbed potato soup, which is followed by The Glens' garden salad. A light sorbet (perhaps a summer lime) will follow. We chose an entree of baked Atlantic salmon wrapped in phyllo and served with a creamy dill sauce, which was accompanied by jumbo shrimp and tri-bell confetti, as well as an order of pan-seared broiled lamb with mint jelly and herbed potatoes. For dessert one of us devoured a rich Southern pecan pie with homemade vanilla ice cream; the other had a chocolate-walnut bourbon pie with homemade cinnamon ice cream.

Following dinner we headed out beyond the pool to one of the hot tubs. We sat under the stars sipping a cool drink and were ever so relaxed as we talked and planned together.

We rose the next morning to see deer, wild turkey, and birds from our deck in the early-morning mist. We had brought our bicycles, and we spent a leisurely morning riding along the C & O Canal Trail. After our return we lazed away the afternoon near the swimming pool. Tomorrow we would play golf.

Both breakfast and dinner are included in the room rate, and the breakfasts are as lavish as dinner. For guests who make arrangements in advance,

Mr. Everhart will have a limousine pick them up and bring them to the inn. The limo is equipped with two televisions and a VCR so that guests can watch a movie both coming and going.

HOW TO GET THERE: Directions given when reservation made.

Hillbrook Inn
Charles Town, West Virginia 25414

INNKEEPER: Gretchen Carroll

ADDRESS/TELEPHONE: Route 13 (mailing address: Route 2, Box 152); (304) 725–4223 or (800) 304–4223; fax (304) 725–4455

ROOMS: 6; all with private bath, telephone, and air conditioning; 2 with fireplace, 1 with whirlpool tub. Not appropriate for children unless they can occupy their own room. Smoking permitted.

RATES: $140 to $300, double occupancy; includes full breakfast (seven-course dinner included first night of stay at $70 per person extra, including wines); procrastinator's special rate of $129 per room if booked after noon on day of stay; midwinter midweek special, $99.

OPEN: All year.

FACILITIES AND ACTIVITIES: On seventeen acres with pond and stream. Dinner (by reservation) for guests not spending the night ($70). Nearby: Charles Town Races, Old Opera House, antiquing, tour Shepherdstown or Harpers Ferry, bicycling, and hiking on C & O Canal Towpath.

*H*ave you ever entered a room to find the fringe on the antique Oriental rug covering the polished oak floors perfectly combed? That's the kind of place Hillbrook Inn is. This urbane, refined, and sophisticated retreat is absolute perfection.

The half-timbered wood-and-stucco Tudor house was built in seven sections. It meanders down its limestone ridge in fifteen different levels. Constructed in the 1920s the original section incorporates the log-and-chink walls of an old log cabin. The house is encircled by leaded and stained-glass windows, stone pathways and terraces, and seventeen acres of gorgeous landscaped grounds that include an English rock garden, two streams, and a pond. One stream is crossed by a 12-foot-wide Bridge of Sighs, a bridge with a Chinese Chippendale design that includes ornate lion's heads. There's a 4-foot-high chess set beside the pond.

The rooms in the inn are exquisitely designed, combining the unique architecture of the inn with Gretchen's eclectic decor that includes objects d'art that she's collected in her worldwide travels. The living room, which has 20-foot ceilings, includes deep terra-cotta walls with exposed white posts and timbers and a woodburning fireplace. There are rich silks on the sofas and chairs. Antique tables and chests display ebony statues, pottery, vases, and figurines. On the lowest level, where the garage used to be, there's now a tavern with natural oak floors placed on the diagonal, boxed beams, and English-style mullioned windows. French doors lead to a stone terrace, and tapestries decorate the walls.

The guest rooms are as distinctive as the common rooms. The Bamford Suite has a private porch and luxurious big chairs before a fireplace. There's a four-poster bed and another sitting area with Victorian furniture. The

Point, a cozy retreat that is adored by everyone who stays here, is entered along a narrow tunnel-like hallway that opens to reveal an antique cannon-ball bed. All the rooms have private baths.

A seven-course dinner is served to inn guests and the general public in the evening. It's a leisurely, relaxed, and very romantic event—each course is served with appropriate wines—with soft classical or Broadway music playing in the background. Couples are seated at individual, candlelit tables, and the food is served on lovely china (much of it is by Lynn Chase) with beautiful silver and crystal. The courses include an appetizer (one night it was smoked trout in puff pastry with a cold dill sauce), a soup (a curried almond, for example), a light pasta (perhaps a farfalle in basil cream sauce), an entree (quail with pilaf one night), a salad, a cheese-and-fruit plate, and dessert (Chocolate Decadence with strawberry coulis) with coffee.

Most of the area surrounding Charles Town and the inn was owned by George Washington, who gave it to his brother, Charles, for whom the town is named. His country estate was located nearby, and some of the original log cabins are still on the property.

HOW TO GET THERE: From I-270 take I-70 west to Route 340 west. Past Harpers Ferry take Route 51 west to Charles Town. Continue on Route 51 west to Route 13 (Summit Point Road), which bears off to the left at the west end of town. Go 4$^8/_{10}$ miles on Route 13 to the inn, which is on your left (past elementary school on right). Watch for stone pillars.

The South

by Carol and Dan Thalimer

*L*adies' hoop skirts and parasols and gentlemen's ivory-handled walking sticks may be forever gone with the wind, but white-columned mansions, steamboats on the Mississippi, moonlight, magnolias, mint juleps, and that famed Southern hospitality remain in abundance to give residents and visitors alike a lively taste of the romance of the Old South. But the South is so much more than its stereotypes. A delightful blend of the old and new, the New South is a land of contradictions where you'll find stately mansions sitting in the shadow of towering rockets. Southerners, as a whole, display a passionate reverence for history and tradition, and they're only too happy to share their fascinating stories with anyone who's interested.

That brings us to where you'll stay whenever and wherever you're visiting in the South. Although the choices are infinite, the most important ingredient is not the place you choose, but the special person you're with. When you're with the right person, any place can be romantic, but being in sync about personal tastes and what gives both of you pleasure goes a long way to creating a memorable amorous experience.

Every duo is different. So start reflecting on what appeals to the two of you in a lodging: a secluded rustic mountaintop lodge or an opulent port city town house, an intimate bed-and-breakfast or a larger resortlike inn with sports facilities, some place inexpensive or a place that costs the national debt, a venerable old hotel or a spanking new contemporary hostelry—or anything in between.

Fortunately for those couples who love history and yearn to stay in a historic lodging (and contrary to legend), General William Tecumseh Sherman didn't burn everything in the South. Many simple to opulent homes that were built from the late 1700s to the first quarter of the twentieth century survive and have been exquisitely restored to operate as small inns and bed-and-breakfasts. These inns make up the majority of the twenty-two extraordinarily romantic Southern inns we've chosen for your consideration, but we've included a variety of other types of inns as well. You can't go wrong with any of them.

The South

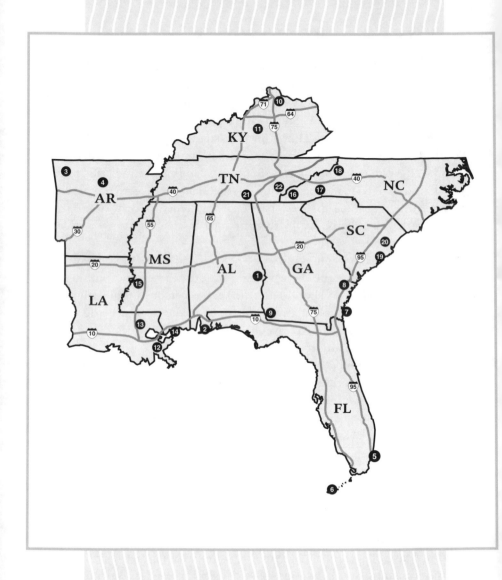

The South

Numbers on map refer to towns numbered below.

Kendall Manor Inn and Bed and Breakfast
Eufaula, Alabama 36027

INNKEEPERS: Barbara and Tim Lubsen

ADDRESS/TELEPHONE: 534 West Broad Street; (334) 687-8847;
fax: (334) 616-0678

E-MAIL: kmanorinn@aol.com

WEB SITE: www.bbonline.com/al/kendallmanor/

ROOMS: 6; all with private baths.

RATES: $95 to $109; includes full breakfast, welcome beverage, afternoon tea, fresh flowers, a sweet with turndown service. No smoking inn.
Children older than age fourteen.

OPEN: Year-round.

FACILITIES AND ACTIVITIES: Upstairs and downstairs porches, sunny
private deck. Dinner served by reservation at additional charge. Nearby:
Seth Lore and Irwinton Historic District, water sports on Lake Eufaula,
Eufaula National Wildlife Refuge, Tom Mann's Fish World, Callaway
Gardens, Auburn University, U.S. Army Aviation Museum, Farley
Nuclear Visitor's Center, Providence Canyon; deer and small-game hunt-
ing, hiking, bicycling, golf, nature trails.

After an ultraromantic stay at Kendall Manor, it will be difficult to
reenter the twentieth century. A National Register of Historic
Places treasure, the mansion is the quintessential wedding-cake
Victorian, built in the 1860s when cotton was king. An architectural masterpiece in the Italianate style, the majestic two stories are festooned with
columns and porches. The mansion is crowned with a graceful towering
belvedere, a tall addition to a house that was put there not for its striking
good looks but to let hot air escape from the house. Do yourself a favor and
make the climb to the belvedere tower. From its tall windows, 75 feet above
the street, you can see for miles in every direction.

Despite the breathtaking view, Kendall Manor's belvedere is special in
another way. Over the more than one hundred years since the house was
built, guests have gathered in the belvedere to see the view and enjoy the cool
breezes. They've left behind graffiti—names, salutations, and anecdotes.
These have never been scrubbed off or painted over. In fact, *graffiti* is not a

dirty word here. As guests, you'll even be invited to leave your own mark by adding your remarks to the collection.

Eufaula is one of the most beautiful towns in the South, with a collection of more than 700 preserved and restored historic buildings. We've always thought Kendall Manor was the most beautiful structure in town, indeed perhaps in the South, and were overjoyed when it opened its doors as an inn. Named one of the Top Fifty All-American Getaways by *Condé Nast Traveler*, the inn offers a warm welcome and the gracious ambience of the Old South as well as exquisite accommodations, delicious food, and exceptional attention to detail. Public rooms and guest chambers showcase 16-foot ceilings, gold-leaf cornices, Italian-marble fireplaces, and ruby-colored glass windows and are opulently decorated in the lavish Victorian style with antiques, period reproductions, and ornate fabrics. Large, light, and airy, with high ceilings and numerous windows, guest rooms blend history with mod-

ern amenities and personal touches. Each individually decorated, in addition to king- or queen-sized beds the well-appointed rooms feature cozy sitting areas and spacious baths.

After an exceptional night's sleep in your romantic bed chamber, you might be tempted to lie in bed indefinitely. The wafting aromas of home-made breads and muffins and a special blend of freshly ground coffee will draw you out of bed and down to a delicious full breakfast, which might include an entree such as Eggs Kendall, orange French toast with berry sauce, or gingerbread pancakes accompanied by coffee, tea, fruits, and juices.

To make your Kendall Manor experience even more special, arrange ahead of time to have an intimate multicourse gourmet dinner for two served by candlelight in the Manor Dining Room or in front of the fireplace in the original Kendall Dining Room.

HOW TO GET THERE: Follow U.S. 431 to Eufaula; at Broad Street turn west. The inn is in the third block on your right.

The Beach House Bed and Breakfast
Gulf Shores, Alabama 36542

INNKEEPERS: Carol and Russell Shackelford

ADDRESS/TELEPHONE: 9218 Dacus Lane; (334) 540–7039 or
(800) 659–6004

WEB SITE: www.bbchannel.com/al

ROOMS: 5; all with private bath.

RATES: Peak Season (Friday before Mother's Day to Thursday after Labor
Day), Long Weekend Plan or Short Week Plan $500 to $695, Full Week
Plan $1,000 to $1,390; Off Season (Friday after Labor Day to Thursday
before Mother's Day), Long Weekend or Short Week Plans $450 to $585,
Full Week $900 to $1,170 (which means the seventh night is free). Rates
are double occupancy and include breakfast, snacks, beverages, afternoon
wine and cheese. No credit cards. Smoking outside only.

OPEN: Eleven months (usually closed from mid-December to mid-January,
but dates change, so be sure to ask).

FACILITIES AND ACTIVITIES: Use of the living room, kitchen, porches,
and hot tub. Nearby: Golfing, bicycling, boating, fishing, hiking, horseback riding, sailing, and tennis. Historic Fort Morgan and Mobile Bay
are only a few miles to the west; the towns of Gulf Shores, Orange
Beach, and Foley with shopping, restaurants, amusement parks, museums, theaters are only a few miles to the east. Take the auto ferry across
the bay to Dauphin Island, Bellingrath Gardens, or the casinos of Biloxi.

For us, there is no better or romantic place to be rejuvenated than
at the beach. So there's nothing we love better than a beach getaway, and when we go we want to stay right at the water's edge so
that all we have to do is step outside our door to swim, sun, take long walks,
or search for shells. Even when we're in our room, we want to be able to open
the doors and windows to see the waves crashing, hear the soothing sounds
of the sea, and watch the vivid displays of color as the sun rises or sets.

The delightful Beach House Bed and Breakfast, a B&B inn near Gulf
Shores on the Alabama Gulf Coast, fulfills our every requirement and desire
for an amorous getaway—even things we hadn't previously realized we
wanted. Owners Carol and Russell Shackelford provide an intimate, friendly
atmosphere with lots of amenities to spoil you outrageously. Their philosophy is to balance "leaving you alone" with "taking care of you." The biggest

decision you'll have to make is whether to relax in one of the hammocks, soak in the hot tub, go to the beach, or leave the property for sight-seeing, shopping, or dinner.

Perched on high dunes directly on the shores of the Gulf of Mexico, the rambling, three-story Beach House sits on the last lot before the Bon Secour National Wildlife Refuge, which guarantees that the vast stretch of dune-backed beach next door will never be developed. This provides you with solitude for intimate tête-a-têtes and hand-in-hand walks on the beach. Although the house is only five years old, the tin-roofed exterior is reminiscent of the grand beach houses built early in this century. A huge screened porch wraps around the front of the first floor. Outdoor stairs lead to the hot tub deck, where you can soak away your tensions—a particularly romantic place to snuggle at night to enjoy the canopy of stars. A smaller second floor screened porch is another popular retreat. Wicker seating, hammocks, and hanging chairs provide numerous choices for unwinding.

Inside, the Beach House is filled with modern amenities. Ample use is made of pine, ceramic tile, and beaded board. Round timbers rise through all floors of the house like the masts of old sailing ships. The living room/kitchen is a large open room with a wall of windows looking out onto the Gulf. Comfortable seating invites guests to settle in, and a large library table is a great place to play games or put together a puzzle. In the kitchen area a guest refrigerator is well stocked. Bookcases in the living room and up the stairways on all three floors are laden with books and magazines on every subject. What you happily won't see are televisions and telephones. In fact, the Shackelfords advertise their home as a "no phone, no TV, no shoes zone." Instead they provide kites and floats, beach chairs, and even flip-flops.

All five luxurious guest rooms have their own distinct personality, indicated by their names: Nags Head, Cape May, Key West, Cumberland Island, and West Indies. Most seductive to couples are the two suite-size rooms on the third floor, which feature seating areas and private Jacuzzies; one has a private deck. All boast fabulous views, pine floors, Oriental rugs, and ceiling fans (air-conditioning is used in particularly hot weather). Private baths are large; some have tub/showers, others have huge walk-in showers, but all are amply supplied with plush towels and bathrobes. Beds are king- or queen-size and feature premium mattresses topped with plump feather beds and use down pillows and luxury linens. With all the reading that goes on in the house, the Shackelfords have thoughtfully provided bedside tables and reading lamps on both sides of the bed—a big plus to our twosome. Two of the rooms open onto the second-floor porch. The two suite-size rooms on the third floor feature seating areas and private Jacuzzis; one has a private deck.

Pampering begins immediately upon afternoon arrival, when you'll be treated to freshly baked goods, assorted spreads, and a beverage. Cool drinks, fruit, and snacks are available all afternoon, followed by wine and cheese in the late afternoon. In the morning you'll awake to freshly brewed imported coffee and chilled juice followed by a hearty breakfast casserole and delicious side items.

Firmly believing that a one-night stay simply isn't sufficient time to unwind and get all the benefits of the ocean, beach, and fresh salt air—as well as the inn itself—the Shackelfords require a minimum three-night stay. Choose a Friday to Monday long-weekend plan, a Monday through Thursday short week, or a full week. Some folks even go all out and choose the week-and-a-half plan by combining a full week with either the long weekend or short week stay. We'd consider that heaven.

HOW TO GET THERE: From I-10 (exit 44), follow Alabama Route 59 south to Gulf Shores. At the fourth traffic light after the bridge over the Intracoastal Waterway, turn right (west) on Route 180 (Fort Morgan Parkway). When you see the Meyer Real Estate office on the left, continue approximately $7/10$ mile and turn left on Veterans Road. Take the second left, onto Dacus Lane. At the end of Dacus Lane, The Beach House is on the right, atop the dunes.

Heartstone Inn and Cottages
Eureka Springs, Arkansas 72632

INNKEEPERS: Iris and Bill Simantel

ADDRESS/TELEPHONE: 35 Kingshighway; (501) 253–8916 or (800) 494–4921; fax (501) 253–6821

E-MAIL: billiris@ipa.net

ROOMS: 10, plus 2 suites and 2 cottages; all with private bath.

RATES: $68 to $125, single or double; includes full breakfast. Inquire about winter discounts.

OPEN: Year-round, except January through February.

FACILITIES AND ACTIVITIES: Gift shop, massage/reflexology therapist available by appointment. Located in the historic district, within walking distance of downtown Eureka Springs tourist activities; golf privileges at private course. Nearby: restaurants.

*T*he Heartstone Inn gets its name from a large, flat, vaguely heart-shaped stone that the Simantels found on the property. They play with the heart theme, using the phrase "Lose your heart in the Ozarks" and a heart-shaped logo in their brochure. The doors have heart-shaped welcome signs. The stone that justi-fies it all rests in the front garden, surrounded by flowers.

As far as we're concerned, the Simantels have such heart they could use the theme even without the stone.

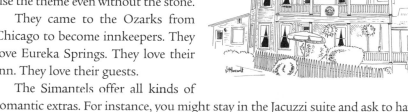

They came to the Ozarks from Chicago to become innkeepers. They love Eureka Springs. They love their inn. They love their guests.

The Simantels offer all kinds of romantic extras. For instance, you might stay in the Jacuzzi suite and ask to have flowers in the room, along with a heart-shaped cake and champagne. Iris will make it happen. Couples celebrating anniversaries often will make appointments for massages in the massage therapy room, often adding perfect relaxation to the romantic mix. Breakfast is always a pampering affair, with such delights as strawberry blintzes and delicate coffee cake, plus several kinds of fruit.

And if you like getting out and around, the Simantels will pack a picnic for you to enjoy on a sunset lake cruise or arrange a carriage ride for you in one of Eureka Spring's white "wedding" carriages.

Of course, the Heartstone is in a romantic town, too. Eureka Springs has become known as a "wedding destination" where hundreds of couples come to be married in one of its wedding chapels. You could say that here romance is always in the air.

The inn is a pretty Edwardian house, painted pink, with a white picket fence and lots of bright pink geraniums and roses all around.

Most of the rooms are furnished with elegant antiques, though a couple are done in country style. One favorite is an especially elegant Jacuzzi suite. Such outdoor niceties as decks and a gazebo mean there are always glorious places for special gatherings such as weddings.

Many couples enjoy the privacy afforded by the two cottages. The smaller one has its own garden with a deck and a garden swing that become your own romantic hideaway. The larger Victoria house has a fireplace in the bedroom.

The Simantels have been enjoying a good bit of "discovery," applause from magazines and newspapers and other innkeepers for doing such a good job. The praise, Iris says, has not gone to their heads. They are still keeping their prices moderate because they don't want to attract snobs who go to places only because they are expensive. Not that Bill and Iris could be snobs if they wanted to. That Simantel humor bubbles too close to the surface. In fact, Iris said, there are lots of new jokes between them, but some, she thinks, may not be suitable for print.

They love jokes and they love to laugh. An inn filled with love and laughter can't help but be romantic.

HOW TO GET THERE: From the west, take the first 62B exit off Route 62: From the east, take the second 62B exit. Follow 62B through town until it becomes Kingshighway.

Oak Tree Inn
Heber Springs, Arkansas 72543

INNKEEPERS: Richard and Susan Burdyshaw

ADDRESS/TELEPHONE: 1802 West Main Street; (501) 362–7731 or (877) 362–7731

WEB SITE: www.bbonline.com/ar/oaktree

ROOMS: 4 in inn; all with private whirlpool bath and fireplace; 3 cottages with fireplace and television; 2 with wheelchair access.

RATES: $85 per room; full breakfast and dessert.

OPEN: Year-round.

FACILITIES AND ACTIVITIES: Nearby: restaurants, area noted for fall foliage and spring dogwood; 45,000-acre Greers Ferry Lake, trout fishing on Little Red River.

*T*he Oaktree is a romantic inn with a difference—the innkeepers. About ten years ago they read an article in the *Air Force Times* about a couple who had retired from the service and opened a B&B. That is when they fell in love with the idea of their own inn. As Richard neared retire-

ment, the idea grew. They took courses, did research, even "inn sat" for a friend to get an idea of what was invloved—they loved it all. So in the Spring of 1998 they bought the Oak Tree Inn and brought their love affair full term. The Burdyshaws want their inn to be a place for couples who wish to escape daily routines and converse without distractions. There are no televisions in the guest rooms, but there are fireplaces and private whirlpool baths inviting you to relaxation and intimate conversation.

For the time when you want some activity away from the inn, the lake is only one block away. Richard and Susan keep a list of restaurants they recommend along with a list of interesting things to see and do in the area. There's plenty. Heber Springs is an easy place to be in. It has a population of approximately 5,000 neighborly people in the foothills of the Ozark Mountains. These are the kind of people who wave when they see you whether they know you or not and slow their cars if they see you're taking a photograph across the road. The inn is close to Greers Ferry Lake—45,000 acres of recreational potential. Also close, Little Red River is stocked with trout. Good hiking trails are nearby. After enjoying the Burdyshaw's generous breakfast of waffles or eggs Benedict or some other treat, you can spend a romantic day playing in the great outdoors, then at the end of the day, return to the inn patio and relax in the shade of huge oak trees with the dessert served by Richard and Susan each evening. Their most popular specialty is homemade hot fudge sauce over ice cream or cake.

HOW TO GET THERE: State Highway 25 Business goes into Heber Springs. From 25, take Highway 110 West, which is also Main Street, to the inn.

Mayfair House Hotel
Coconut Grove, Florida 33133

INNKEEPER: Amauri Biedra, general manager

ADDRESS/TELEPHONE: 3000 Florida Avenue; (305) 441–0000 or
(800) 433–4555; fax (305) 447–9173

E-MAIL: coryf@bellsouth.net.

WEB SITE: www.mayfairhousehotel.com

ROOMS: 179 suites; all with private bath, hair dryer, cable television
with VCR, central stereo system, telephone, minibar, indoor or outdoor
Jacuzzi.

RATES: $199 to $269 for standard suites; $249 to $279 for executive
suites, double occupancy. Ask about Weekend Break rates, which are
applicable for stays of two nights or more between Friday and Sunday
inclusive and include breakfast and added value benefits such as complimentary use of sports and leisure facilities.

OPEN: Year-round.

FACILITIES AND ACTIVITIES: Room service, valet parking, concierge,
fitness center, pool, spa, restaurant, champagne bar, laundry service, car
rental, facilities for the disabled. Nearby: restaurants, movie theaters,
boutique shopping, Key Biscayne beaches, Viscaya Museum, University
of Miami.

*A*fter several trips to Miami where we stayed amid the constant
hubbub of South Beach, we were looking for a small, quiet,
romantic hideaway in the area and wondered if *small, quiet hideaway* and *Miami area* weren't an oxymoron. Much to our delight we found
just what we were looking for in glamorous Coconut Grove—an exquisite
low-key hostelry where we had a hot tub on the secluded balcony of our suite
and easy access to a champagne bar, gourmet restaurant, and fitness facilities. What is this paragon among intimate inns? The elegant Mayfair House
Hotel. Located in the quaint shopping district of Coconut Grove across the
street from the exciting Cocowalk, this first-class, five-story inn comes as a
surprise. Above the first floor of shops, an ivy-covered structure rises. It isn't
immediately apparent whether it's a parking deck, an office building, a
department store, or a hotel. You'll be well rewarded by finding out what's
inside. Awarded four stars and four diamonds by the major hotel rating services, the all-suite Mayfair House Hotel offers unsurpassed service in exquisite surroundings. Beautifully appointed, the mahogany-furnished suites

boast either a Japanese spa tub nestled on a private veranda hidden behind the ivy or an indoor marble Roman tub Jacuzzi. Either provide just the right setting for indulging your romantic fantasies.

American contemporary cuisine is served in the exquisite white-linen restaurant, where seafood is a specialty. Begin your epicurean feast with an appetizer such as Chardonnay-steamed white clams, garlic-grilled squid, or pan-fried lump crabcakes, then move on to an entree such as Florida snapper, grilled veal steak, grilled tenderloin of Sterling beef, or rosemary-roasted rack of lamb—but save room for the specialty desserts of the day.

The well-trained, friendly staff, who help impart the feeling of an upscale inn, are always ready to give you directions to the many sights in the area, other places to eat, the best nightspots, or the quietest beach where you and your beloved can stroll hand in hand in the warm glow of moonlight.

HOW TO GET THERE: I-95 becomes U.S. 1, which you will take south to Unity Boulevard. Continue south to Tigertail Avenue, turn right and go to May Street. Turn left on May and go 1 block to Florida Avenue. Turn right on Florida; the hotel is on your right.

Little Palm Island
Little Torch Key, Florida 33042

INNKEEPERS: Ben Woodson, owner; Paul Royall, director

ADDRESS/TELEPHONE: 28500 Overseas Highway; (305) 872-2524, (800) 343-8567, or (800) 3-GET-LOST; fax (305) 872-4843

E-MAIL: littlepalm@relaischateaux.fr

WEB SITE: www.littlepalmisland.com

ROOMS: 30 suites; all with private bath with Jacuzzi, private sundeck, ceiling fan, air-conditioning, coffeemaker, wet bar/minibar, outdoor shower.

RATES: $350 to $850 per couple per night, depending on the season, includes launch service to and from the island, daily newspaper, and use of swimming pool, sauna, exercise room, kayaks and canoes, windsurfers and instruction, Hobie day-sailers, snorkel and fishing gear, beach lounges, towels, and floats. Suites will sleep four adults, additional persons, $100 per night. Full American dining plan is available for $140 per person per day; modified American plan $125 per person per day. Holiday meals may be subject to a meal plan surcharge.

OPEN: Year-round.

FACILITIES AND ACTIVITIES: Sauna, Jacuzzi, spa, beauty salon, water sports, fishing tournaments, scuba diving and certification, snorkeling, cruises aboard the *First Lady*—a Columbia 42-foot yacht—sailing courses and certification, deep-sea fishing charters, backcountry and flats fishing, pontoon boat rental, natural history backcountry ecotours.

*D*oes Bali Hai exist? Do you and your partner have to travel to the South Pacific or deep into the Caribbean to find and enjoy complete relaxation amid unspoiled natural tropical surroundings? The answers to these questions are yes and no. You can find your very own Bali Hai paradise at Little Palm Island—a five-acre private island resort located 3 miles offshore Little Torch Key midway down the Florida Keys. Named one of the twelve most romantic hotels in the country, it's all so exotic and seductive—and accessible only by boat, sure to please any romantic adventurers among you.

Within the lush grounds of the Jamaican coconut palm–ringed island are flamboyant bougainvillea, oleander, hibiscus, and other vibrant tropical blooms. Scattered among this profuse vegetation, and very subdued in contrast, are fourteen thatched-roof villas on stilts—like charming treehouses. Designed for seclusion, each villa houses two luxurious ocean-view suites. The interior of each features a sitting room and bedroom decorated and furnished as a tropical retreat with bold, bright colors, plantation shutters, and ceiling fans and a luxurious bath with a Jacuzzi. You'll love the romantic mosquito netting draped over the bed. Although the villas are air-conditioned, with an average year-round temperature of 76.8 degrees, you'll prefer to enjoy the fresh air and natural breezes.

The island's location at the entrance to Newfound Harbor and its fast-running tides created a white sandy beach and deepwater dockage that serve as the heart of the island's activities. Our idea of a really strenuous day is breakfast on our deck, then spending some time on the pristine white beach with a good book, followed by a dip in the aquamarine Gulf waters or the lagoon-style freshwater pool with its tinkling waterfall, followed by a nap in a hammock strung between two palms, punctuated by a snack or a cool drink, and finally ending the day snuggling on our private veranda sipping a frosty cocktail while contemplating the sunset—all the while serenaded by colorful birds and fanned by ocean breezes. Another day, maybe, we'll have a massage in the massage treehouse, where fresh breezes and birdsong blow through the windows or avail ourselves of some spa services.

We could stand on the main dock looking west to Loggerhead Key, where 2,000 Rhesus monkeys live, or watch the wading birds such as the roseate spoonbill, or wait quietly in the evening to see the endangered Key deer feeding on the hibiscus and the herbs in the kitchen garden.

For those who are more active, there's plenty to do. You can snorkel or dive to explore Looe Key reef where the HMS *Looe* sank in 1744 after hitting the reef—one of the prettiest in the world. Looe Key National Marine Sanctuary is rated as one of the top-ten reefs in the world and is the only living reef in North America. Scuba and sailing certification courses are offered, as are fishing charters and pontoon boat rentals. Environmentalists will appreciate a visit to bird rookeries and wilderness sanctuaries in the backcountry of the Great White Heron National Wildlife Refuge.

The only problem we experience with all this inactivity is the calories that don't get burned off from the award-winning French cuisine accented with Caribbean flavors. Meals are served in the spacious, airy dining room, on the terrace or, more romantic to us, right on the beach. Chef Michel creates a six-course gourmet feast each Thursday and is renowned for his Sunday brunch and holiday offerings. Because the island is so close to the mainland, folks come over by boat to dine at Little Palm Island (by reservation only). Every night reveals a new delicacy to savor such as lobster and stone crab soup, smoked salmon parfait with Belgian endive and green apple, Chef Michel's signature rack of lamb, or duck breast—all culminated by a mouthwatering dessert such as coconut cream–filled chocolate ravioli with praline sauce.

At this exclusive hideaway, you and the most important person in your life can experience a memorable romantic rendevous of a lifetime.

HOW TO GET THERE: Take U.S. 1 from Miami through the Keys to Little Torch Key, then the ferry to Little Palm Island.

Greyfield Inn
Cumberland Island, Georgia

INNKEEPER: Brycea Merrill

ADDRESS/TELEPHONE: For reservations, contact 8 North Second Street, Box 900, Fernandina Beach, Florida 32035-0900; (904) 261-6408

WEB SITE: www.greyfieldinn.com.

ROOMS: 11, plus 4 suites; only 6 rooms have private en-suite bath; 2 others have adjoining bath; the remainder share baths; the only shower is in an outside bathhouse; rooms vary in size and have twin, double, queen- or king-sized beds.

RATES: Rooms range from $275 to $350; $375 to $395 for suites; all double occupancy; includes three meals, naturalist's tour, bicycles, and ferry transportation to and from Fernandina Beach. Weekends require a two-night minimum.

OPEN: Year-round.

FACILITIES AND ACTIVITIES: Dining room, bar, bicycles, nature tours.

*J*ohn F. Kennedy, Jr., chose a tiny chapel on this supersecluded island for his top-secret wedding to Carolyn Bessette. How much more romantic can you get? As writers, isolated Cumberland Island and the exclusive Greyfield Inn have always presented us with a great dilemma. Do we tout their many attractions to our readers or keep one of the best-kept secrets on the East Coast all to ourselves? Well, once *the* wedding of the nineties became public that decision was taken out of our hands. Pictures and information about the island and the inn were immediately splashed around the world.

Fortunately, restrictions on visitation to Cumberland Island keep it peaceful and untamed. Healthy dunes, oceans of sea oats, long stretches of deserted beach, and dense, scrubby maritime forests characterize Cumberland Island—one of the most pristine islands in America. For almost one hundred years, the Manhattan-size island was owned and used by the wealthy Thomas Carnegie family as their exclusive retreat. In 1972 the family donated all but 1,300 acres of Cumberland Island and all but Greyfield mansion to the United States, and the island was designated a National Seashore to preserve and protect it from development. The island is overseen by the National Park Service and visitation is limited to 300 day-trippers and campers per day. The National Park Service ferry operates between the island and St. Marys, Georgia, once or twice a day depending on the season. Greyfield Inn operates its own ferry, which makes three exclusive runs between the island and Fernandina Beach on Amelia Island, Florida.

Thomas Carnegie's granddaughter, Lucy Ferguson, opened Greyfield Inn in the 1960s as an elite refuge from the hectic everyday world. Lucy's children and grandchildren operate the inn now as if they were welcoming old friends into their home. At Greyfield, you can easily imagine you're in the illustrious company of such as the Carnegies and Kennedys at leisure—a throwback to a gentler time. Expect eccentric charm, but not a decorator look. The inn is furnished with family heirlooms and antiques, many of them original to the house, and some of them suffer from the passage of time and exposure to the salt sea air.

Although it isn't visible from the house, endless vistas of deserted beach are only steps away. For nonbeach time, our favorite place to relax is on the spacious front veranda. Heavily shaded by deep overhangs and further sheltered by ancient live oaks and cooled by a gentle sea breeze, the veranda is furnished with comfortable rockers, but even better yet, with two immense porch swings—the perfect place to read a good book, snuggle with your love, sip a cool drink, or take an afternoon nap.

Simple guest accommodations are found in eleven rooms and four suites, which vary in size and feature twin, double, queen- or king-size beds. Only six rooms have private en-suite bath; two others have an adjoining bath and the remainder share baths. The only shower is in an outside bathhouse. For most of its existence, Greyfield was closed each August. Recent addition of air-conditioning permits the inn to remain open year-round. During the winter, fires blaze from the living room and dining room fireplaces; cooler temperatures make vigorous hiking, biking, and beach walks more pleasant; and there are fewer visitors. The romantic adventure of a stay here with that special someone more than makes up for the lack of luxuries.

Fine dining is an integral part of the Greyfield experience, and all meals are included in the price. A full country breakfast is served in the dining room each morning. Picnic lunches are packed into knapsacks or baskets for you to enjoy whenever and wherever you please. Be sure to be back in time for hors d'oeuvres before dinner. The evening meal is served in the dining room with candlelight and flowers, and gentlemen are asked to wear jackets. The centerpiece of the gourmet meal might be seafood, Cornish hen, lamb, or beef, but it will be accompanied by a delicious array of homemade breads and fresh vegetables and topped off by a mouth-watering dessert. Although limited in choice, the wine list is excellent. The inn maintains a well-stocked bar in the old gun room where guests help themselves on the honor system.

Some things to be aware of before you go: the only telephone is a radio-phone to the mainland reserved exclusively for emergencies. There are no stores on Cumberland Island, so bring everything you think you will need.

If you've been searching for a place where it's more than OK to do nothing but lose yourselves in each other, this is it.

HOW TO GET THERE: Get specific directions when you make your reservations—you can only get to the inn via their ferry from Fernandina Beach on Amelia Island, Florida.

Ballastone Inn
Savannah, Georgia 31401

INNKEEPER: Jean Hagens

ADDRESS/TELEPHONE: 14 East Oglethorpe Avenue; (912) 236–1484 or (800) 822–4553; fax (912) 236–4626

ROOMS: 13, plus 3 suites; all with private bath, telephone, television, and VCR; 11 with working fireplace and Jacuzzi; some with wheelchair access.

RATES: $195 to $225 standard, $255 to $285 superior, and $315 to $345 suites ($60 more during high season and for special events such as St. Patrick's Day); includes full breakfast, high tea, hors d'oeuvres, brandy, and chocolates.

OPEN: Year-round.

FACILITIES AND ACTIVITIES: Full-service bar, landscaped courtyard. Located in Savannah historic district. Nearby: restaurants, antiques shops, Savannah riverfront, historic sites.

Whenever you're looking for an extraspecial place to take that very special partner, consider a romantic liaison at the Ballastone Inn. Considered to be among the Tiffanys of Savannah's many inns and bed-and-breakfasts, the luxurious Ballastone Inn is housed in an exquisitely restored 1853 Italianate mansion. Originally constructed as a wealthy shipper's home, over the intervening years the building has served as an apartment house and even a bordello. Loaded with accolades, the gemlike inn has been named one of the most romantic inns in the nation by *Bride's Magazine* and *Glamour*.

Like many other old buildings in Savannah, the inn has been restored with special attention to authenticity, using Scalamandré fabrics and Savannah Spectrum colors. The colors were developed by chipping old buildings down to the original paint and matching it. The most impressive thing about the inn is the absolute faithfulness with which the fabric, carpet, and eighteenth- and nineteenth-century furniture and art have been combined to fit the period of the house.

The formal atmosphere of the high-ceilinged guest rooms on the upper stories of the mansion is enhanced with four-poster and canopy rice beds, marble-topped tables and dressers, cheval mirrors, comfortable loveseats, and wing chairs. Bed chambers on the garden level have low ceilings, exposed brick walls, and country primitive decor and furnishings. No matter where your comfortable haven is located, it features all the modern conveniences: private bath, ceiling fan, television, and VCR. Most rooms offer a king- or queen-sized bed and a working or decorative fireplace. The most romantic of all boast whirlpool tubs and a wet bar. To give you a better idea of the rooms, consider the one called Scarlett's Retreat, a popular room at the Ballastone. It has an English canopy bed, a small sitting area, and a gas fireplace. The walls are painted spruce green and the drapes and bedding blend softly in more shades of green and white. The hardwood floors are set off with Oriental rugs.

The Ballastone is the kind of place that indulges the whims and idiosyncrasies of even the most crotchety traveler. Each time we stay we're impressed with the good humor and ease with which the staff carry in extra luggage, rearrange schedules, and hasten check-in for a group of what we consider unusually demanding guests.

A few other nice things the staff will do for you include serving your breakfast at whatever time you choose—either in your room, in the tea or main parlor, or in the courtyard—and arranging everything from restaurant reservations and theater tickets to sight-seeing tours and airline flights. They'll even polish your shoes if you leave them outside your door at night.

The Ballastone also upgraded their food service over the past year. They now serve a full breakfast (you select what you want and where you want it served the night before), high tea at 4:00 P.M. each day, hors d'oeuvres at 6:30 P.M., and chocolates and brandy at bedtime.

HOW TO GET THERE: Take I-16 east to its end in downtown Savannah, where it merges into Montgomery Street. Turn right at the second stoplight onto Oglethorpe Avenue. Go 4 blocks to Bull Street. The inn is next to the Juliette Gordon Low House.

Melhana, The Grand Plantation Resort
Thomasville, Georgia 31792

INNKEEPERS: Fran and Charlie Lewis

ADDRESS/TELEPHONE: 301 Showboat Lane; (912) 226–2290 or (888) 920–3030; fax (912) 226–4585

E-MAIL: info@melhana.com

WEB SITE: www.melhana.com

ROOMS: 25, plus 4 suites and honeymoon cottage; all with king- or queen-sized beds and private bath (two are down the hall), plush bathrobes, television, desk, computer dataport, and multiline phone with conferencing capabilities; some with fireplace, whirlpool bath; twenty-four-hour concierge. The entire interior of the facility is non-smoking.

RATES: Rooms and suites in the Pink House are $250 to $450, the Hibernia Cottage is $450, and rooms in the Village section are $250 to $650; includes breakfast, afternoon tea, and use of recreational facilities. Ask about special packages—especially the Plantation Honeymoon, Swept Away, and Moonlight and Roses packages and those for Thanksgiving, Christmas, and New Year's; discounted rates are available from October 1 through December 30.

OPEN: Year-round.

FACILITIES AND ACTIVITIES: Complimentary airport shuttle service, heated pool, clay tennis court, croquet, fitness facility with personal trainer available by appointment, massage available by appointment, horse-drawn carriage rides on weekend evenings or by appointment. Nearby: historic Thomasville—the Rose City, Tallahassee, golf courses, skeet shooting, quail hunts in season, horseback riding, Birdsong Nature Center, Tall Timber Research Station, Maclay Gardens State Park, the Museum of History and Natural Science.

What better place for you and the love of your life to get away for an amorous rendevous than at an authentic Southern plantation? Happily, now you can experience for yourselves the gracious, luxurious, romantic Old South way of life. Melhana Plantation is a truly magical place where your everyday cares will melt away in its luxurious surroundings.

The heart of the sprawling pink Greek Revival mansion was built in 1825 and it has been added onto various times over its long life, creating the graceful manor house you see today. Seven exquisite guest rooms and four opulent suites grace the manor house—now known as the Pink House. Each ultraromantic high-ceilinged guest chamber is uniquely furnished and decorated to ensure its own distinct personality, but each is appointed with lovely antiques and/or period reproductions as well as opulent fabrics and every possible amenity such as down comforters. Hibernia Cottage, a honeymoon hideaway in the fanciest creamery we've ever seen, guarantees complete seclusion for newlyweds or other romantics, and eighteen other guest chambers have been fashioned out of the many splendid Greek Revival outbuildings.

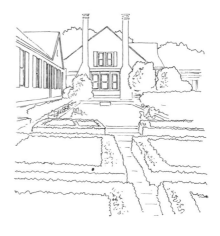

A docent gives tours of the extensive property. Our favorite spot was the stately poolhouse. Stretching back from the brick facade and enclosed in glass is a heated pool surrounded by comfortable seating and hothouse plants, men's and ladies' dressing rooms, a brick and marble walled courtyard, and a sitting area with a fireplace. Had we been able to stay longer than one night, this is where we would have spent most of our time.

Another treat at the plantation is the Showboat—not a boat at all. What looks like a typical Southern mansion on the outside reveals a private theater inside where the first private screening of *Gone with the Wind* was shown in 1939. The extensive gardens include a walled vegetable garden where fresh herbs and vegetables are raised for use in the restaurant, a winter garden, sunken garden, marble goldfish pond with koi, and endless borders blooming flamboyantly depending on the season. Peacocks and hens strut their stuff for your entertainment.

White-gloved waiters serve you with élan in the princely Chapin Dining Room restaurant. Since this is a plantation, we expected that the fare would be Southern and we weren't disappointed, but the innovative, updated cuisine offers sophisticated surprises. One of us began our meal with traditional fried green tomatoes with the unexpected addition of a topping of grilled Gulf shrimp and Vidalia onion and tomato relish, while the other feasted on pan-fried soft-shell crab. Then we shared cold zucchini soup and lobster bisque. Although it was extremely difficult to pass up the duck breast and roasted quail, we opted to try the New Zealand rack of lamb and the baked stuffed Gulf grouper combined with fresh Maryland jumbo lump crab meat. Regretfully, we had to pass on dessert: buttermilk pie, chilled seared pears with raspberry sorbet and chocolate sauce, carrot cake, or marble cheesecake with Amaretto sauce. Reservations and jackets for gentlemen are required.

After such a gargantuan dinner followed by a fabulous night's sleep in our four-poster bed, we were surprised to be hungry the next morning. It must have been the fresh air and clean living, because we managed to put away respectable portions of the signature breakfast pinwheel omelette accompanied by sweet potatoes, grits, hash browns, and biscuits.

HOW TO GET THERE: Follow U.S. 319 (Tallahassee/Thomasville Road) south from Thomasville 4 miles; watch for the sign on your right.

The Amos Shinkle Townhouse
Covington, Kentucky 41011

INNKEEPERS: Don Nash and Bernie Moorman

ADDRESS/TELEPHONE: 215 Garrard Street; (606) 431–2118 or (800) 972–7012; fax (606) 491–4551

WEB SITE: www.bbonline.com/ky/shinkle

ROOMS: 7, three in main house, four in carriage house; all with private bath and television. Smoking and no-smoking rooms available.

RATES: $79 to $140, double; $10 less, single; includes full breakfast.

OPEN: Year-round.

FACILITIES AND ACTIVITIES: Located in historic district across the bridge from downtown Cincinnati. Meeting space for groups up to fifteen. Nearby: walking distance to restaurants; Ohio River recreation, boating, cruises.

*I*f you share the preservationist's enthusiam for the romance of fine old architecture in excellent condition, you'll enjoy a stay at the Amos Shinkle Townhouse. This is the house the entrepreneur Amos Shinkle and his family lived in during the Civil War while his castle was being finished. A tour brochure for the historic district calls the structure a "modest Italianate home." Compared to a castle, maybe. But unless you are accustomed to castle life, you'll find The Amos Shinkle Townhouse posh.

The ceilings in this B&B inn are 16 feet high, with Rococo Revival chandeliers, plaster moldings, and cornices. Beyond the front entry a mahogany staircase, still with the original murals on the walls and crown moldings that continue on the second-floor landing, ascends to guest rooms furnished with antiques. The master bedroom has a fireplace, a four-poster bed, and a maroon-tiled bath with a crystal chandelier and a whirlpool tub.

Downstairs, comfortable couches and chairs clustered near the fireplaces make elegant places to read or chat. You're welcome to play the baby grand piano, too.

Behind the main house in the carriage house are simpler rooms decorated in Early American style. This building served as stable quarters in the 1800s. The horse stalls have been turned into sleeping accommodations for children.

A brick-and-grass courtyard between the two buildings includes places to sit under umbrellas when the weather is nice. During the growing season, pots of geraniums, petunias, and black-eyed Susans brighten the area. Tall hollyhocks and mature shrubs soften the austere lines of the carriage house.

Quite apart from the visual and architectural interest of the town house, staying here evokes a sense of old Southern hospitality. Be sure to spend some time talking with the resident innkeeper, Bernie Moorman. He used to be the mayor and maintains active involvement with the community. He likes to tell guests how special the area is historically and culturally, and he'll do almost anything to make sure you like it here. Bernie said that everyone at the inn will help you arrange everything from restaurants to tickets for the horse races.

Even breakfast reflects their willingness to cater to your schedule. You order from a full menu anytime from 7:00 to 9:30 A.M. during the week or 8:00 to 10:00 A.M. on weekends. Your eggs, pancakes, French toast, or whatever come to you cooked to order. Be sure to try the goetta, a regional sausage-like dish of cooked ground pork, pinhead oatmeal, and spices. Bernie said their goetta, made by Dick Fink, is the best in the area. We say if you wanta spenda day in romantic luxury you gotta getta night here.

If your love affair extends to baseball, the Cincinnati ballpark is only a ten-to fifteen-minute walk (or a forty-five minute car trip) from the house.

HOW TO GET THERE: From I–75/71 take exit 192 onto Fifth Street, which is one-way going east. Drive 9 blocks to where Fifth Street ends at Garrard Street. Turn left and go 2½ blocks north. The inn is on the left.

Bed and Breakfast at Sills Inn
Versailles, Kentucky 40383

INNKEEPERS: Tony Sills and Glen Blind

ADDRESS/TELEPHONE: 270 Montgomery Avenue; (606) 873–4478 or (800) 526–9801; fax (606) 873–7099

E-MAIL: SillsInn@aol.com

WEB SITE: www.sillsinn.com

ROOMS: 12 rooms and suites; all with private bath, cable television, VCR, stereo CD player, and telephone; 9 with whirlpool bath; some with sitting room, porch, and/or deck.

RATES: $69 to $89 for guest rooms, $99 to $159 for suites, single or double occupancy; includes full gourmet breakfast, complimentary snacks, newspaper; $20 for each additional person.

OPEN: Year-round.

FACILITIES AND ACTIVITIES: Porch, library, two-person whirlpools. Nearby: antiques shops, Nostalgia Station Toy and Train Museum,

Bluegrass Railroad Museum, Buckley Wildlife Sanctuary, Jack Jouett House, Labrot and Graham Distillery, Shakertown Village at Pleasant Hill, Keeneland Race Course, Kentucky Horse Park.

*U*ltraromantics will find many things to love about the Sills Inn. First of all, most of the inn's superb rooms are located in an elegant three-story 1911 Queen Anne Victorian mansion with its big inviting wraparound porch. Second, nine of the nostalgic accommodations boast a two-person whirlpool tub—some heart-shaped. Is this just the place for an amorous couple to kindle or rekindle their love life or what? And not to be neglected, we must mention the food, the attentive staff, and the location in historic downtown Versailles.

High ceilings, tall windows, opulent Victorian-era antiques, and king- or queen-sized beds characterize the guest rooms in the main house. The Tara and Victorian suites in the main house feature gorgeous sitting rooms, and the Penthouse suite has a private deck. The English, French, and Oriental suites in the modern annex boast a sitting area, private porch, and wet bar with a microwave and refrigerator. Considered the most romantic of all, for one thing because it is the most secluded, the French suite features a crystal chandelier, French antiques, king-size bed, two-person whirlpool and two-person shower, and a private porch.

Breakfast is a substantial affair served in the formal dining room or on the delightful sunporch. Fresh fruit and juices as well as freshly baked muffins accompany an entree such as Eggs del Sol, eggs Benedict, baked stuffed French toast, or spinach soufflé.

One of the things we love about the inn is the lobby library, which is packed with books on Kentucky history, horses, and genealogy and an astounding collection of 1,500 cookbooks. Items with a horse theme as well as local arts and crafts are for sale in the sunporch gift shop.

HOW TO GET THERE: Exit from I–75 at exit 115 and head west on KY 922. Turn west (right) on New Circle Road, then turn west (right) on KY 60 at exit 5-B (it is approximately ten minutes to Versailles). Follow the business route to downtown, and at the courthouse turn left onto Main Street. At the second traffic light turn left at Montgomery Avenue. The inn is 2 blocks ahead on the right. Pull into the driveway and park in the back.

Delta Queen
New Orleans, Louisiana 70130

INNKEEPERS: Various captains of the Delta Queen Steamboat Co.

ADDRESS/TELEPHONE: Robin Street Wharf, 1380 Port of New Orleans Place; (504) 586–0631 or (800) 543–1949; fax (504) 585–0630

WEB SITE: www.deltaqueen.com

ROOMS: 87 staterooms; all with private bath.

RATES: Approximately $200 per night per person; includes all three meals daily, snacks, and entertainment, depending on the season and itinerary.

OPEN: Year-round.

FACILITIES AND ACTIVITIES: Betty Blake and Forward Cabin Lounges, Orleans Room restaurant and theater, Texas Lounge bar, gift shop.

*A*t one time more than 11,000 steam-powered paddle wheelers plied the inland waterways which served as highways in the 1800s. Today only a few of these extraordinary boats remain and most of those are used as sight-seeing tour boats. Only three—one a genuine antique, the other two of new construction—offer overnight accommodations. Listed on the National Register of Historic Places and included as one of the National Trust for Historic Preservation's prestigious Historic Hotels of America, the *Delta Queen* is even a post office with its own postmark.

Fed on Twain stories and movies such as *Showboat*, we wanted to re-create the ambience of the steamboating paddle-wheel era—the soul-stirring patriotic fervor, the slow pace of another era—for ourselves when we took our first cruise aboard the *Delta Queen*. That trip from New Orleans to Vicksburg and back to New Orleans created indelible, precious memories and friendships and provided a fantasy boost to our relationship. All our expectations were surpassed. We totally agree with the company's slogan that a voyage aboard the *Delta Queen* is an "antidote to overstimulated lives." The soft swoosh, swoosh of the great steam pistons driving the enormous paddle wheel lulls you into a complete sense of well-being and detachment.

Constructed in 1926, the *Delta Queen* worked a shuttle route on the Sacramento River with her twin, the *Delta King*. Commandeered by the U.S. Navy and painted gray during World War II, the boats ferried military personnel to ships in San Francisco Bay. After their heyday, they languished at the docks and even operated as a restaurant.

Then the Greene Line Steamers of New Orleans had the bright idea of providing overnight accommodations on the Mississippi River, sometimes called the American Nile. The *Delta Queen* was completely overhauled and refurbished (using many parts salvaged from the *Delta King*) and put into service. The military gray paint has been removed and the interior restored. Gleaming teak handrails line the decks, Tiffany windows sparkle in the brilliant sunlight or in the soft glow of lamp light, and crystal chandeliers sway gently as the vessel proceeds at her languid, almost silent, 5-mile-per-hour pace. Your surroundings are like those of a warm yet elegant nineteenth-century Victorian home, with paneling and a grand teak and brass staircase. Public spaces and most staterooms are filled with period furnishings—many of them genuine antiques—and opulent velvet- and tapestry-covered upholstered pieces. The small number of public rooms enhances the intimacy. You really get to know your fellow passengers and the crew.

Each stateroom has an individual Victorian personality that exudes charm and elegance enhanced by homespun touches such as patchwork quilts, collectibles, brass fittings, and wood-shuttered windows.

Your cruise, whether it be three days or two weeks, includes four sumptuous meals a day, including a fabulous five-course dinner each night, moonlight buffet, other snacks and treats throughout the day, professional showboat-style entertainment nightly, lectures, craft lessons, and calliope concerts (you can even learn to play a few notes on the difficult steam-powered instrument and get a certificate to take home to impress your family and friends). Drinks and shore excursions at many of America's most charming river cities and small towns are extra.

HOW TO GET THERE: You may board the *Delta Queen* at any of dozens of cities from New Orleans to Minneapolis/St. Paul or Pittsburgh to Galveston. Specific directions will be given with your cruise documents.

Nottoway Plantation Inn
White Castle, Louisiana 70788

INNKEEPER: Cindy A. Hidalgo

ADDRESS/TELEPHONE: P.O. Box 160 (River Road, LA 1);
(504) 545–2730; fax (504) 545–8632

E-MAIL: nottoway@worldnet.att.net

WEB SITE: www.louisianatravel.com/nottoway/

ROOMS: 13; all with private bath, telephone, television.

RATES: $125–$250, double occupancy; includes prebreakfast wake-up
call, full breakfast, fresh flowers, tour of mansion.

OPEN: Year-round except Christmas Day.

FACILITIES AND ACTIVITIES: Tour of mansion, swimming pool,
restaurant serving lunch and dinner, meeting space. Nearby: Baton
Rouge museums, Old and New Capitols, USS *Kidd*, casinos,
restaurants, nightlife, shops, galleries.

*N*ottoway Plantation is a genuine romantic's dream come true.
When we saw the monumental plantation house for the first time,
it rose from the fog obscuring the tranquil surface of the Mississippi River and its banks like a mysterious castle floating on the clouds.
That's how the big white mansion appeared to us the first time we saw Nottoway Plantation house from aboard the *Delta Queen*, cruising upriver from
New Orleans. Little wonder that the few remaining antebellum homes along
the river are dubbed "Ghosts along the Mississippi." Later, when we landed
for a tour, the fog burned off and the sun came out, transforming the mansion into a gigantic wedding cake. It's little wonder that this relatively unin-
habited area has taken the name White Castle from the plantation house
that dominates it.

As hard as it is to believe, when this magnificent neoclassical mansion
was completed by John Randolph in 1859 with modern innovations such as
hot and cold running water and a gas lighting system, it wasn't the largest
plantation home in the South.

Only a few years after the mansion's completion, the Civil War raged in
the area and the mansion might have met the same unfortunate fate as many
other opulent homes of the extravagantly wealthy planter class—being
burned to the ground by Union troops. Legend has it that a Union gunboat
fired on the mansion, but when Mrs. Randolph appeared on the front
gallery, the captain recognized her and the house where he had been a guest

before the war. He came ashore and offered her protection. As a result, Nottoway is now the largest surviving plantation home in the South. Soaring two-story columns across the front support vast verandas on both levels. Magnificently detailed paneling, molding, and plaster frieze work as well as original hand-painted Dresden doorknobs, marble fireplaces, Baccarat crystal chandeliers, and exquisite furnishings characterize the interior.

You can hardly imagine rooms more romantic than Nottoway's stunning white double parlors, so it's only natural that many weddings are held there. How ultrasentimental—to be married at Nottoway and then to spend your honeymoon there, perhaps in the Bridal Suite, which features a private courtyard and a swimming pool, or in Cornelia's Room on the third floor of the mansion with sweeping views of the river.

Guest accommodations are located in the mansion and the connected annexes, which once served as children's rooms or servants' quarters, as well as in an overseer's cottage and the honeymoon cottage. Those in the main house (two on the first floor, four on the second floor, and two suites on the third floor) are the most elegant. Four rooms located in the overseer's cottage aren't quite as formal.

No matter where your bed chamber may be located, you'll be pleasantly awakened by what the staff calls a prebreakfast wake-up call consisting of hot sweet-potato muffins, coffee, and juice delivered to your room to tide you over until you're dressed and ready for breakfast in the formal dining

room. The generous full breakfast consists of such items as eggs, sausage, grits, cereal, waffles, juices, fruits, and hot beverages. Other amenities include fresh flowers in all the guest accommodations and chilled champagne in the suites or a carafe of sherry in the other guest rooms.

Use the inn as a base from which to explore the many plantations in the surrounding area, or stay on the property and do little or nothing. Tour the house, of course. Spend time sitting on the verandas, watching the slow-paced river traffic glide by or reading a good book. Stroll hand in hand through the acres of lawns shaded by the broad canopies of ancient oaks. Swim or sun yourself around the pool. When hunger strikes, Randolph Hall, a restaurant located on the grounds, serves Cajun and Southern cuisine for lunch and dinner.

HOW TO GET THERE: From Baton Rouge, take I-10 west to the Plaquemine exit, then take LA 1 south for 20 miles. The inn is on the left.

The Father Ryan House
Bed & Breakfast Inn
Biloxi, Mississippi 39530

INNKEEPER: Rosanne McKenney

ADDRESS/TELEPHONE: 1196 Beach Boulevard; (228) 435–1189 or (800) 295–1189; fax (228) 435–1189

E-MAIL: reservations@frryan.com

WEB SITE: www.frryan.com

ROOMS: 9 in main house, 4 in cottages; all with private bath, cable television, coffeemakers, and telephone. Smoking outside only.

RATES: $92 to $165, double; single $15 less; $15 for each additional guest; includes full breakfast.

OPEN: Year-round.

FACILITIES AND ACTIVITIES: Swimming pool, Gulf of Mexico ocean beach. Nearby: restaurants, Biloxi Lighthouse, Keesler Air Force Base, Jefferson Davis home at Beauvoir, Gulf Shores National Seashore, golf courses, floating gambling casinos, art galleries and museums.

*P*oetry is the language of romance. Here is an inn devoted to the memory of its resident poet and embellished by a bright decor and lots of creature comforts that will make you feel romantic even if you don't care about poetry.

> *Just a hundred feet away*
> *Seaward, flows and ebbs the tide;*
> *And the wavelets, blue and grey*
> *moan, and white sails windward glide*
> *o'er the ever restless sea.*
>
> —Father Abram Ryan, Sea Rest

*S*o Father Ryan described this place. He was the poet laureate of the Confederacy and a close friend of Jefferson Davis, president of the Confederacy. Father Ryan wrote some of his best-known poetry while he lived in this house, which was built about 1841. Legend has it that when Father Ryan was in residence, he erected a cross on the front steps to indicate that a priest lived there. When he left for the last time, the cross was blown away in a storm, but a palm seed took hold in its place. Towering over the house today and known as the Rather Ryan Palm, it extends a welcome to visitors.

Standing just 20 feet from the beach, but across a busy highway, this is one of the oldest remaining structures on the Gulf Coast, and it has been faithfully restored according to information in Father Ryan's letters and other contemporary sources.

To further heighten the mood, his poetry, written in calligraphy, is displayed throughout the house, as are books about him, some of his letters, and more poetry. Margaret Mitchell's *Gone with the Wind* lies open to her mention of Father Ryan's visit.

But don't suppose that the historicity of the house means it's dark and gloomy. In fact one guest who saw it for the first time said, "How did you make it so light?"

Windows, mainly. Roseanne said that the English architect who added the second and third floors at the turn of the century "went crazy with windows," an uncommon approach at the time because homes were taxed according to the number and size of their windows. "Apparently it didn't matter," Roseanne said.

The guest rooms in the house, including the ones that once would have been Father Ryan's bedroom, study, and a room for an orphan boy he took in, are quietly elegant, almost understated, furnished with handcrafted beds and antiques dating back to the early 1800s. All the comforters and pillows are of down. If you are into water sports, ask for one of the rooms with a whirlpool tub.

Concessions to modern travelers include private bathrobes, cable television, and telephone with dataports. Some guest chambers boast whirlpool tubs. Four additional rooms are available in the historic cottages next door and behind the pool.

The inn has several appealing common areas. Upstairs a large room that runs all the way from the north to the south side of the house overlooks the Gulf on one side and the courtyard and swimming pool on the other. The library has floor-to-ceiling shelves filled with books, including many about the South and Mississippi. Rolling ladders help you reach the high shelves.

Empire furniture from the 1860s, upholstered in a light cream-colored fabric, lends dignity without being overbearing. In addition to a formal dining room, there is the Lemon Room—a bright closed-in porch with Mexican tile floors, high ceilings, and antique converted brass gaslight fixtures—where breakfast is served unless you request (free) room service.

No matter where you take your breakfast, it will be special. Anita, the chef, was trained in San Francisco and brings a California flair and expertise with herbs to the kitchen. Each breakfast includes a savory or fruit bread, fruit prepared in various ways—poached pears or yogurt-fruit soup, for instance—and a main dish that may be anything from cheese blintzes to puffy oven pancakes with fruit. That's a breakfast that gives you zing for a romantic day.

HOW TO GET THERE: The inn is on Highway 90, 6 blocks west of the I–110 off ramp, 4 blocks west of the Biloxi Lighthouse, and 2 blocks east of the main Keesler Air Force Base entrance. You will receive a brochure with a map when you make a reservation.

Cedar Grove Mansion Inn
Vicksburg, Mississippi 39180

INNKEEPERS: Ted and Estelle Mackey

ADDRESS/TELEPHONE: 2200 Oak Street; (601) 636–1000 or (800) 862–1300; fax (601) 634–6126

WEB SITE: www.cedargroveinn.com

E-MAIL: info@cedargroveinn.com

ROOMS: 14 in the mansion, 2 in the pool house, 8 suites in the carriage house, 5 cottages; all with private bath, cable television, and telephone; some with patio; some with fireplace, whirlpool tub, wheelchair access.

RATES: $85 to $165, double; 10 percent less for single; includes full plantation breakfast and tour of mansion.

OPEN: Year-round.

FACILITIES AND ACTIVITIES: Full cocktail service with piano and gourmet candlelight dining at 6:00 P.M. Rooftop garden overlooking Mississippi River; swimming pool and Jacuzzi set in a courtyard with five acres of formal gardens, gazebos, fountains. Nearby: restaurants, Mississippi riverboat tours, historic sites in Vicksburg.

*V*oted the Best Antebellum Home in Vicksburg, this magnificent estate makes a perfect place to capture *Gone With the Wind* elegance and romance.

The place smells like dried rose petals when you enter. Just as you start thinking that there was a softness about the atmosphere that most antebellum tour houses lack, you see the cannonball lodged in the parlor wall, a patch in the door, and a ragged hole in the parlor floor that has been framed and covered with heavy glass so that you could see through to the rooms below.

What is all this?

"Union gunboat cannonball, from the Civil War," the innkeeper said. "It came through the door and hit the parlor wall. Mrs. Klein, the owner of the house, insisted on leaving it there as a reminder after the war."

And the hole?

"War damage. After the fall of Vicksburg, Grant slept here for three nights. He turned the servants' quarters down below into a Union hospital for his soldiers. The Kleins were in residence at the time."

The present owners' and innkeeper's familiarity and personal fascination with the history of the house provide them with little stories to tell about every room of the mansion and adds a human note to the Civil War that you'll never get from reading plaques in museums or touring military memorials.

Ted and Estelle Mackey, the owners, have been working steadily assembling the furnishings, buffing the house, and manicuring the lawns to bring the property up to its pre-Civil War glory. The Greek Revival home was built about 1840 by John A. Klein as a wedding present for his bride. The house survived the Civil War because it was used as a Union hospital and, it's rumored, because Mrs. Klein had family ties to General Sherman—a fact that caused her to be rejected by Vicksburg society during the war.

Superior guest accommodations are found in the main house, the two-story carriage house, or several humble restored cottages scattered around the five-acre grounds—some of them poolside. Each is lavishly decorated and furnished with period antiques and reproductions. Some of these furnishings are original to the house and were collected by the Kleins on their year-long European honeymoon. Romantic canopy and half-tester beds grace many guest chambers.

It's impossible to describe all twenty-nine rooms and suites here, but we must mention a few of the most exceptional bed chambers—many of which are named for Civil War heroes or *Gone with the Wind* characters.

Perhaps the two of you would like to sleep in the very room and the very bed where General Grant spent three nights after the fall of Vicksburg. This room features a heavily carved and opulently draped canopy bed, original rosewood and cherry antiques, a Prudence Mallard armoire bearing the master craftsman's signature mallard egg, and a marble bath with a whirlpool tub.

The two-story Library Suite is located in the original library. A spiral iron staircase connects the extravagant scarlet Victorian sitting room with the bedroom. The General Lee Suite boasts a king-sized bed, working fireplace, entertainment center with surround sound, and private patio with a fountain.

We enjoyed staying in the grand, white-columned carriage house. We had a separate sitting room and easy access to our second-story veranda, where we could relax with a cool drink on comfortable wicker while we surveyed the main house, gardens, statuary, fountains; original Italianate ironwork gazebo, catfish pond, greenhouse, arbors, courtyards, and swimming pool as well as view the Mississippi River in the distance. If we hadn't had such a wonderful vantage point, we could have gone up to the terraced garden on the roof of the big house to enjoy the views.

Bask in the luxury of the Old South and let the dedicated staff spoil you. Awaken to the sounds of Mozart and the aroma of fresh coffee, followed by a full Southern plantation breakfast. In the late afternoon or evening, relax to live piano music in the Mansion Bar, then enjoy a romantic candlelight dinner of New Orleans cuisine accompanied by fine wines in the cozy garden atmosphere of Andre's, an elegant restaurant voted the Best Restaurant in Vicksburg (additional charge). Delicacies include such mouthwatering dishes as New Orleans catfish off the grill and topped with Cajun crawfish étouffée or sushi-grade yellowfin tuna marinated in champagne with Andre's Creole seasoning, topped with crumbled hickory-smoked bacon, and served with lemon caper hollandaise sauce. Cap your meal with cappuccino and brandy bread pudding. Chef Andre's herb olive oil and cookbooks are for sale in the gift shop.

HOW TO GET THERE: From I-20, take the 1A Washington Street exit. Go north about 2 miles. Turn left onto Klein.

Innisfree Victorian Inn
Glenville, North Carolina 28736

INNKEEPERS: Teri Federico and Brenda Crickenger; Henry Hoche, owner

ADDRESS/TELEPHONE: Highway 107 North (P.O. Box 469); (828) 743-2946

WEB SITE: www.innisfreeinn.com.

ROOMS: 10 rooms and suites; all with private bath, clock radio, ceiling fan; some with fireplace or woodstove, whirlpool tub, telephone, television with VCR, refrigerator.

RATES: Rates for the rooms in the main house are $119 to $249 week nights and during the off-season (November through May) and $150 to $290 for weekends and the peak season; $159-$239 week nights and off-season and $175 to $275 weekends and peak season for suites in the Garden House; includes candle-light breakfast in the tower for inn guests or breakfast delivered to the suite for Garden House guests, afternoon hospitality hour, Irish coffee by the fireplace in the evening, and Godiva chocolates; weekends require a two-night minimum, holidays a three-night minimum; wedding, honeymoon, and anniversary packages.

OPEN: Year-round.

FACILITIES AND ACTIVITIES: Gardens, verandas, walking trails, hammock, gazebo, private beach, games, small gift shop. Nearby: water sports, boat rentals, fishing, tennis, golf, hiking, snow skiing, antiques and crafts shopping, restaurants.

To us there's just something about the opulent exuberance of the architecture and furnishings of the Victorian era that exudes romance, and we've rarely visited a Victorian inn that disappointed us. Some, however, outshine the others and one of these is Innisfree. We're crazy about Christmas, so you can just imagine how enchanted we were to see the lavish Victorian decorations at Innisfree. Our first glimpse was of what seemed like miles of garlands draped around two stories of wraparound verandas and decks. Inside, a magnificent Christmas tree reached to the cathedral ceiling.

Even if you're not lucky enough to visit Innisfree at Christmastime, there are plenty of Victorian furnishings and accessories to admire. First, the stately house itself. Although it was built in 1989, it has many of the Victorian characteristics you'd expect—gables, verandas, gingerbread, and, the most obvious, a three-story turret. Perched on a hillside on twelve acres, the house boasts walls of windows overlooking Lake Glenville—the highest lake east of the Rockies—with the Blue Ridge Mountains providing a backdrop.

The cathedral ceiling in the great room simulates the high ceilings of yore, and the marble mantelpiece is just as grand as any you'd see in a century-old house. Exuberantly furnished, the great room, breakfast room, and guest rooms feature antiques and reproductions, Oriental carpets, and carefully chosen accessories from years of world travel. Under the eaves is an informal observatory/TV/game room equipped with binoculars. Guest chambers are divided between the main house and a smaller garden house.

Every guest room or suite features a firm mattress, fine linens, plush towels, and good reading light, but each has its own charms. In the main house, rooms are named for Queen Victoria and Prince Albert as well as the English cities of Cambridge, Canterbury, and Windsor. The Queen Victoria Suite, the grandest of them all, boasts a tray ceiling; bay window; massive, ornate canopy bed; whirlpool bath; and even a bidet. The Windsor Room has a fireplace and an Italian lavatory with hand-painted blue irises and gilded dolphin faucets. Exotic Chinese headboards are the focal point in the Prince Albert Suite and Canterbury Room. The Cambridge Room features a private porch and separate entrance.

The Garden House, a small Dutch Colonial–style house with its own turret, located down the hill from the main house, contains five suites named for English authors: Lord Tennyson, Elizabeth Barrett, Emily Brontë, Charles Dickens, and Robert Browning. Offering more privacy and romantic accou-  trements than the big house, these suites boast a fireplace, wet bar, refrigerator, telephone (although why would you want one?), and a fireplace—some of them double-sided so that you can enjoy the fire in your bedroom and, the height of luxury, in your bathroom. Several offer garden tubs for two with spectacular views out the window. Because the tower dining area won't accommodate more guests than those staying in the main house, breakfast and evening liqueurs are brought to the Garden House Suites. If lovers want to be at all sociable, they can gather with fellow guests for afternoon refreshments on the veranda in good weather or around a crackling fire in the great room in inclement weather.

Open to its rafters and surrounded with stained-glass windows, the tower is the striking setting for the ample breakfast of egg dishes, breakfast meats, juices, fruits, special breads, and hot beverages. You'll feel like royalty feasting by candlelight under the ornate chandelier. After you return from dinner Irish coffee and hot chocolate are waiting, and you'll find a Godiva chocolate on your pillow at bedtime.

HOW TO GET THERE: From U.S. 64 in Cashiers, turn north on NC 107 and go 6 miles. Watch for the signs to the inn on the left.

Greystone Inn
Lake Toxaway, North Carolina 28747

OWNERS: Tim and Bobo Lovelace

ADDRESS/TELEPHONE: Greystone Lane; (704) 966–4700 or (800) 824–5766; fax (828) 862–5689

WEB SITE: www.greystoneinn.com

E-MAIL: greystone@citcom.net

ROOMS: 33; all with private bath, Jacuzzi, television, and telephone; some with fireplace and private balcony.

RATES: $265 to $525, per couple; includes breakfast and dinner, afternoon tea and cakes, hors d'oeuvres, and all recreational activities except golf fees (greens fees waved weekends shoulder season). Inquire about children's rates. Off-season rates and several packages are available. Thanksgiving and Christmas are magical.

OPEN: Year-round.

FACILITIES AND ACTIVITIES: Library-lounge with full bar service. Lake for swimming, boating, waterskiing, and fishing; heated swimming pool, golf course, tennis courts, croquet, horseshoes, lawn games, use of boats, and spa. Nearby: hiking, scenic drives, antiques and resort shops.

Ringed by an exclusive resort community, placid Lake Toxaway sits among several thousand acres of heavily wooded highlands. Driving past beautiful lakeshore homes and a golf club, tennis courts, and swimming pool, we followed the road for quite some way before we ultimately came to the centerpiece of the community—the historic Swiss revival–style, four-star Greystone Inn and its new additions perched on a promontory overlooking the lake. In addition to the mansion, there are several two-story almost motellike buildings, although they do blend in architecturally with the historic house—that contain upscale rooms and suites and another structure that houses the Lakeside Dining Room, which offers a panorama of the lake.

Enter the inn through the enclosed sunporch, where white wicker entices you to relax to watch the activities on the lake, read a good book, visit with fellow guests, or even steal a nap alongside your sweetheart. This is also the location of a delightful afternoon tea. Just beyond the sunporch is the first of two handsomely paneled lounges where you check in and a small gift shop. Behind the first lounge is a second one, which serves as a library and a cozy bar. In winter, fires blaze in both lounges. In good weather guests throw open the sets of French doors in the library and step out onto the stone ter-

race. Just picture you and your mate snuggled together, drinks in hand, watching the breeze play across the deep blue water of this pristine mountain lake.

Early in this century the Grey-stone was built as the private mansion of Lucy Moltz. When she first decided that she wanted to build a summer place in the woods beside Lake Toxaway, her husband, apparently a practical man, suggested that she camp out there for a while first to see if she really liked it. This she did—in a tent with hardwood floors staffed with eleven servants. After a successful season of "roughing it," she had the 16,000-square-foot mansion called Hillmont built.

Owner Tim Lovelace has worked hard to keep the intimate feeling of visiting a private home, but make no mistake—most of us don't visit private homes as luxurious as this. Every room in the inn has a magnificent view of the lake or grounds and is furnished in antiques and period reproductions similar to the furniture Mrs. Moltz had. The television sets are hidden in armoires. The rooms are named after the wealthy and famous people who used to visit Lake Toxaway.

Although we're partial to the quaint charm and eccentricities of the sumptuous rooms in the mansion, those in the Hillmont and Lakeside Suites buildings have their own considerable appeal. They're very spacious and contain a large seating area or separate sitting room, as well as a fireplace, whirlpool tub, ceiling fan, and private porch—some of them screened.

Guests dine in the Lakeside Dining Room, where every table has a great view of the water and the cuisine is gourmet. Breakfast and dinner are included in the nightly rate. Lunch is available at the golf club for an additional cost. During the peak season, jackets are required for gentlemen at dinner.

But as lovely as everything is inside the inn, the outdoor activities thrilled us more. In good weather, Tim is available to lead hikes along Horse Pasture River past three magnificent waterfalls. During the warmer months, he takes guests out on the lake on the party boat to watch the sunset. What could be more romantic than a champagne cruise before dinner? When the leaves are in color, the beauty of sailing or canoeing along the lake's 13 miles of shore-line can be an almost religious experience.

HOW TO GET THERE: The inn is in western North Carolina, 50 miles south of Asheville. It is off U.S. 64, 10 miles east of Cashiers and 17 miles west of Brevard. Turn into the Lake Toxaway entrance. It is clearly marked. Follow the signs 4 miles to the inn. Because you are driving steep, winding roads, it will feel longer, but keep going.

The Swag
Waynesville, North Carolina 28786

INNKEEPER: Deener Matthews

ADDRESS/TELEPHONE: 2300 Swag Road; (828) 926-0430 or (800) 789-7672; fax (828) 926-2036

E-MAIL: dianem@theswag.com

WEB SITE: www.theswag.com

ROOMS: 16 rooms, plus 3 cabins; all with private bath; 9 with fireplace or woodstove; some with whirlpool or steam shower, 2 with wheelchair access. No smoking inn.

RATES: $240 to $510 single or double, includes three meals daily, tea-time cookies, and an hour of hors d'oeuvres. Two-night minimum stay.

OPEN: May through November (closed weekend before Thanksgiving).

FACILITIES AND ACTIVITIES: Restaurant, brown bagging permitted. Gift shop, library, racquetball court, sauna, croquet, badminton, pond, 3 miles of hiking trails with marked plants and trees on Swag property, special interest events, entrance to hiking trails in Great Smoky Mountains National Park. Nearby: Asheville and Biltmore Estate, Maggie Valley.

"God lives here!" a guest told us when we visited this spectacular getaway. And we can readily believe it. First of all, we had twisted and turned up dozens of hairpin turns while climbing the incredibly steep dirt road to finally reach the lofty elevation of 5,000 feet. Once we got there, we were so close to the sky, we could easily believe that God was within easy reach. Second, on a clear day (and most of them are) the vista from this 250-acre privately owned mountaintop is more than 50 miles.

The inn is a collection of pioneer buildings that, back in the early 1970s, were hauled up the mountain, where they were grouped about vast, grassy grounds right at the edge of the Great Smoky Mountains National Park.

Everything is set up to make the most of the views and the outdoors: big windows and porches, rockers and hammocks, picnic nooks, a path, and several overlooks. We dropped into a pair of Adirondack chairs arranged along the brow of the mountain to contemplate the view, and we were mesmerized. You will be, too. As professional photographers, we found many spectacular shots to take—and we've sold quite a few of them. Be sure to get someone to take a picture of the two of you with the dramatic mountain background.

Inside, the public and guest rooms vary in detail but have in common rough wood walls, exposed beams, and wood floors. The rustic ambience contrasts with such luxuries as coffee grinders, coffeemakers, hair dryers, terry-cloth robes, and handmade covers and rugs. Many of the rooms offer a view of the mountains from your windows or your private porch.

Accommodations are also offered in several cabins, including Chestnut Lodge. Recently this lodge was gutted so that its three guest rooms could be

converted to two "super" rooms. Each of these new-and-improved accommodations now boasts a sleeping loft with a sofa, reading lamps, and a view as well as two bathrooms, one of which sports a whirlpool and separate steam shower and the other of which has a skylight shower—the perfect hideaway for you lovebirds. The lodge's common living room, which is often used for lectures in the special events series, has a new library loft with a Putnam rolling ladder to reach the high shelves.

You find more contrasts in the dining room. The room itself is rustic, with more wood walls and floors, plus tables that were handmade by a Tennessee furniture maker. Yet the service is professional. The food is sophisticated enough to include shredded jicama in a salad and simple enough to offer fresh trout without unnecessary extra trappings.

The library is filled with books stashed in old, stacked wooden crates, organized by category, and has an honor borrowing system. The collection ranges from local history to philosophy, with lots of mysteries, science fiction, and nature books as well. The inn also has a theological library.

What will come as a complete surprise to you is that deep in the bowels of the inn, burrowed into the mountain, is a racquetball court. So those Type-A personalities, to whom a stiff competition of some sort is their only idea of relaxation, won't have to worry about being bored. And when they're finished torturing their bodies, they can sweat off some more calories in the sauna.

The innkeeper's husband, Dan, is an Episcopalian priest in New York City; he's around infrequently. Throughout the inn you see extraordinarily good art with a religious theme. None of it is sentimental, nor do guests who are not Christian ever seem to find it bothersome. Without bowing to any dogma, The Swag practices hospitality as a joyful ministry.

You could drive down the mountain to find a church on Sunday, and you could drive to any number of tourist attractions in the area—but it seems to us that once you get up to the top of this mountain, walk in the woods, and look down on range after range of mountains following one another into the clouds, you've got all the entertainment and all the spiritual renewal you could possibly need.

HOW TO GET THERE: From I–40, take exit 20. Go south on Route 276 for 2 8/10 miles, turn right on Hemphill Road, and drive about 4 miles to the private road that winds up the mountain to the inn. The road is narrow and rough; it's only a few miles long, but will feel much longer.

Ansonborough Inn
Charleston, South Carolina 29401

INNKEEPER: Kevin Eichman

ADDRESS/TELEPHONE: 21 Hasell Street; (843) 723-1655 or
(800) 522-2073; fax (843) 577-6888

E-MAIL: ansonboroughinn@cchat.com

WEB SITE: www.aesir.com/ansonboroughinn

ROOMS: 37 suites; all with private bath, telephone, television, and
kitchen. No smoking inn.

RATES: Spring and fall, $139 to $199, double; summer and winter,
$109 to $139, double; includes continental breakfast and afternoon
wine and cheese. Inquire about discounts.

OPEN: Year-round.

FACILITIES AND ACTIVITIES: Free off-street parking. In heart of waterfront historic district. Nearby: historic sites, restaurants, shuttle transportation to visitor center. Walking distance to antiques shops and
downtown Charleston.

*L*ike so many Charleston inns, this one had a different function in its
earlier time. It was a three-story stationer's warehouse built about
1900. The building's renovation not only kept the heart-of-pine
beams and locally fired red brick, which are typical of the period, but actually emphasized them. The lobby soars three stories high, with skylights; the
original huge, rough beams are fully visible, an important part of the decor.

The original plan to
use the renovated building
as a condo complex didn't
work out, which probably
was bad news for some
investors; but it's great for
inn guests now, because
the rooms, which are really
suites, are huge. At least
one wall in each features
the exposed old brick. The
ceilings are about 20 feet

high. Because all the rooms were fit into an existing shell, no two rooms are exactly the same shape or size. Nothing is exactly predictable. The resulting little quirks, nooks, lofts, and alcoves add a lot of interest.

The living rooms are furnished in period reproductions with comfortable chairs and sleeper sofas to accommodate extra people. What's more, you really can cook in the kitchens. If you ask for place settings and basic kitchen utensils when you make your reservations, the kitchen will be ready when you arrive. The inn is just across the road from an excellent Harris Teeter supermarket housed in an old railroad station. I don't think it would be appropriate to whip up corned beef and cabbage or deep-fried chitlins in this environment, but the arrangement is great for preparing light meals—a good way to save your calories and your dollars for some sumptuous dinners in Charleston's excellent restaurants.

Clearly this isn't the kind of place where everyone sits around the breakfast table comparing notes about dinner the night before, but the continental breakfast (with sweetbreads baked at a plantation in Walterboro) and the evening wine and cheese are set up in the lobby so that guests can sit in conversational clusters. If someone on the staff thinks that you may have something in common with another guest, he or she will take the trouble to introduce you. Indeed, the staff here is personable and helpful—attitudes you don't always encounter in Charleston hostelries. A visitor from a Scandinavian country said that if this is Southern hospitality, he likes it.

HOW TO GET THERE: From I-26 east, take the Meeting Street/Visitor Center exit. Go 1²/₁₀ miles to Hasell Street. Turn left and go through the next traffic signal. From Route 17 south, take the East Bay Street exit, go 1³/₁₀ miles to Hasell and turn left. From Route 17 north, after crossing the Ashley River, exit to the right and go through the first traffic signal onto Calhoun Street. Drive 1⁴/₁₀ miles to Easy Bay Street, turn right, and go to the second traffic signal (Hassell Street) and turn left. The inn is on your right.

Woodlands Resort and Inn
Summerville, South Carolina 29483

INNKEEPER: Joe Whitmore

ADDRESS/TELEPHONE: 125 Parsons Road; (843) 875–2600 or (800) 774–9999; fax (843) 875–2603

E-MAIL: groupsales@woodlandsinn.com

WEB SITE: www.woodlandsinn.com

ROOMS: 19, including 9 executive suites, 4 junior suites, and 6 superior rooms; all with private bath, two telephones, television with VCR, alarm/radio, in-room safe, and robes; some with fireplace and/or whirlpool bath and heated towel racks. Three rooms are accessible to the disabled.

RATES: $295 for superior rooms, $325 for junior suites $350 for executive suites; includes afternoon tea upon request, turndown service, valet parking, and leisure activities; meals and spa services extra. Call about special packages.

OPEN: Year-round.

FACILITIES AND ACTIVITIES: Breakfast, lunch, and dinner in dining room; bar, conservatory, all-natural day spa; two English clay lighted tennis courts, professional croquet lawn, seasonally heated outdoor swimming pool with poolside food and beverage service; nature trails, bicycles. Facilities for weddings. Nearby: historic Summerville and Charleston, plantations, many golf courses, ocean beaches, seasonal theater, antiques shopping, galleries.

*T*he estate sanctuary at Woodlands is the perfect place for a honeymoon, anniversary, or other special occasion—or just because the two of you deserve a special getaway. Our experience is typical of what lovers might expect. It was after dark, but we knew we were in for a treat from the moment we wended our way through the towering pines and up the circular driveway to the clearing dominated by an imposing, white-columned neoclassical mansion. Spotlights on the exterior and lights blazing from the windows cast a welcoming glow. Alighting at the foot of the stairs sweeping up to the expansive veranda and turning our car over to valet parking, our royal treatment, based on quintessential Southern hospitality, began.

Built in 1906 and a luxurious private home until 1993, Woodlands was renovated and expanded to become an exquisite inn in 1995. The original house provides space for a delightful formal parlor and sumptuous guest

rooms. Wings added to both sides of the main house blend perfectly with the original structure and create room for suites, a restaurant, a lounge, and a conservatory. Elegantly appointed, without succumbing to the decorator look, public rooms and guest rooms reflect the Anglo-Indian and West Indian styles that so influenced the Low Country in past centuries. You feel that you are in a gracious home rather than a hotel.

You'll be thrilled with whichever lavish, spacious guest room or suite you're lucky enough to be assigned. Each has a distinct personality, but all are created with an eye to style and creature comforts with magnificent furnishings, four-poster or canopy king- or queen-sized rice beds, upscale amenities, and all the modern conveniences. Some rooms boast sitting areas, gas-log fireplaces, whirlpool baths and separate showers, or heated towel racks.

You'll know you're in for an unparalleled romantic experience from the moment you enter your bed chamber. For starters, fresh flowers—usually signature yellow roses—as well as a split of iced Perrier-Jouet champagne await you, so kick off your shoes and relax in a deep chair while you imbibe this extravagant welcome. So enticing are the guest rooms that you may never want to leave yours, but the resort offers many inducements to draw you out to explore and enjoy.

The resort tempts guests with a variety of activities in the relaxed gentility of the countryside. Sit in a rocker on the veranda with a good book, exercise vigorously on the tennis courts, play a leisurely round of croquet on the professional lawn, swim in the pool, play badminton or pitch horseshoes, or enjoy the forty-two acres of grounds by bicycling or strolling the nature trails. After exercise, perhaps you can pamper yourself with the services of the spa: facials, manicures, pedicures, herbal body wraps or sea-salt glows, or massage therapy. Fresh fruit, honey, and cocoa butter are a few of the natural ingredients used to create the delightful treatments, which are performed by candlelight. If your afternoon schedule permits, request afternoon tea in the luxurious Winter Garden, a cheery conservatory furnished with wicker.

Dining is a gastronomic experience at Woodlands and should be savored. You dine while listening to the lilting strains emanating from the grand piano. Chef Ken Vedrinski's innovative, sophisticated contemporary regional cuisine with an Asian influence has been recognized each year since 1997 with the AAA Five Diamond Award for Culinary Excellence—an award shared by only a few other restaurants in America; Woodlands is the only one so honored in South Carolina. The stunning circular formal dining room seats seventy-five and offers many windowside or tucked-away tables perfect for lovers. Those who want to watch Chef Vedrinski at work may request a seat at the chef's table in the kitchen. Menus change daily, and you may order your dinner in three to five fixed-price courses. Presentation and service are exemplary. You can accompany your feast with a selection from the award-winning wine list. When you return to your bed chamber, you'll find that nightly turndown service includes chocolates or cookies handmade by Woodlands' pastry chef. Sweet dreams for you and your honey are guaranteed.

All this, as well as impeccable service and attention to detail, has earned the one-of-a-kind resort the designation as one of only seventeen AAA Five Diamond Resorts and Restaurants in the country in 1997, 1998, and 1999. It is also a member of the prestigious world-renowned Relais & Chateaux collection of exquisite hotels—one of only four in the Southeast.

HOW TO GET THERE: Take exit 199A off I–26 to Summerville (Highway 17A, Main Street). After you cross the railroad tracks, watch for the town square; turn right (north) onto Route 165 (West Richardson Avenue) and follow it to Parsons Road (on left). Turn left; Woodlands is on your left.

Richmont Inn
Townsend, Tennessee 37882

INNKEEPERS: Susan and Jim Hind and Jim, Jr., and Hilda Hind

ADDRESS/TELEPHONE: 220 Winterberry Lane; (423) 448-6751;
fax: (423) 448-6480

E-MAIL: richmontinn@worldnet.att.net

WEB SITE: www.thesmokies.com/richmont–inn/

ROOMS: 10 rooms; all with private bath, robes, piped-in music,
coffeemaker, hair dryer, refrigerator; most with double-sized whirlpool
tub, fireplace, and balcony; one room with wheelchair access.

RATES: $105 to $150 includes full breakfast, afternoon coffee and tea,
and evening gourmet desserts.

OPEN: Year-round.

FACILITIES AND ACTIVITIES: Sitting room, dining area, potting shed,
greenhouse, chapel. Nearby: Great Smoky Mountains National Park,
hiking, biking, fishing, horseback riding, whitewater rafting, golf,
swimming, historic tours, antiques and mountain crafts shopping.

*T*he Richmont Inn is a perfect example of the adage that you can't
tell a book—even a love story—by its cover. Who would ever think
that this rustic barnlike structure conceals spacious, comfortable
guest rooms, most of which boast romantic accoutrements such as a wood-
burning or gas-log fireplace, double-size spa tub, and private balcony.

As we did, you'll drive through deep woods and pull up in front of what
appears to be an unusual weathered gray barn—not just any barn, but one
where the square upper story overhangs the smaller lower story. In fact, the
B&B inn is modeled after the Appalachian cantilever barn, which is a hall-
mark of nearby Cades Cove and indigenous to the mountainous areas of
eastern Tennessee and western North Carolina. With its ideal, secluded
location facing Laurel Valley and towering Rich Mountain, for which it is
named, we knew the inn would make a perfect getaway.

We were warmly greeted by Susan and Jim Hind, who explained the barn's
style to us and told us that farmers often chose that design because the overhang provided shelter for animals in bad weather. Asked why they had chosen to model their bed-and-breakfast after these interesting structures, Jim
said simply, "I've always loved barns."

Our first impression was that the interior would be as rustic as the exterior, but we were partially wrong. True, the main living/dining area does have

mortar-chinked barn-wood walls, the 13-foot-high ceilings are open to the exposed beams, and broad planks and gray slates cover the floors. But the fireplace wall is formally paneled in white and is embellished with fine moldings and a graceful mantel. Antiques, traditional furnishings, comfortable overstuffed sofas and chairs, original sculpture, and French paintings create an upscale total look.

A huge corner window in the dining area permits an unparalleled panorama of the valley and mountains. The stunning view from here is everchanging, depending on the time of day, the season of the year, and the weather. What a perfect place for the two of you to enjoy a gourmet breakfast, which might be something scrumptious such as an egg-and-sausage casserole or apple-cinnamon pancakes with fresh fruit and maple syrup. When darkness settles, candles are lit and the room is transformed into a romantic scene where you can gaze deeply into each others eyes while you savor sinful desserts.

Considering that the exterior of the inn gives the impression that there are few windows, you might be surprised to find that each guest room actually has windows that admit an amazing amount of light as well as stunning views. Guest chambers are named for obscure and unselfish men and women who made major contributions to the history and culture of the Great Smoky Mountains. Each chamber is decorated in a manner that pays homage to its namesake. Old barn paneling, folk art, canopy beds, a stainedglass window, log walls, and Native American art set each room apart from every other. Each, however, brims with modern comforts and conveniences such as a private bath, a king- or queen-sized bed, piped-in music, hair dryer, coffeemaker, and lounging robes. Most boast a wood-burning or gas-log fireplace, double-size spa tub, and private balcony.

The Hinds recognize that many visitors love the property and its sur-roundings so much that they'd prefer not to leave at all, so they can provide some other meal options at an additional fee. An adjacent building serves from spring through fall as a casual cafe where you can enjoy a fondue din-ner. They will also provide dinner baskets so that you can enjoy a private "pic-nic" in your room. This basket might be filled with such delicacies as cold chicken breast, smoked trout, salad, fruit, Brie, and bread. They'll prepare similar picnics for you to take on hikes and other outings. Look for more additions and surprises at this sentimental inn in the future.

HOW TO GET THERE: As you enter Townsend at mile marker 26 from Maryville on U.S. 321 North, take the first right onto Old Tuckaleechee Road. Turn right on Laurel Valley, the next paved road, and go ⁸/₁₀ mile through the stone wall entrance. Go to the crest of the hill and turn left.

Blackberry Farm
Walland, Tennessee 37886

INNKEEPERS: Brian Lee; Kreis and Sandy Beall, owners

ADDRESS/TELEPHONE: 1471 West Millers Cove; (423) 984–8166; fax (423) 983–5708

E-MAIL: info@blackberryfarm.com

WEB SITE: www.blackberryfarm.com

ROOMS: 23 estate rooms and 16 cottage suites; all with private bath, feather bed, television, VCR, and telephone; suites with whirlpool bath and fireplace. Wheelchair accessible.

RATES: $395 to $550 for rooms, $650 for cottage suites; includes all meals, afternoon tea, and recreational equipment and amenities; deduct $100 during winter months. A two-night minimum is required for all stays; Friday and Saturday may not be split unless reserved one week prior to arrival and space is available; a three-night minimum is required in October.

OPEN: Year-round.

FACILITIES AND ACTIVITIES: Restaurant, outdoor heated pool, tennis courts, stocked fishing ponds, putting green, hiking and nature trails, bicycles, fully equipped fitness room. Nearby: Great Smoky Mountains National Park, antiques and crafts shops.

*L*overs of all ages and length of union proclaim the gemlike inn at Blackberry Farm to be a place of unparalleled accommodations, extraordinary personal service, and exquisite culinary experiences. A few days at this sumptuous romantic hideaway are guaranteed to lull you into the "Blackberry state of mind" and to create glorious sentimental memories. Don't wait for a honeymoon or anniversary to indulge in this one-of-a-kind fairy-tale estate.

The resort's reputation whet our appetite for a visit and our anticipation mounted as we traveled a country road meandering through a valley, or cove, of neat-as-a-pin farmsteads before coming to the stately Virginia fence and gateway to Blackberry Farm. After driving up the heavily wooded hill, we emerged at the stunning frame-and-stone country house perched at the top.

We were welcomed at the front door of this inn as if we were long-lost relatives returning to a beautiful family home. Our luggage was whisked inside and our car spirited off and we were escorted to our room in the elegant Guest House next door, which blends so perfectly with the restored manor house that you'd swear they were built at the same time. Recently, Holly Glade Cottages of suites have been added, scattered throughout the grounds. In all the resort boasts forty-two luxurious accommodations, including those in the historic main house.

This sophisticated and gracious country inn is the centerpiece of an 1,100-acre estate bordering the Great Smoky Mountains National Park. A stylish ambience reminiscent of great English country houses is achieved in all the public rooms and guest chambers by the lavish use of English and American antiques, period reproductions, floral chintz fabrics, opulent window treat-

ments, and carefully selected art. Sumptuous, intensely romantic guest rooms in the main house and guest house are spacious, comfortable, and opulently decorated. Canopy or four-poster beds topped with feather mattresses, fresh flowers, and plush robes create an idyllic surroundings in which to kindle your relationship. If you need even more seductive surroundings, the new knock-your-socks-off Cottage Suites are even larger and boast a king-sized feather bed, whirlpool bath, woodburning fireplace, entertainment center, stocked refrigerator/pantry, and covered porch.

When we want to spend some quiet time appreciating each other, one of our favorite activities is simply to pull up a pair of rocking chairs from the ones lined up across the stone patio so that we can gaze out at the vast expanses of forests and rolling lawns. We never get tired of the glorious panorama because it's always changing, depending on the season, weather, and time of day. More likely than not, early morning reveals a heavy mist draped over the peaks, educating you as to why Native Americans called the ridges the Smoky Mountains. Gradually the veils of mist lift, revealing not only the forests but also birds and wildlife. If you've forgotten binoculars, borrow a pair from the collection sitting on the windowsill. On the occasional inclement day or during the winter season, the public lounges are filled with books, magazines, and games to help you enjoy your time of utter relaxation by a blazing fireplace.

Although the attractions of the national park, as well as several small towns filled with antiques and crafts shops, may entice you off the property, you may opt not to leave it at all. A splendid restaurant specializing in creative Southern cuisine allows you to eat all your meals on the property. A pool, tennis courts, fishing ponds, putting green, shuffleboard, and bicycles attract more active guests, as do hiking along secluded mountain trails crossing burbling streams and canoeing. Orvis-certified instructors provide free fly-fishing demonstrations on Saturdays, and all fly rods and flies are provided. Try your hand in the stocked pond or in Hesse Creek, which flows out of the national park. Cooking schools are scheduled periodically throughout the year. Christmas at Blackberry Farm is a never-to-be-forgotten experience.

HOW TO GET THERE: From I–75, exit onto U.S. 321 east to Walland; just past Walland watch for West Miller Cove Road, turn right and follow the signs to the inn.

The Midwest

by Bob Puhala

Whether you prefer classic romance like *Romeo and Juliet* or modern love tales such as the *Horse Whisperer*, it's obvious that love is what makes your world go round. But did you realize that the Midwest holds tremendous romantic potential for those searching out a getaway rendezvous?

From restored farmhouses given new life as a couples' getaway to renowned Victorian hotels elegantly restored to their former 1800s grandeur, Midwest wanderers will discover hideaway retreats featuring all kinds of romantic ambience—from cozy rooms boasting roaring fireplaces to suites offering huge whirlpool baths, see-through hearths, and king-sized canopy beds.

And the only reason for all this pampering is so that you and your special someone can rediscover your romantic potential that's often left at the front door of your hurly-burly, whirlwind lives.

Two of the most romantic retreats my wife, Debbie, and I have ever visited are located in the Midwest. Canoe Bay, a sixteen-room masterpiece in Chetek, Wisconsin, combines its 280 acres of private, natural wonderlands with some of the most luxurious and elegant inn rooms of the Midwest. In fact, it is the first Midwest lodging to become a member of the prestigious Paris-based *Relais et Châteaux,* which includes many of the finest hotels and lodgings in the world. At the other end of the size-scale is The American Club in Kohler, Wisconsin, boasting 236 rooms and a five-star rating—the only such rated resort hotel in the region. It more resembles a baronial estate than a hotel—with all the finery and lavishness you'd expect at a titled English retreat.

But it's not just the surroundings that make an inn score high on the romance scale. There's ambience and pampering, too. Some inns offer breakfast baskets delivered right to your door. Others boast candlelight breakfast meals in a formal and highly romantic atmosphere—and that includes a crackling fireplace nearby.

Yes, there are many opportunities for couples to enjoy a romantic rendezvous in the Midwest. And here are some of the best places I know.

The rest is up to you!

The Midwest

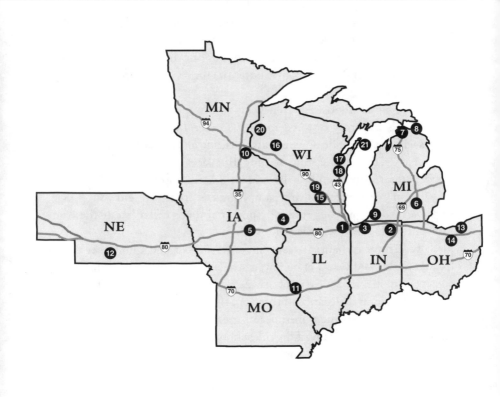

The Midwest

Numbers on map refer to towns numbered below.

The Wheaton Inn
Wheaton, Illinois 60187

INNKEEPER: Dennis Stevens

ADDRESS/TELEPHONE: 301 West Roosevelt Road; (630) 690–2600

ROOMS: 16; all with private bath and air-conditioning; some with Jacuzzi. Wheelchair access.

RATES: $99 to $215, single or double; EPB. Weekend packages.

OPEN: Year-round.

FACILITIES AND ACTIVITIES: Patio, lawn area with croquet course and gardens, sitting room, dining area. Nearby: McCormick's Cantigny war museum, Prairie Path hike and bike trail; Herrick Lake paddle boating and fishing; Wheaton Water Park; Fox River and Geneva famous shopping districts; horseback riding; Morton Arboretum; Wheaton College's Billy Graham Center; golf courses; tennis courts; polo grounds. Also a short drive to Drury Lane Theatres.

With a little imagination, romantic nights can be yours at the Wheaton Inn, which weaves so well today's sophistication with yesterday's elegance. Completed in 1987, it relies on opulence in the Colonial Williamsburg tradition for its distinctive flair.

Attractive rooms are named after famous Wheaton citizens. Cuddlers note that eleven have gas fireplaces, many boast Jacuzzi tubs, and each has an elegantly distinctive personality. All have European towel warmers in their bathrooms—another thoughtful touch, especially for coosome twosomes who venture out in Chicago winters.

Rooms have oversized styles often found in European concierge hotels. The Woodward Room is one of my favorites, with its Jacuzzi situated in front of a large bay window that overlooks the inn's gardens. (Go ahead and use your imagination.) The fireplace marble came from the face of Marshall Field's department store in downtown Chicago. (By the way, the room's namesake, Judge Alfred Woodward, is the father of newspaperman Bob Woodward, who broke the Watergate scandal for the *Washington Post* along with Carl Bernstein.)

Vaulted ceilings in the third-floor McCormick Room, along with its huge four-poster bed and windows overlooking the garden, make this a "romance" favorite. Another charmer is the Morton Room, with its alcoved ceiling, cozy fireplace, and 4½-foot-deep Jacuzzi, perfect for couples who yearn for a relaxing soak.

Especially romantic nights can be yours in the Rice Room, where a Jacuzzi sits almost in the middle of the room, in front of a fireplace, and two skylights let you gaze at the stars above.

Only the Ottoson Room, named after the inn architect, departs from the Williamsburg theme. A brass-topped black iron-rail bed is dwarfed by cathedral ceilings that harbor a skylight.

In a cheery, window-lit breakfast room, couples enjoy the innkeeper's European-style buffet of imported coffee and teas, hot egg dishes, seasonal fruits, and delicious pastries and muffins. Personal service is a trademark here, so expect amenities like afternoon cheese and crackers, freshly baked cookies and milk, twenty-four-hour coffee, and bedtime turndown service with chocolate treats left on your pillow.

Other "personal" service is up to you!

HOW TO GET THERE: From Chicago, take I-294 to Roosevelt Road, then go west to the inn.

The Checkerberry Inn
Goshen, Indiana 46526

INNKEEPERS: John and Susan Graff, owners; Sheila Reed, manager

ADDRESS/TELEPHONE: 62644 County Road 37; (219) 642-4445

ROOMS: 13, including 3 suites; all with private bath and air-conditioning. Wheelchair access.

RATES: Sunday through Thursday, $112 to $260; Friday and Saturday, $140 to $325; single or double; continental breakfast.

OPEN: May through December; limited time February through April; closed January.

FACILITIES AND ACTIVITIES: Full-service dining room, swimming pool, arbor, croquet course, tennis court, hiking trails, cross-country ski area. In the midst of Amish farmlands; offers horse-drawn buggy tours of Amish surroundings, sleigh rides in winter. Near Shipshewana auctions, Middlebury festivals.

"We wanted to create a European feel to the inn," Susan said. "After all, being surrounded on all sides by Amish farmlands is more than enough country ambience."

The fine appointments of this northern Indiana inn do remind me of intimate, romantic European hotels I've stayed at. In fact, the handsome photographs adorning inn walls were taken by John during his travels in the French Bordeaux region.

Amish straw hats hang over beds, lending a cozy regional touch to luxurious guest rooms that boast fine-arts prints, furniture with definite European flair, wide windows that allow views of the rolling countryside, and amenities like Swiss goat's milk soap in the baths. Rooms are named for flowers; my favorite is Foxglove, with its sitting-room fireplace, whirlpool bath, and six windows—an almost perfect lovers' retreat.

Queen Anne's Lace is another handsome room; its most interesting feature is a primitive secretary, made in the 1850s. It consists of 1,200 individual pieces, and it took three years to complete. Its geometric designs put that craftsman far ahead of his time.

The inn's restaurant leans toward country-French and contemporary cuisine. Four-course meals begin with a fresh garden salad, followed by a fresh fruit sorbet, entree, and dessert. An inn specialty is double duck breast sautéed and served over sweet onions, topped with an orange and port wine sauce, accompanied by *pommes Anna* and a bouquet of fresh vegetables. The vegetables, herbs, and spices are grown specially for the inn. Other favorites include chicken basil, veal medallions, and rack of lamb served off the bone with herb cream-and-garlic cheese.

Checkerberry sits on one hundred acres, so there's plenty of quiet and relaxation. It's just a walk through French doors to the swimming pool, and the woods contain numerous hiking trails. The inn provides Indiana's only professional croquet course, so now is the time to perfect your game.

Unless you're too busy enjoying each other.

HOW TO GET THERE: From Chicago, take the Indiana Toll Road (I–80/90) to the Middlebury exit (#107). Go south on Indiana 13, turn west on Indiana 4, then go south on County Road 37 to the inn. It's 14 miles from the toll-road exit to the inn.

Creekwood Inn
Michigan City, Indiana 46360

INNKEEPER: Mary Lou Linnen

ADDRESS/TELEPHONE: Route 20/35 at Interstate 94; (219) 872–8357

ROOMS: 13, including 1 suite; all with private bath and air conditioning. Wheelchair access.

RATES: $143 to $168, double, weekends; $123 to $148, double, weekdays. Subtract $10 for single; $133, suite; continental breakfast.

OPEN: All year except two weeks in mid-March and Christmas Day.

FACILITIES AND ACTIVITIES: A short drive to southeastern shore of Lake Michigan, Indiana Dunes State Park, Warren Dunes State Park in Michigan. Charter fishing, swimming, boating; antiquing in nearby lakeside communities; area winery tours; Old Lighthouse Museum; "Fruit Belt" for fruit and vegetable farms.

The Creekwood Inn is nestled amid thirty-three acres of walnut, oak, and pine trees near a fork in tiny Walnut Creek. The winding wooded roadway leading to the inn is breathtaking, especially in the fall, when nature paints the trees in glorious colors.

Done in English Cottage design, the inn is romantic, cozy, and classically gracious. Massive hand-hewn wooden ceiling beams on the main floor were taken from an old area toll bridge by the original owner, who built the home in the 1930s. The parlor has a large fireplace, surrounded by comfortable sofas and chairs—a perfect setting for afternoon tea or intimate midnight conversation. Wood planking makes up the floors, and you can gaze out a bay window that overlooks the estate's lovely grounds.

Mary Lou said she wanted to combine the ambience of a country inn with the romantic pampering that people have come to expect. She has done better than that; she has established a first-class retreat. Twelve large guest rooms and a suite are tastefully decorated in a mixture of styles; incurable romantics should note that some have fireplaces and terraces. All have huge beds, overstuffed chairs, and minirefrigerators.

Couples should visit the Conservatory, overlooking the inn's pond and gardens, which offers both a comfy spot to enjoy nature and a chance to luxuriate in the whirlpool or hit the exercise room.

Mary Lou visited Oxford, England, and was inspired to plant an English perennial garden on the east side of the inn. Things just keep getting better.

One winter my wife and I stayed here during an especially snowy stretch. We simply walked out the front door, slipped on our touring skis, and beat a path to the inn's private cross-country trails, which wind through deep woods and

past Lake Spencer, the inn's private lake. Average skiers, we completed the loops in about twenty minutes, returning with a hearty breakfast appetite. Mary Lou served us a tasty continental breakfast of freshly baked breads, pastries, fruit, and coffee. It was one of the most romantic winter mornings we ever spent together.

Late-afternoon tea in the parlor offers cookies and some delicious pastries. You may even have a cup of hot chocolate at bedtime on a blustery winter night, stretching before the fire with your partner and toasting your toes.

Mary Lou now serves dinner every night at the inn's American Grille. Be prepared for savory delights from chef Kathy deFuniak, who came from Ambria's in Chicago's Lincoln Park. These might include New Zealand lamb loin with basil whipped potatoes and summer tomato salad; crispy soft-shell crab with citrus vinaigrette; portobello mushroom lasagna; herb-roasted chicken with sweet corn and garlic polenta; and much more.

Desserts might include anything from simple fresh-fruit tarts to "gooey chocolate" treats—her husband's favorite.

HOW TO GET THERE: Heading northeast to Michigan City on I-94, take exit 40B. Then take an immediate left turn onto 600W, and turn into the first drive on the left. The inn is at Route 20/35, just off the interstate.

Squiers Manor
Maquoketa, Iowa 52060

INNKEEPERS: Cathy and Virl Banowetz

ADDRESS/TELEPHONE: 418 West Pleasant Street; (319) 652–6961

ROOMS: 8, including 3 suites; all with private bath and air-conditioning.

RATES: $75 to $110, single or double; $160 to $195, suites; EPB.

OPEN: Year-round.

FACILITIES AND ACTIVITIES: Library, parlor, porch. Nearby: A short drive to Mississippi River towns; Dubuque, site of low-stakes riverboat casino gambling; and Galena, Illinois, a Civil War–era architectural wonderland.

*N*othing prepares you for the romantic splendor of this 1882 house, listed on the National Register of Historic Places. The handsome Queen Anne home boasts fine wood everywhere. There's a walnut parlor, a cherry dining room, and butternut throughout the rest of the house.

Fine antiques are everywhere, too; some, such as the 1820s Federal four-poster mahogany bed in the Harriet Squiers Room, are of museum quality.

That's not surprising, since Cathy and Virg also own a nationally renowned antiques store just a few miles out of town. But enough about architecture and antiques . . . let's get down to the things that really matter.

Romantics should try the Jeannie Mitchel Bridal Suite. Its canopied brass bed stands more than 7 feet tall. (Note the mother-of-pearl on the footboard.)

And the Victorian Renaissance dresser with marble top is another treasure.

Did I mention that the suite has a double whirlpool bath?

So does the J. E. Squiers Room; there a green marble floor creates a path leading to a cozy corner whirlpool for two. What better way to spend an evening on a romantic getaway.

And Opal's Parlor (named after a longtime resident of the manor when it rented its rooms as apartments) features not only 1860s antiques and hand-crocheted bedspreads but also a Swiss shower that acts "like a human car wash," said Cathy. (Create your own romantic fantasies here.)

Every common room bespeaks luxury and splendor. The parlor's fireplace, with tiles depicting characters in Roman mythology, is unusual. Look at the fabulous hand-carved cherry buffet in the dining room. The dining room's 10-foot-tall hand-carved jewelers' clock is another conversation starter.

And the library, an enclave done entirely in butternut paneling and graced with its original fireplace, is flat-out gorgeous.

Not only do you get great atmosphere; Cathy's breakfasts are terrific, too. Consider pumpkin-pecan muffins, black-walnut bread, eggs Katrina, pecan-stuffed French toast, seafood quiches, apple pudding, and more.

A romantic wrinkle is "candlelight evening desserts." Imagine nibbling on Cathy's chocolate bourbon pecan pie, delicious tortes, or Grandma Annie's bread pudding, a guest favorite. Other kinds of nibbling are optional.

And there are two fantastic new suites reclaimed from the house's grand ballroom. The Loft boasts a gas-log fireplace for instant romance, a 6-by-4-foot whirlpool tub, and a wicker sitting room—with breakfast delivered to your bedchamber.

The Ballroom (that's the other suite's name) is an incredible 1,100 square feet of luxury, with a whirlpool tub nestled in a "garden" setting, king-sized bed, cathedral ceiling, massive sitting room, reading nook, and lots more surprises.

Maybe this is your own "Garden of Eden."

HOW TO GET THERE: From Dubuque, take U.S. 61 south to U.S. 64, then turn east into town. One block past the second stoplight, turn right, then go 1 block to the inn.

La Corsette Maison Inn
Newton, Iowa 50208

INNKEEPER: Kay Owen

ADDRESS/TELEPHONE: 629 First Avenue; (515) 792–6833

ROOMS: 5, including 2 suites; all with private bath and air-conditioning. No smoking inn.

RATES: $75 to $110, single or double; $145 to $170, suites; Sister Inn, 2 bedchambers, $145 and $170; EPB. Multinight minimum during Pella, Iowa, Tulip Festival and some other special events. Pets allowed by pre-arrangement.

OPEN: Year-round.

FACILITIES AND ACTIVITIES: Gourmet five-course dinners. Two sitting rooms with fireplace; porch. Nearby: Maytag Company tours, tennis courts, golf courses, horseback riding, cross-country skiing. A short drive to Trainland, U.S.A., Prairie Meadows Horse Track, Krumm Nature Preserve.

My wife, Debbie, and I sat in front of a roaring fire in an elegant parlor, enjoying a romantic gourmet-style breakfast. First Kay brought us a delightful fresh-fruit compote of pink grapefruit, mandarin orange slices, grapes, and kiwi. Her home-baked apple muffins with strudel were next. (We could have eaten four apiece, they were so delicious.)

We sipped on raspberry and orange juice, which washed down authentic English scones, another of Kay's specialties. Then came a wonderful frittata with two cheeses—and some special La Corsette French bread.

It was one of the ultimate bed-and-breakfast experiences for lovers.

It's also no wonder that Kay's inn has received a four-and-one-half-star rating from the *Des Moines Register* and has been hailed as a "gleaming jewel in the crown of fine restaurants."

The mansion itself is a 1909 Mission-style masterpiece built by an early Iowa state senator. Not much has changed in the intervening years. Gleaming Mission-oak woodwork, Art Nouveau stained-glass windows, and other turn-of-the-century architectural flourishes make La Corsette a special place.

We overnighted in the Windsor Hunt Suite; the massive bedchamber has a huge four-poster bed (you use a stepstool to reach the high mattress), and the sitting room boasts its own fireplace—which we used for a romantic end to the day—as well as a two-person whirlpool bath.

Other rooms are imbued with their own particular charms. The Penthouse bedchambers, for instance, are located in the tower and surrounded by beveled-glass windows. Use your imagination here.

Kay's romantic five-course gourmet-style dinners, prepared by both herself and a new chef (a graduate of the Culinary Institute of America, by the way), are

renowned. The first person to make reservations for the evening sets the night's menu. Choices include the likes of French veal in cream, broccoli-stuffed game hen with Mornay sauce, and roast loin of pork with prune chutney.

Maybe you'd rather have a romantic basket dinner delivered to your door during weekday visits. This three-course treat might included stuffed pork chops, fancy veggies, home-baked breads, and more.

Or choose to stay at the one-hundred-year-old Sister Inn next door. Here Kay features double whirlpools and antique soaking tubs. Imagine the fun. . . .

HOW TO GET THERE: From the Quad Cities, take I–80 to Newton (exit 164), and go north until the second light (Highway 6); then turn right and continue 7 blocks to the inn.

Pine Ridge Inn
Fenton, Michigan 48430

INNKEEPER: Jim and Val Soldan

ADDRESS/TELEPHONE: N-10345 Old U.S. 23; (810) 629–8911 or (800) 353–8911

ROOMS: 4; all with private bath, whirlpool tub, and fireplace.

RATES: $145, single or double, Monday through Thursday; $195, single or double, Friday through Sunday and holidays; continental breakfast.

OPEN: Year-round.

FACILITIES AND ACTIVITIES: Walking paths through forest and by pond. Nearby: Less than an hour's drive to Pontiac Silverdome, Henry Ford Museum and Greenfield Village, and metro Detroit.

*I*f ever there was a setting for privacy and romance, this is it. Secluded in a very remote forty acres amid swaying pine trees and rolling hills, the Pine Ridge Inn is an exclusive hideaway. No phones. No pets. Just you and your honey for a luxurious and romantic interlude.

Guest rooms are elegant and huge, with lovey-dovey relaxation kept in mind. Those king-sized beds are actually firm waterbeds. Whirlpools are massive, measuring 7 by 7 feet. And a romantic fire in the hearth is only a fingertip away, thanks to gas-log fireplaces that light up the room with a very romantic glow.

They say you "never have to leave your room" at the Pine Ridge. Sure enough. A gourmet snack tray is delivered to your bedchamber each evening. And a deli-

cious continental breakfast tray will be found at your door come morning.

For those who do venture outside, walk along a cozy forest path marked with red hearts. Or gaze longingly at the inn's pond. Winter visitors might cross-country ski on a blanket of newly fallen snow.

But when your guest room has all the above, plus stereo and remote-control television, why bother ever leaving until it's time to leave?

HOW TO GET THERE: From east or west, take I–96 to U.S. 23. Turn north and continue to White Lake Road exit; turn left, then turn left immediately onto Old U.S. 23, and continue to inn.

Kimberly Country Estate
Harbor Springs, Michigan 49740

INNKEEPERS: Ronn and Billie Serba

ADDRESS/TELEPHONE: 2287 Bester Road; (616) 526–7646 or 526–9502

ROOMS: 6, including 3 suites; all with private bath. Wheelchair access.

RATES: $145 to $235, single or double; EPB and afternoon tea. Two-night minimum on weekends. Special packages. No smoking inn.

OPEN: Year-round.

FACILITIES AND ACTIVITIES: Living room, library, lower-level entertainment room, terrace, swimming pool. Nearby: golf, biking, hiking; sailing and other water activities on Little Traverse Bay; a short drive to chic shops in Harbor Springs; downhill skiing at Boyne Highlands and Nubs Nob.

*R*onn and Billie's inn could be a romantic showcase for *House Beautiful.* That's not surprising, I guess; Ronn, an interior designer, has transformed this Southern plantation–style home into an elegant retreat that offers some of the most extraordinarily luxurious inn surroundings possible.

We got the red-carpet treatment (literally) as we mounted steps to the house, set atop a gentle hill and surrounded by fields and farms.

Inside, Chippendale and Queen Anne–style furniture, Battenburg linens, Laura Ashley fabrics, and exquisite antiques collected by the innkeepers over forty years add to the elegance.

The Lexington Suite is the epitome of romanticism, with its four-poster bed and Battenburg linens lending touches of sophistication; this room also has its

own sitting area, wood-burning fireplace, and Jacuzzi.

Le Soleil is another of our favorites, with its walls of windows, sunny yellow color, and hand stenciling. And four of the rooms open onto a shaded veranda overlooking the inn's 22-by-40-foot swimming pool.

The library is a most stunning common room. It's entirely paneled with North Carolina black walnut—milled on the spot as the house was built, Billie told me.

Pampering is legion here. Guests find a decanter of sherry in their rooms upon arrival, with an invitation to join Ronn and Billie for afternoon tea and hors d'oeuvres—sometimes at poolside in good weather. At night they return to their rooms to discover beds turned down and chocolate truffles on the pillows.

Weekend breakfasts are another Southern-tinged plantation treat. Billie might serve fresh fruit compote, scrambled eggs, smoked turkey sausage, home-baked muffins, and more.

If you want to experience the "estate of the art" in romantic country inn living, make your reservations now.

HOW TO GET THERE: From Petoskey, take U.S. 31 north to Michigan 119; continue north toward Harbor Springs. Turn right at Emmet Heights Road, then left on Bester Road, and continue to the inn.

Grand Hotel
Mackinac Island, Michigan 49757

INNKEEPER: R. D. Musser III, corporation president

ADDRESS/TELEPHONE: Mackinac Island; (906) 847–3331 or
(800) 334–7263 (reservations)

ROOMS: 324; all with private bath.

RATES: $160 to $485 per person, May through mid-June; $180 to $525
mid-June through late October. Children in same room with two persons, $25 to $99 per child; MAP. Special packages available.

OPEN: Mid-May to late October.

FACILITIES AND ACTIVITIES: Main dining room, Geranium Bar, Grand
Stand (food and drink), Audubon Bar, Carleton's Tea Store, pool grill;
magnificent swimming pool, private golf course, bike rentals, saddle
horses, tennis courts, exercise trail; carriage tours, dancing, movies.
Expansive grounds, spectacular veranda with wonderful lake vistas.
Nearby: museums, historic Fort Mackinac, Mackinac Island State Park,
and other sites, guided tours; specialty shops. There are no motor vehi-
cles allowed on historic Mackinac Island; visitors walk or rent horses,
horse-drawn carriages and taxis, and bicycles.

The Grand Hotel, built in 1887, has been called one of the great hotels
of the railroad and Great Lakes steamer era. Its location high on an
island bluff provides magnificent vistas over the Straits of Mackinac
waters. And it also was the location for one of the most romantic period movies
ever made—*Somewhere in Time*—which still draws fans to the historic hostelry.

Its incredible, many-columned veranda is 660 feet
long (it claims to be the longest in the world) and
is decorated with huge American flags snap-
ping in the wind, bright yellow awnings
that catch the color of the sun,
and colorful red geraniums
hanging everywhere. Many
guests simply sit in generous
rockers, sip on a drink, relax,
and enjoy cooling lake breezes.
We also like to admire the hotel's acres of
woodland and lawns, finely manicured with exquisite flower gardens and greenery arrangements.

At the Grand Hotel, guests feel immersed in a long-ago era of luxury and romance. Even the attire of hotel attendants harkens back to a long-ago era; they're dressed in long red coats and black bow ties. Once Debbie and I rode the hotel's elegant horse-drawn carriage (the driver wore a black top hat and formal "pink" hunting jacket) from the ferry docks, up the long hill, to the grand portico. That was one of the most romantic journeys we've ever taken.

Inside, the hotel boasts Victorian-era colors and decor—greens, yellows, and whites, with balloon draperies on the windows, high-back chairs and sofas everywhere in numerous public rooms, and a healthy dash of yesteryear memorabilia hanging on hallway walls. (One 1889 breakfast menu especially caught my eye, listing an extraordinary selection of foods, including lamb chops, lake fish, stewed potatoes in cream, and sweetbreads.)

Special services are legion and include complimentary morning coffee, concerts during afternoon tea, romantic horse-drawn-carriage island tours, hold-me-close dinner dances, and much more. It seems as if the pampering never stops.

Many of the guest rooms have spectacular lake views that induce lots of lovey-dovey musings. Rates include breakfast and candlelight dinners, with Lake Superior whitefish an evening specialty. A dessert treat—the Grand pecan ball with hot fudge sauce—is a sweet confection best shared with your special honey. The rest of the evening's romantic bliss is up to you. Oh yes . . . you can indulge in the ultimate romantic getaway by making reservations for the "Somewhere in Time" weekend, during which guests get swept away in Victorian elegance.

HOW TO GET THERE: From either Mackinaw City from the Lower Peninsula or from St. Ignace on the Upper Peninsula, a thirty-minute ferry ride brings you to Mackinac Island. Dock porters will greet your boat. There's an island airstrip for chartered flights and private planes.

Pine Garth Inn
Union Pier, Michigan 49129

INNKEEPERS: Russ and Paula Bulin

ADDRESS/TELEPHONE: 15790 Lakeshore Road (mailing address: P.O. Box 347); (616) 469–1642

ROOMS: 7; all with private bath. No smoking inn.

RATES: $125 to $170, single or double; EPB.

OPEN: Year-round.

FACILITIES AND ACTIVITIES: Gathering room, screened porch, five decks overlooking Lake Michigan, 200 feet of private sugar-sand beach with beach chairs. Neraby: short drive to New Buffalo arts and antiques stores, skiing, water sports, restaurants.

RECOMMENDED COUNTRY INNS® TRAVELERS' CLUB BENEFIT: Stay two nights, get third night free, Sunday to Thursday, November to April, excluding holidays, subject to availability.

When we first came to this stretch of shifting sands in southwestern Michigan almost twenty years ago, all we found was an empty Lake Michigan shoreline, sleepy towns, and small cottages.

How times have changed.

Now there's a huge marina crammed with massive cabin cruisers, luxury town houses stacked one atop the other, and a small-town "Main Street" that's increasingly filled with tony shops to lure big-city spendthrifts.

And those small cottages—they're more likely to have four-bedroom summer mansions as next door neighbors than somebody's clapboard cabin.

Yet Harbor Country, a 50-mile swath of white-sand beaches stretching from Michigan City, Indiana, to Harbert, Michigan (and beyond), somehow manages to retain its small-town charm and be a big attraction (especially for stressed-out Chicago folks) at the same time.

In fact, Harbor Country is now the cool weekend place to be, with a wave of lodgings, stores, and restaurants hitting the beaches and environs.

One of the best ways to enjoy the region is by staying at the romantic Pine Garth Inn—the only bed-and-breakfast in Harbor Country nestled on the lakeshore. Located on a high bluff, six of the seven rooms in the 1905 inn offer breathtaking vistas of Lake Michigan and the hostelry's private white-sand beach below.

Rachel's Room boasts flamingos perching on the headboard and an entire wall of windows overlooking Lake Michigan—and opening out to a private terrace.

Or go upstairs to Melissa's Room, done in Laura Ashley blues and yellows. Another favorite of guests because "it's so romantic," it features a canopied bed and deck overlooking the lake. Even the bathroom boasts a lake view.

Of course, all lovers understand the lure of the private beach, reached by walking down a terrace of stairs clinging to the bluff. We looked for shells and ran around in the sand. Spending time together—life can't get much better than that.

HOW TO GET THERE: Take the I–94 to Michigan exit 6, which is the Union Pier exit. Turn right (on Towline Road) and proceed west toward the lake and go to the flashing red light, which is Red Arrow Highway. *Do not turn.* Continue on Townline Road to the next stop sign, which is Lakeshore Road. Turn right and proceed about ¼ mile to the inn (it'll be on your left).

Rosewood Inn
Hastings, Minnesota 55033

INNKEEPERS: Pam and Dick Thorsen

ADDRESS/TELEPHONE: Seventh and Ramsey; (612) 437–3297

ROOMS: 8, with 4 suites; all with private bath and air-conditioning; TV and phone upon request. No smoking inn.

RATES: $97 to $217, single or double; EPB. Two-night minimum on weekends. Special packages available.

OPEN: Year-round.

FACILITIES AND ACTIVITIES: Dinner by reservation. Sitting room, parlor, library, porch. Nearby: historic river-town architecture, arts and crafts stores, antiques shops, specialty boutiques, Mississippi River water activities, bluff touring on bikes and hikes, St. Croix Valley Nature Center, Alexis Bailly vineyard winery; downhill and cross-country skiing, snowshoeing, golf.

*T*his handsome Queen Anne, built in 1878, now houses one of the most romantic getaways imaginable. That's not really surprising, since Pam and Dick's other Hastings hideaway (the Thorwood Inn) reflects similar pampering-inspired luxuries.

As soon as you see Rebecca's Room, you'll get the idea. This is a stirring romantic retreat, with a marvelous all-marble bathroom highlighted by a double whirlpool bath resting in front of its own fireplace. There's a second fireplace opposite an inviting four-poster antique bed. And a four-season porch offers views of the inn's rose garden.

Or consider the Vermillion Room, with a see-through fireplace that warms both an ornate brass bed and a sunken double whirlpool bath.

If you want shameful opulence, try the Mississippi Room. As large as an apartment, it offers skylights over a sleigh bed, its own fireplace, baby grand piano, bathroom with both a copper tub and double whirlpool, and a meditation room where "people can either relax or be creative," said the innkeeper. "We've  even had several guests do paintings here." A collection of some of those works are hanging about the room.

The breakfasts are added treats. And the mealtime flexibility is unusual: They'll serve whenever guests are hungry, between 6:00 and 11:00 A.M. Eat in one of the dining areas, on the porch, in your room, or in bed—the choice is yours.

The feast might include homemade breads and blueberry muffins, cheese strata, wild-rice gratiné, cherry strudel, raspberry coffee cake. . . . Aren't you hungry just thinking about all this food?

Another chance to feast: The inn offers gourmet dinners in the formal parlor—or in your room. The meal might feature delights such as beef Wellington and a raspberry strudel with chocolate and vanilla sauce. The cost is around $50 per couple.

The innkeepers are also happy to arrange an in-room "hat box" supper or to package a delightful evening with dinner at one of the town's fine restaurants, including limousine service. And they occasionally arrange dinner at the inn featuring Minnesota-accented recipes accompanied by live chamber music.

HOW TO GET THERE: From the Twin Cities, take U.S. 61 south into Hastings and exit at Seventh Street; then turn left and proceed 1½ blocks to the inn.

Thorwood Inn
Hastings, Minnesota 55033

INNKEEPERS: Pam and Dick Thorsen

ADDRESS/TELEPHONE: Fourth and Pine; (612) 437-3297

ROOMS: 7; all with private bath and air-conditioning. Wheelchair access. No smoking inn.

RATES: $97 to $167, single or double; EPB. Can arrange for pet-sitters. Special package rates available.

OPEN: Year-round.

FACILITIES AND ACTIVITIES: "Hat box" dinners in your room. Nearby: walking tour of historical area just blocks away. Quaint Mississippi River town with specialty and antiques shops, several good restaurants. Parks and nature trails; also river, streams, lakes, and all sorts of summer and winter sports.

Perhaps Thorwood's ultimate romantic retreat is the Steeple Room, with its see-through fireplace and double whirlpool—set in the house's steeple. The steeple rises 23 feet above the tub and boasts a ball chandelier hanging from the pinnacle. Ooh, la la!

Others swear by Sarah's Room, with its bedroom-sized loft, window views of the Mississippi River Valley, and skylight over a queen-sized brass bed, or Maureen's Room, with its unusual rag-rug head-board, fireplace, country-quilted bed, and double whirlpool bath.

However, my favorite lovers' lair is Captain Anthony's, named for the original owner's son-in-law, who operated a line of steamboats on the Mississippi. It has a canopied four-poster brass bed and Victorian rose, teal, and blue Laura Ashley fabrics. Though the Lullaby Room (the house's historic nursery) with its double whirlpool bath is a close runner-up.

The house itself, fashioned in ornate Second Empire style and completed in 1880, is a testament to the innkeepers' restoration prowess and romantic notions. When I saw the marble fireplaces, ornate rosettes and plaster moldings on the ceilings, and elegant antiques and surroundings, it was difficult to imagine that the house had once been cut up into several apartments. For more fine detail, just look to the music room. Pam said that maple instead of oak was used for flooring because it provided better resonance for live piano concerts, popular with society crowds at the turn of the century.

There's lots of special pampering, too. A complimentary bottle of wine from the local Alexis Bailly vineyards and snacks of fruits and pastries await guests. Then there are those breakfast baskets.

"People seem to enjoy the morning breakfast baskets more than anything else," Pam told me as we sat in the parlor of her gracious inn. "It has grown into quite a tradition." Once when she mentioned to a repeat couple that she'd been thinking of changing that practice, "They immediately spun around, with dismayed looks on their faces, and said, 'You wouldn't!' I knew right then we could never change."

Lucky for us. The breakfast basket, delivered to the door of your room, is stuffed with platters of fresh fruits, omelettes or quiches, pull-apart pastries and rolls, home-baked breads, coffee, juice, and more. As Dick says, "Pace yourself."

HOW TO GET THERE: From LaCrosse, take U.S. 61 north to Hastings; turn left on Fourth Street and proceed to inn.

St. Charles House
St. Charles, Missouri 63301

INNKEEPERS: Patricia and Lionel York

ADDRESS/TELEPHONE: 338 South Main Street; (314) 946–6221 or (800) 366–2427 via town Tourism Center

ROOMS: 1 suite with sitting room, porch overlooking Missouri River, and private bath; one two-bedroom guest cottage with two baths, dining room, small porch. No smoking inn.

RATES: $120 weekdays, $150 Friday and Saturday; deluxe continental breakfast.

OPEN: Year-round.

FACILITIES AND ACTIVITIES: Walk to quaint shops, restaurants, riverboat cruises, tours of the first state capital. Nearby: a short drive to downtown St. Louis and the Arch, St. Louis Art Museum, restored Union Station, Opera House, Powell Symphony Hall, and Fox Theatre.

*O*pen the door to this re-created 1800s brick building within sight of the lazing Missouri River, and you step back into a setting of nineteenth-century luxury and romance.

The inn sits on Main Street of Missouri's first state capital, a street lined with more than one hundred historic brick buildings dating to the late nineteenth century (and today largely inhabited by arts and antiques shops).

It's a lovingly restored retreat from the bustle of visitors that can overwhelm the tiny hamlet. The replica house looks fit for a prosperous frontier businessman, sporting spacious rooms, fine antiques, and elegant surroundings.

"All of our antiques pre-date 1850," said Patti. Many were purchased in Denver, some right in town. Especially noteworthy is a massive Austrian buffet with intricate hand carving and a 9-foot-tall French walnut armoire.

The house's open floor plan includes a four-columned foyer and a bedchamber complete with oak hardwood floors, queen-sized canopy bed, and original Mary Gregory table lamp.

An elegant sitting area offers Oriental-style rugs and a place to relax. There's even a minirefrigerator in an antique side buffet along with a small wet bar.

Walk downstairs to reach the bath. Behind handsome double doors is a claw-footed tub under a crystal chandelier in a huge room decorated in pink and blues. Just outside is another Victorian-style sitting room. (Insert your own fantasies here.)

Hard to believe, but "it took only three days to buy all our pieces," Patti said. "We went on an antiques-buying spree, and every place we stopped just happened to have exactly what we wanted."

Antiques aside, the St. Charles House may be best suited for "getting to know you" adventures.

HOW TO GET THERE: From St. Louis or Kansas City, exit I–70 at First Capital Drive, and follow that north, then east to Main Street; turn right and continue to the inn.

The Cambridge Inn
Cambridge, Nebraska 69022

INNKEEPERS: Mike and Elaine Calabro

ADDRESS/TELEPHONE: 606 Parker (mailing address: P. O. Box 239);
(308) 697–3220

ROOMS: 5; 3 with private bath. No smoking inn.

RATES: $55, single; $50 to $75, double; EPB.

OPEN: Year-round.

FACILITIES AND ACTIVITIES: Lunch and dinner available by arrangement. Parlor, library, dining room, front porch. Nearby: golf, museums,
antiques stores; Medicine Creek State Recreation Area, hunting, fishing,
boating, biking.

"We always said it'd take a lot to get us out of Colorado," noted Elaine.
"But once we stepped inside this house, we knew it had to be ours."
"It" is The Cambridge Inn, a historic 1907 Neoclassical Revival
house that's been a landmark in Cambridge for as long as anyone can remember. Built by W. H. and Anna Faling (he helped incorporate the town), the mag-
nificient house retains the elegant features of an era long past.

These include luxurious cherry, oak, and pine woodwork; stained and
beveled glass; and hand-grained walls and ceilings created by Danish craftsmen.

Actually, it was Mike who first spotted the house, then for sale, on a return
trip from visiting his son's college in Galesburg, Illinois. He drove around the

block a few times, then told
Elaine about it on his return
home to Colorado. They made
the five-hour drive from Loveland on a pleasant day in October, walked inside the house . . .
"And that was it," Elaine said.

The innkeepers have fash-
ioned an elegant inn full of Victorian charm and romance. An
entrance hall showcases a magnificent oak staircase leading to
second-floor guest rooms; above the landing is an incredible stained-glass window original to the house. Memorable breakfasts in the dining room, itself a
showplace, with its 10-foot-tall built-in fruitwood and leaded-glass sideboard,

might include French toast stuffed with cream cheese and walnuts, fruit plates, and more. And the parlor features twin oak columns at least 10 feet high.

Among the guest rooms, Ivy Court is my favorite. Originally the home's master bedroom, it retains a high Victorian ambience. Its antique furnishings include a writing desk. There's a sitting room and a bay window gussied up with lace curtains. Its private bath also claims the home's original "water closet"—a claw-footed tub, pedestal sink, and unusual foot bath.

Choose Morningside and you'll get a quilt-covered bed and antique oak armoire (see if you can find the signatures of those Danish workmen who crafted all the house's wood-grain appearances out of common oak). Or opt for the more simple Goldenrod, once the maid's room but now a bright, cozy retreat decorated with patterns of wildflowers.

And make sure to get out and explore the region during your stay here. The inn is located in the heart of the Republican River Valley of the Prairie Lakes region in Southwest Nebraska—a spot noted for boating as well as biking across its gently rolling hills.

HOW TO GET THERE: Take U.S. 6/34 into Cambridge (whose name changes to Nasby Street in town). Follow the road to the intersection of Nasby and Parker; the inn sits on the corner.

The Inn at Chagrin Falls
Chagrin Falls, Ohio 44022

INNKEEPER: Mary Beth O'Donnell

ADDRESS/TELEPHONE: 87 West Street; (440) 247–1200, fax (440) 247–2122

ROOMS: 15, with 4 suites; all with private bath; several with fireplace and whirlpool. No smoking in rooms.

RATES: $130 to $205, double; subtract $10 for single; continental breakfast.

OPEN: Year-round.

FACILITIES AND ACTIVITIES: Gathering room with fireplace; Gamekeeper's Taverne for fine dining. Nearby: walk to falls, browse quaint village shops, hike in Western Reserve surroundings. Eastern suburb of Cleveland; only a short ride to Rock 'n' Roll Hall of Fame, Jacob's Field, home of the Cleveland Indians; Severance Center, home to Cleveland Orchestra; The Flats, Cleveland's riverfront nightlife; Sea World.

*D*riving into Chagrin Falls, I thought I'd entered a cinema time warp and arrived at Bedford Falls, home to Jimmy Stewart in the movie *It's a Wonderful Life*. See if you don't get the same feeling when you first arrive.

The inn is an elegant retreat fashioned from the historic Crane's Canary Cottage. Built in 1927, it still sports canary-colored clapboards that give a light and airy touch to the surroundings.

Inside, guests first reach the Gathering Room. It boasts English-style antiques, including my favorite—a plump, King George wing chair. There's also a Victorian round-back sofa fronting the large hearth, whose fire always seems to be going.

Guest rooms are exquisitely fashioned with antique reproductions of fine furniture houses such as Colonial Williamsburg, Drexel, and Baker. Romantics should choose the Crane Suite, with its king-sized bed, Jacuzzi, and a (now gas-burning) fireplace, original to the home, that has a massive hearth; it must measure at least 6 feet long and 4 feet high.

The Philomethian Suite is another beauty, offering a four-poster mahogany bed, plantation-shuttered windows, corner fireplace, and whirlpool.

You can enjoy breakfast in a handsome pine-paneled dining room that features oak refectory tables and high-backed Windsor chairs. Morning fare usually consists of cereals, seasonal fruits, English muffins with fresh jams, and the inn's specialty—sour-cream coffee cake.

Do try dinner at Gamekeeper's Taverne, attached to the inn. Where else might you sample char-grilled blackwing ostrich fillet, black buck antelope, or sautéed elk tenderloin? Other delicious entrees include herb-crusted rib pork chop, cedar-planked salmon, and penne pasta with smoked venison sausage.

Of course, no visit to the inn would be complete without a hand-holding walk among the boutiques of this quaint, picture-perfect village. And why not partake in a village tradition on your visit: Buy an ice cream cone and relax by the falls!

HOW TO GET THERE: From Cleveland, take I–77 south to I–480 east, then follow U.S. 271 north. The first exit on 271 is Chagrin Boulevard; get off and go east 9 miles to reach Chagrin Falls. As you come into town there will be a large hill; before reaching the stoplight at the bottom of the hill, turn right on West Street to the inn. If you pass the stoplight, turn around.

The Inn at Brandywine Falls
Sagamore Hills, Ohio 44067

INNKEEPERS: George and Katie Hoy

ADDRESS/TELEPHONE: 8230 Brandywine Road; (330) 467–1812 or 650–4965

ROOMS: 6, with 3 suites; all with private bath. Wheelchair access. No smoking inn.

RATES: $94 to $185, double; for single, subtract $5; EPB.

OPEN: Year-round.

FACILITIES AND ACTIVITIES: Located on 33,000 acres of parkland known as Cuyahoga Valley National Park. Porch swings, chairs overlooking gorge. Short hike to boardwalk to falls and down into gorge. Biking and hiking trails yards away.

There's nothing more romantic than a waterfall. And Brandywine Falls check in at 67 feet. But the hike on the boardwalk to the falls, and then down deep into the gorge itself, seems much greater.

Maybe that's because of the grandeur of nature at Brandywine Falls, part of the massive Cuyahoga Valley National Park. We had been marveling at the natural beauty for miles before we came upon this handsome inn.

The Inn at Brandywine Falls turned out to be among our favorites on our swing through eastern Ohio. Not only does it boast a waterfall but also hiking and biking trails and expansive grounds perfect for romantic nature walks with your partner.

The inn, a Greek Revival beauty built in 1848 by James Wallace, was the centerpiece of a once-thriving pioneer community with a sawmill and gristmill, thriving businesses along the falls.

Today, all that is left of that village are some mill foundations and the inn. But the inn (and the falls) are more than enough!

Inn suites are among *my* favorites on the Midwest country inn landscape. For a complete, reclusive getaway, the Granary offers towering windows overlooking a hemlock grove and rustic, wide-plank pine floors and hand-hewn wooden beams. Then there are the king-sized bed, wood-burning stove, two-person whirlpool, microwave, and fridge.

Another good choice is the Loft, which began as a small barn in the 1800s; it has been transformed into another rustic wonder with a wall of windows overlooking that hemlock grove, as well as a romantic loft area with bed and oversized whirlpool.

Downstairs, you can marvel at all the country geegaws decorating the suite. There's even a model train that circles the ceiling.

In the main house, the James Wallace Parlor has an elegant double sleigh bed luxuriating on Axminster carpeting, English armoire, handpainted lamp shades, and an antique chair (oldest original piece of furniture in the house) that came from 1820s Maryland.

But I might opt for Adeline's Retreat, a charming and romantic second-floor room with double sleigh bed and claw-footed tub; it's the only guest quarters with glimpses of the falls.

Guests take breakfast in the dining room, where a portrait of James Wallace gazes down over the festivities. Goodies might include fruited oatmeal soup, fresh juices, homebaked breads, and hot beverages.

Did I mention that it's a candlelight breakfast?

Most important, however, is that a visit to Brandywine Falls offers you a chance to walk, listen, and marvel at nature. Relax. Visit the falls. Doze in the sun. Breathe in the aroma of wildflowers and the forest.

Just be. Together.

HOW TO GET THERE: From the Ohio Turnpike, take exit 12, then continue on Highway 8 for 1½ miles to Twinsburg Road. Turn west (left) and drive another 1½ miles to a dead end at Brandywine Road. Turn right and cross the bridge. The inn is on the left.

Cameo Rose Bed and Breakfast
Belleville, Wisconsin 53508

INNKEEPERS: Dawn, Gary, and Jennifer Bahr

ADDRESS/TELEPHONE: 1090 Severson Road; (608) 424–6340

ROOMS: 5; all with private bath. No smoking inn.

RATES: $95 to $145, single or double; EPB.

OPEN: Year-round.

FACILITIES AND ACTIVITIES: Cathedral great room, porches, rose gazebo, flower gardens, 120 acres of hills, woods, hiking trails. Nearby: fifteen minutes from Madison, the University of Wisconsin, the State Capitol, State Street (shops and specialty stores), Dane County Coliseum; golf courses, water sports on Lakes Medota and Monona.

*I*f there is a more attractive Victorian-style inn than this one, let me know about it. But I'll put my money on the Cameo Rose, a hostelry that's blossoming into one of the finest little romantic getaways in the Midwest.

"We built the house specifically for a bed-and-breakfast," Dawn told me. It was completed in 1991, though it has the Victorian-era complement of ornate gingerbread, slashing gables, and an imposing tower.

Inside, you'll find modern elegance. The "foyer" is two stories high, incredibly decorated to the season, with stairs leading to second-floor guest rooms. But first enjoy the guest parlor, with skylights gracing a cathedral ceiling and looking as if a *House Beautiful* layout has come alive.

Dawn does all the decorating—and it is exquisite. Of course, romantic roses are everywhere, especially in the Tower Room, graced with Cameo Rose wall coverings, Battenburg lace, handsome quilts, and a double whirlpool whose window looks out over the surrounding valley.

Is there a more enticing spot for a romantic rendezvous?

I also loved the Rose Arbor room, with its rococo reproductions (such as that antique fainting couch). And all guest rooms have televisions and VCRs; the inn's film library contains more than 700 titles.

Dawn's breakfasts are elegant, too. Served in the formal dining room on antique china with crystal goblets, consider hot breakfast fruit compote, eggs Benedict, berry struesel muffins ("Wild berries grow everywhere around here," Dawn said), and homemade cinnamon rolls—a house specialty.

The inn is located on 120 acres of hills and trees. Part of the renowned Ice Age Trail edges across the property. There are also miles of hiking paths that loop to hilltops, through maple and oak groves, and into the valley. Or relax among Dawn's rose and flower gardens, a blaze of colors in the growing season.

The Cameo Rose is a special place. But don't take my word. See for yourself.

HOW TO GET THERE: The inn is located 5 miles south of Verona, 3 miles north of Belleville (and about 12 miles southwest of Madison) in unincorporated Basco. From Madison, take Highway 151 (Verona Road) west and use the Paoli exit. Basco, the town, is basically a sign and a small group of houses at Henry Road along Highway 69 about 1 mile past Paoli on the way to Belleville. You'll see the Cameo Rose to the left on a hill, a bit more than 1 mile down Henry Road.

Canoe Bay
Chetek, Wisconsin 54728

INNKEEPERS: Dan and Lisa Dobrowolski

ADDRESS/TELEPHONE: W16065 Hogback Road; (715) 924–4594 or (800) 568–1995

E-MAIL: mail@canoebay.com

WEB SITE: www.canoebay.com

ROOMS: 16 in seven buildings, including inn and lodge rooms and deluxe cottages; all with private bath, double whirlpool, air-conditioning, and audiovideo centers. No smoking inn.

RATES: $225 to $375, single or double; EPB. Gourmet dinners $42.50 per person.

OPEN: Year-round

FACILITIES AND ACTIVITIES: Located on private 280 acres; two private lakes, hiking paths, nature trails, cross-country ski trails, cross-country rentals, bike rentals, fishing, swimming, canoes, rowboats, and more. Sitting room, video room, library. Spa services: theraputic massage, body wraps, facials, hand and foot care. About forty-five minutes west of St. Paul, Minnesota.

*D*an and Lisa Dobrowolski's inn has perhaps set new standards in romantic luxury. I've always considered this elegant country retreat possibly the best Mid-America has to offer discerning guests, but don't take *my* word for it.

Canoe Bay is the first Midwest lodging establishment to become a member of the prestigious Paris-based association *Relais et Chateaux,* which includes many of the finest hotels and lodgings in the world. The inn also has received a four-star rating from the *Mobil Travel Guide,* the only lodging in the Midwest to be so honored.

Now you can't have any doubts when I say Canoe Bay is an experience that shouldn't be missed.

Dan (a former TV weatherman for WFLD–Channel 32 in Chicago) and Lisa built their inn on the shore of crystal-clear Lake Wahdoon, a fifty-acre spring-fed body of water surrounded by 280 acres of private oak, aspen, and maple forests. The inn provides breathtaking views, incomparable service, and complete privacy besides many opportunities for outdoor recreation and relaxation, including wildlife watching.

The main building's centerpiece is a great room, with soaring natural-cedar cathedral ceilings, a wall of windows, and a 30-foot-tall, hand-constructed fieldstone fireplace. Inn rooms here are exquisite, like something out of *Architectural Digest*.

Also sprinkled through this grand country estate are luxurious cottage suites, featuring Frank Lloyd Wright's signature Prairie-style architecture along with "every possible creature comfort with the ultimate in privacy."

The innkeepers spared no expense in re-creating the great architect's distinctive style. For example, the Oak Park Suite boasts a 14-foot-high wall of casement windows overlooking the lake; the Wood Grove Suite allows guests to observe natural surroundings from their platform two-person Jacuzzi through wraparound windows. Also count on a river-rock fireplace, a stereo/TV/VCR/CD, a wet bar with refrigerator and microwave oven, and a huge private deck.

Or how about a dream cottage with a see-through fireplace next to the whirlpool, plus lake views?

Mornings bring pampering, with breakfast baskets delivered to your room or brought out to the patio overlooking the lake, where you can enjoy scores of chirping songbirds. Canoe Bay also offers dinner featuring gourmet cuisine that would be difficult to beat even when considering Chicago or Minneapolis's best restaurants, thanks to Culinary Institute of America trained staff.

The inn's standout season could be autumn, with its incomparable colors, but holidays receive special treatment, too. Thanksgiving and New Year's Day guests can enjoy guided cross-country ski tours, ice skating, ice fishing, and a 14-foot-tall Christmas tree with all the trimmings.

Then, again, anytime at Canoe Bay is special. You might even receive a free personal weather forecast from prognosticator Dan, who's often heard to say, "If there's a better place on Earth, I don't know it."

Forget Earth. This is heaven.

HOW TO GET THERE: Once in Chetek, Highway 53 becomes Second Street. Follow that through town, over a bridge, and turn right on County Road D (there's a cemetery at this intersection). Go about 1½ miles to Hogback Road (look for a CANOE BAY sign here); turn left and continue for about 7 miles to the inn.

The Astor House
Green Bay, Wisconsin 54301

INNKEEPERS: Doug Landwehr and Nan Nelson

ADDRESS/TELEPHONE: 637 South Monroe Avenue; (920) 432–3585

ROOMS: 5 suites; all with private bath. No smoking inn.

RATES: Weekend, $109 to $149, single or double; weekdays, $79 to $99, single or double; continental breakfast.

OPEN: Year-round

FACILITIES AND ACTIVITIES: Guest parlor, wraparound veranda. Located in Astor Historic District—take self-guided walking tour of notable homes. Nearby: Short drive to Lambeau Field, Green Bay Packer Hall of Fame, Heritage Hill State Park, Oneida Casino, Weidner Center for the Performing Arts, Bay Beach Wildlife Sanctuary, Arena Expo Center.

*G*reen Bay's only bed-and-breakfast inn boasts a tony three-diamond rating. Not hard to understand once you've visited this gracious 1888 Victorian beauty.

Just look at the craftsmanship: The exterior boasts fishscale shingles, vertical boards, sunbursts, and circle motifs—all decidedly Victorian. Inside, there are leaded glass, 9-foot-tall oak pocket doors, original silver crystal chandelier, and a grand staircase with octagonal-carved spindles.

Doug Landwehr took me on a tour. The Marseilles Garden suite, he said, is like a Monet flower garden come to life and perfect for lovers. Consider its ivy-laced headboard, arbor trellis, gas-log fireplace, and double-whirlpool room.

The Hong Kong Retreat is nearly 4,000 square feet of space, reached by a spiral staircase leading to the third floor. Luxuriate in the double jade whirlpool; the black-tile fireplace is guaranteed to keep things cozy.

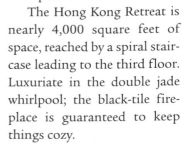

The Vienna Balconies is a two-level suite with another double whirlpool in its bedroom and a private third-floor balcony overlooking the gardens.

Breakfast is delivered to your room or may be taken in the guest parlor. It might include scones, apple tortes, and baked apples and pears. Recipes are taken from renowned bed-and-breakfast cookbooks.

There's even turndown service at the Astor House. Finally, a reason for this rabid Chicago Bears fan to think of Green Bay and not envision those evil Packers.

HOW TO GET THERE: Located at the junction of Highways 54 and 57, 8 blocks from Green Bay's City Centre. From Milwaukee (Port Washington), take Wisconsin 57 north into Green Bay; it turns into Monroe Street in town. Watch for Wisconsin 54, and the inn.

The American Club
Kohler, Wisconsin 53044

INNKEEPERS: Susan Porter Green, vice-president; Alice Hubbard, general manager

ADDRESS/TELEPHONE: Highland Drive; (920) 457-8000 or (800) 344-2838; fax (920) 457-0299

ROOMS: 236; all with private whirlpool bath, air-conditioning, TV, and phone. Wheelchair access.

RATES: $210 to $780, single or double, Sunday to Thursday; $235 to $805, Friday and Saturday; peak season. Off-season rates available. Two-night minimum on weekends from July through September. Several packages available.

OPEN: Year-round.

FACILITIES AND ACTIVITIES: Nine restaurants and full-service dining rooms. Renowned for extravagant buffets, special-event and holiday feasts; large Sunday brunch. Ballroom. Sports Core, a world-class health club. River Wildlife, 500 acres of private woods for hiking, horseback riding, hunting, fishing, trapshooting, canoeing. Cross-country skiing and ice skating. Also Kohler Design Center, shops at Woodlake, Kohler Arts Center, Waelderhaus. Nearby: antiquing, lake charter fishing, Kettle Moraine State Forest, Road America (auto racing).

*J*ust 4 miles from the shoreline of Lake Michigan, amid tall pines, patches of white birch, scrubbed farmhouses, and black soil, is one of Wisconsin's most romantic retreats.

There's an uncommonly European ambience at the elegant American Club. With its Tudor-style appointments of gleaming brass, custom-crafted oak furniture, crystal chandeliers, and quality antique furnishings, it looks like a finely manicured baronial estate. It's also the only five-diamond resort hotel in the Midwest.

Built in 1918 as a temporary home for immigrant workers of the Kohler Company (a renowned plumbing manufacturer, still located across the street), the "boardinghouse" served as a meeting place where English and citizenship classes were taught—a genuine American Club.

Talk about romance: Some rooms feature a four-poster canopied brass bed and huge marble-lined whirlpool bath. Special suites contain a saunalike environmental enclosure with a push-button choice of weather—from bright sun and gentle breezes to misty rain showers. And consider guest pamperings: fluffy bathrobes, twice-daily maid service, daily newspapers—the list goes on!

The inn's showcase restaurant is The Immigrant, a romantic hideaway where we dined on a four-course gourmet meal that included smoked Irish salmon. The wine list is impressive, too. For dessert we walked to the Greenhouse, in the courtyard. This antique English solarium is a perfect spot for chocolate torte and other Viennese delights.

Not to mention your late-night rendezvous with your special sweetheart.

HOW TO GET THERE: From Chicago, take I–94 north and continue north on I–43, just outside of Milwaukee. Exit on Wisconsin 23 west (exit 53B). Take 23 to County Trunk Y and continue south into Kohler. The inn is on the right.

From the west, take I–94 south to Wisconsin 21 and go east to U.S. 41. Go south on 41 to Wisconsin 23; then head east into Kohler.

Victorian Treasure Bed and Breakfast
Lodi, Wisconsin 53555

INNKEEPERS: Kimberly and Todd Seidl

ADDRESS/TELEPHONE: 115 Prairie Street; (608) 592–5199

Rooms: 8, including 4 suites; all with private bath and air-conditioning. No smoking inn.

RATES: $85 to $169, single or double; EPB, afternoon wine, cheese, and fruit.

OPEN: Year-round.

FACILITIES AND ACTIVITIES: Sitting rooms, porch. Nearby: water activities on Wisconsin River and Lake Wisconsin. Hiking, rock climbing, bird-watching on Baraboo Range. Restaurants; downhill and cross-country skiing; Devil's Lake State Park, with 500-foot bluffs; American Players (Shakespearean) Theater in outdoor amphitheater; Taliesin, home of Frank Lloyd Wright; golf; bald eagle watching.

imberly and Todd have done a remarkable job transforming this 1897 Victorian into an elegant, romantic getaway that everyone wants to return to again and again.

Little Wonder. Polished chandeliers, brass door fittings, and natural woodwork harken back to a more elegant era. A grand staircase leads to a wide hallway ushering guests to the bedchambers. Then, there's Kimberly and Todd

themselves—two of the most affable and pampering innkeepers around.

What else is special here? How about the Queen Anne's Lace Room, with its queen-sized four-poster canopy bed draped with antique lace panels for privacy? Did I forget to mention its expansive bath featuring a two-person whirlpool?

Then there's the Wild Ginger Room, boasting not only a hand-carved walnut bed but also a private porch perfect for coosome-twosome stargazing.

Any room you choose here is bathed in romance—all beds possess cozy down comforters, four pillows, luxurious linens—real European romantic style.

Lovers of food will savor Kimberly's five-course gourmet breakfasts; they might include fresh fruit with ginger syrup, home-baked nut breads and cinnamon rolls, vegetable fritatta, omelettes, locally "grown" sausages, and more. Perhaps you'll even be served the house specialty: pecan cream cheese-stuffed French toast topped with fruit sauces.

There's lots more. Another choice at the Victorian Treasure is whether to overnight at the inn's other property: the Palmer House. This bit of elegance is an 1893 Queen Anne with four additional luxury suites that include whirlpool bath, fireplace, stereo, and wet bar.

A romantic's favorite is the Angelica suite, perhaps the inn's finest. It boasts three rooms of its own, a mahogany tester bed, double whirlpool—even a private front porch. Imagine the delights.

HOW TO GET THERE: From Chicago and Milwaukee, take I–90/94 to Wisconsin 60 and go west into Lodi. In town take Route 60 (now called Lodi Street) 1 block west, then turn right on Prairie Street. It's the first house on the left.

St. Croix River Inn
Osceola, Wisconsin 54020

INNKEEPER: Bev Johnson

ADDRESS/TELEPHONE: 305 River Street; (715) 294-4248

ROOMS: 7; all with private bath and air-conditioning; 2 with TV.

RATES: Friday and Saturday, $100 to $200; Sunday through Thursday, $85 to $150; single or double; EPB. Gift certificates available.

OPEN: Year-round.

FACILITIES AND ACTIVITIES: Outdoor porch, sitting room overlooking St. Croix River. Nearby: several area antiques shops, canoeing, fishing, downhill and cross-country skiing at Wild Mountain or Trollhaugen. A short drive to restaurants and Taylors Falls, Minnesota—a lovely little river town with historic-homes tours and cruises on old-fashioned paddle wheelers.

This eighty-plus-year-old stone house is poised high on a bluff overlooking the scenic St. Croix River. It allows unsurpassed breathtaking views while providing one of the most romantic lodgings in the entire Midwest.

I'm especially fond of a suite with a huge whirlpool bath set in front of windows, allowing you to float visually down the river while pampering yourself in a bubble bath.

"The house was built from limestone quarried near here," Bev said. "It belonged to the owner of the town's pharmacy and remained in his family until a few years ago."

Now let's get right to the rooms (suites, really), which are named for riverboats built in Osceola. Perhaps (and this is a *big* perhaps) Jennie Hays is my all-time favorite inn room. It is simply exquisite, with appointments that remind me of exclusive European hotels. I continue to rave about a magnificent four-poster canopy bed that feels as good as it looks and a decorative tile fireplace that soothes the psyche as well as chilly limbs on crackling-cool autumn or frigid winter nights.

Then there is the view! I'm almost at a loss for words. A huge Palladian window, stretching from floor to ceiling, overlooks the river from the inn's blufftop perch. It provides a romantic and rewarding setting that would be hard to surpass anywhere in the Midwest. The room has a whirlpool tub, and there's a private balcony with more great river views.

The G. B. Knapp Room is more of the same: a huge suite with a four-poster canopy bed adorned with a floral quilt, tall armoire, its own working gas fireplace, and a whirlpool tub. Then walk through a door to the enclosed porch (more like a private sitting room), with windows overlooking the river. There are also exquisite stenciling, bull's-eye moldings, and private balconies.

Pampering continues at breakfast, which Bev serves in your room or in bed. It might include fresh fruit and juices, omelettes, waffles, French toast or puff pastries stuffed with ham and cheese, and French bread and pound cake.

Bev also delivers to your room a pot of steaming coffee and the morning paper a half hour before your morning meal. She can recommend a great place for dinner, but you simply may never want to leave your quarters.

Let's face it: This is one of the Midwest's most romantic retreats—pure grace and elegance.

HOW TO GET THERE: From downtown Osceola, turn west on Third Avenue and follow it past a hospital and historic Episcopal church (dating from 1854, with four turreted steeples). The inn is located on the river side of River Street.

White Lace Inn
Sturgeon Bay, Wisconsin 54235

INNKEEPERS: Bonnie and Dennis Statz

ADDRESS/TELEPHONE: 16 North Fifth Avenue; (414) 743–1105

ROOMS: 19, in four historic houses; all with private bath and air-conditioning; some with fireplace, whirlpool, TV, and wheelchair access.

RATES: $99 to $179, single or double, weekdays; $109 to $199, Friday and Saturday; continental breakfast. Special winter or spring fireside rates and packages available November through May.

OPEN: Year-round.

FACILITIES AND ACTIVITIES: Five blocks to bay shore. Nearby: specialty and antiques shops, restaurants, Door County Museum, Miller Art Center; swimming, tennis, and horseback riding. A short drive to Whitefish Dunes and Potawatomi state parks, Peninsula Players Summer Theater, Birch Creek Music Festival. Crosscountry skiing and ice skating in winter. Gateway to the peninsula.

*B*onnie and Dennis Statz call their award-winning inn "a romantic fireside getaway." I can't think of a better place to spend a cozy, pampered weekend for two.

And things have only gotten better since my last visit. Now the White Lace Inn resembles a private Victorian-era park, with three handsome historic buildings connected by a red-brick pathway that winds through landscaped grounds filled with stately trees, wildflower gardens, and a rose garden featuring varieties dating from the 1700s. You will also enjoy the Vixen Hill gazebo, a great place to pause among the inn's many gardens; it is a beauty from Pennsylvania.

The Main House was built for a local lawyer in 1903; what's surprising is the extensive oak woodwork put in for a man of such modest means. Stepping into the entryway, I was surrounded by magnificent hand-carved oak paneling.

Bonnie has a degree in interior design and has created guest rooms with a warm feel, mixing Laura Ashley wallpaper and fabrics with imposing, yet comfortable, antique furnishings like rich Oriental rugs and high-back walnut and canopied beds. Fluffy down pillows are provided, handmade comforters and quilts brighten large beds, and lacy curtains adorn tall windows.

The 1880s Garden House has rooms with their own fireplace. They're done in myriad styles, from country elegant to the grand boldness of oversized Empire furniture.

This time my wife and I stayed in the Washburn House, another "old" addition to the White Lace. All rooms here are luxurious; ours had a canopy brass bed with down comforter, fireplace, and two-person whirlpool. It was graced with soft pastel floral chintz fabric and white-on-white Carol Gresco fabrics that tell a story (in fact, some of her work is part of the Smithsonian Design Institution collection). The bath's Ralph Lauren towels are heavenly.

And next time, we want a room in the Hadley House—maybe one with a huge whirlpool, fireplace, and private balcony.

Back in the main house, Bonnie's homemade muffins are the breakfast treat, along with juice, coffee, and delicious Scandinavian fruit soup (a tasty concoction served cold) or old-fashioned rice pudding. Blueberry soup and apple crisps are summer specials. It's a great time to swap Door County stories.

HOW TO GET THERE: From Milwaukee, take U.S. 41 north to Wisconsin 42, toward Sturgeon Bay. Just outside the city, take Business 42/57 and follow it into town, cross the bridge, and you'll come to Michigan Street. Follow Michigan to Fifth Avenue and turn left. White Lace Inn is on the right side of the street. Or you can take the 42/51 bypass across the new bridge to Michigan Street. Turn left on Michigan, go to Fifth Avenue, and take a right on Fifth to the inn.

The Southwest

by Eleanor S. Morris

A h, romance! Who can define it? Dictionaries try. *Webster's* defines romance as "extraordinary life, not real or familiar," adding "colloquially, to make love." *Thorndike Barnhard* agrees; its definition reads, "a love affair, an interest in adventure and love." *Collins Gem* (a French dictionary) declares it *"poesie"* and *"idylle,"* and *Cassell's New Compact French Dictionary* says romance is not only *"amourette"* and *"aventure"* (love and adventure), it is also *"inventer à plaisir"*: to imagine a pleasure, a delight.

So, is it more of a feeling we bring to a place, or can the place itself be romantic, engendering romantic feelings in us? I think it's both; I like the way the French say that romance means to invent a delight. Imagination inspires us to look for surroundings that will complement and enhance romance.

Herein are twenty-two inns of the Southwest that provide a delightful ambience of *"idylle et poesie."* Although they help keep romance alive, part of their magic comes from what you bring along with you. Whether it's romance amid the opulence of a Victorian mansion, in an eagle's aerie in the mountains, or in the pampered Southern comfort of an antebellum plantation, these inns provide the perfect setting for a wonderful experience of romance.

The rest is up to you.

The Southwest

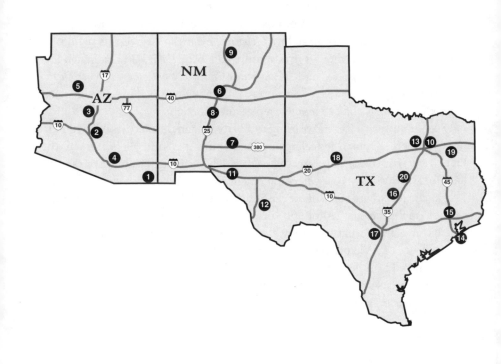

The Southwest

Numbers on map refer to towns numbered below.

Bisbee Grand Hotel
Bisbee, Arizona 85603

INNKEEPER: Bill Thomas

ADDRESS/TELEPHONE: 61 Main Street (mailing address: P.O. Box 825); (520) 432–5900

ROOMS: 11; all with private bath. No smoking inn.

RATES: $52 to $115, double; $15 extra person; EPB.

OPEN: All year.

FACILITIES AND ACTIVITIES: Grand Western Saloon with complimentary snacks, pool table, large TV screen, and Ladies' Parlor; Murder Mystery weekends. Nearby: Old Bisbee Tour, City Mine Tour, Bisbee Mining and Historical Museum, antiques shops, art galleries.

Opulence, extraordinary almost-out-of-the-world opulence, is what we found at the well-named Bisbee Grand. Grand is a perfect adjective for this inn—so is elegant. From the red-velvet Victorian Suite to the other-worldly Oriental Suite, exotic luxury abounds in this posh, treasure-filled inn.

The modest, small black marquee over the double doors, squeezed in between two storefronts, hardly prepared us for what awaited as we climbed the red-carpeted stairs leading from the narrow entrance to the second floor and the inn rooms. Once there, faced with an iridescent stuffed peacock at the head of the stairs, we found ourselves in a world we certainly had never expected in the quaint and charming Old West mining town of Bisbee.

Each of the seven guest rooms is a world in itself, full of beautiful furniture and decorative details. "These antiques were collected for thirty years," innkeeper Bill says with justifiable pride. The three suites are extravaganzas—excitingly imaginative and full of unexpected appointments, such as a working fountain next to a lovely large flower arrangement in the Garden Suite.

We chose the unashamedly opulent Oriental Suite, with walls covered in black, pink, and gold fabric depicting Chinese scenes. The brass bed is adorned with onyx and alabaster. "It's a unique, one-of-a-kind honeymoon bed," Bill explained. It's wide and high, with an oval mirror and paintings; bronze dragon vases and black lacquer vie with other choice collectibles in the room.

The Victorian Suite is dripping with deep-red-velvet hangings, not only on

the windows but also making a cozy nest of the canopied bed. The Garden Suite is a bower of flowers; as for the rest of the rooms, like the Coral and the Gray rooms, Deer Springs and Crow Canyon, well, any one is a perfect place for a romantic getaway.

On the main floor, adjacent to the Grand Western Saloon, the inn's old-fashioned Victorian parlor has an antique piano that you may play if you're careful. The saloon's 35-foot bar came from Wyatt Earp's Oriental Bar by way of the Wells Fargo Museum.

Breakfast will satisfy both the most eager gourmet and the health food aficionado. "All our food is from Tucson Cooperative Warehouses," Bill noted, "and we recycle and compost everything." The fruit course consisted of watermelon, cantaloupe, pineapple, and green grapes; the delicious quiche was full of cheese and mushrooms, with ham on the side; the homemade bread was delicious; and for sweets, there were cheese Danish and cinnamon rolls.

"We treat our guests very special, with all the grace and elegance of the best of a Victorian mining town," Bill said. Morning coffee, hot tea, iced tea, and a plateful of ginger snaps, lemon bars, and peanut butter and chocolate chip cookies are available in the saloon practically round the clock. Not the least of the pleasures of this small, elegant inn is watching together the sunset, or the rainbow after it rains, over the mountains facing the front balcony.

HOW TO GET THERE: From Highway 80 east take Tombstone Canyon Road for approximately 2½ miles until it becomes Main Street. You can't miss the Bisbee Grand on the left.

The Inn at the Citadel
Scottsdale, Arizona 85255

INNKEEPERS: Kelly Keyes, Jane De Beer, and Adam Wilson

ADDRESS/TELEPHONE: 8700 East Pinnacle Peak Road; (602) 994–8700 or (800) 927–8367

ROOMS: 11; all with private bath; wheelchair accessible. No smoking inn.

RATES: $295, double, continental breakfast.

OPEN: All year.

FACILITIES AND ACTIVITIES: Two restaurants, piano bar, limo tours of the desert, health and beauty spa facilities, boutiques. Nearby: hiking to Pinnacle Peak; golf.

"Everything has family meaning," Kelly Keyes said of this posh, family-built inn in chic Scottsdale, at the foot of outstanding Pinnacle Peak. "It's all been built in threes and fives; those three arches over there are for three daughters—me and my two sisters."

The sentiment goes beyond the immediate family. Kelly pointed out that the brands decorating the Marque Bar are those of everyone who had anything to do with the building of the inn. "Architects, builders, my parents—theirs is the flying double K," she explained.

The inn had a propitious beginning. It was built on Hopi Indian land, and the Hopis were invited to a blessing of the land. "Everyone, even the children, came. It was a black-tie-and-jeans event, jeans and boots."

This is a pretty sumptuous establishment for the casual Southwest, more like a fine European-style hotel than a country inn, but "we try to put guests at their ease," Adam Wilson said. "Sometimes they're a little taken aback, awed by the location." This is grand country, with Pinnacle Peak just overhead.

Kelly's mother, Anita Keyes, is an interior designer, and each of the eleven rooms is decorated with careful detail, down to the smallest item. Original artwork by such artists as Jonathan Sobel and Armond Laura hang on the walls, and antiques are used extensively. The armoires in six of the rooms were painted by local Arizona artists Liz Henretta, Skip Bennett, Sherry Stewart, and Carolyn Baer.

Rooms have safes, robes, hair dryers, bath amenities, and an honor bar, stocked with premium liquors, wine, champagne, and playing cards, along with the expected soft drinks, crackers, and candy bars.

Fresh hot coffee comes along with the complimentary newspaper each morning. A massage, facial, or manicure can come to your room, too, if you wish. Each room has cable television with HBO.

The larger rooms are more like suites, with large sitting areas and desks. The king-sized beds are covered with quilted satiny spreads, and the pillow shams match the dust ruffles.

Actually, the Citadel is not just an inn. It's a restaurant and shopping complex in a shady courtyard complete with a pond and a bubbling waterfall. The continental breakfast is served either in The Market or in your room, which we preferred. Fresh-squeezed orange juice is followed by a large serving of seasonal fresh fruit—we had raspberries—and then moist zucchini, bran, or corn muffins and, of course, coffee or tea.

We surfaced for The Market, where you can get anything from blue-corn waffles to hamburgers, pastas, salads, and enchiladas, and it's all deliciously fresh and nicely served. The award-winning 8700 at the Citadel really goes all out, with the finest regional American cuisine. One of chef Leonard Rubin's specialties is roast rack of black buck antelope. "It's pretty popular," Adam said. The menu also features 8700 Mixed Grill, poached salmon, and coffee toffee crunch cake, so we wined and dined in great style.

HOW TO GET THERE: From I–17 take Bell Road 30 miles east to Scottsdale Road, then go north 4 miles to Pinnacle Peak Road and east 2 miles to the inn.

Apple Orchard Inn
Sedona, Arizona 86336

INNKEEPERS: Paula and Bob Glass

ADDRESS/TELEPHONE: 66 Jordan Road; (520) 282–5328 or
(800) 663–6968; fax (520) 204–0044

ROOMS: 7; all with private bath; wheelchair accessible. No smoking inn.

RATES: $135 to $195, double; $20 extra person; EPB; lunch and dinner
if the entire inn is booked by one group.

OPEN: All year.

FACILITIES AND ACTIVITIES: Massage room and masseuse on call; private tour guide; hiking trails; VCRs and videos. Nearby: half a mile from shops, galleries, and restaurants; Sedona Heritage Museum; airplane, helicopter, balloon rides; tours; horseback riding, jeeps, train rides, tennis; Grand Canyon 110 miles north.

*I*t's hard to beat the setting of this romantic inn. Part of the Historic Jordan Apple Farm, these inn grounds cover two acres of the great outdoors, covered with piñon pine, juniper, and Arizona spruce. Wilson Mountain and Steamboat Rock—orange and red, ragged and craggy—loom protectively over the back of the inn, providing a romantic backdrop.

Paula and Bob say they are working hard to be an "upscale" inn. Committed to the spirit of personal hospitality, they offer such amenities as minirefrigerators in each room, filled with complimentary water, juice, and sodas. The turndown service comes with a chocolate on your pillow; there are bathrobes and hair dryers in the guest rooms. Most rooms have patios and/or fireplaces; all have showers and whirlpool tubs.

Since romance means a departure from the mundane, each guest room is different. The only thing they have in common (aside from comfort) is imagination, and you can match your imagination to the room. The Victorian is a plush, romantic room; the Wild Bill Room celebrates the spirit of the West; Old Barn Sides sports a headboard and an armoire fashioned from barn wood. In Old Mission you can sleep in an authentic Mission-style Stickley queen bed, or you can hide in The Hideaway, the inn's most private room. The Sedona Room, of course, has beautiful views of those famous red rocks, as does Steamboat Rock.

The large Great Room, with a rock fireplace, is furnished with an eclectic assortment of comfortable chairs and colorful Southwest rugs on the wide-plank wood floor. Breakfast is prepared by two chefs, John Paul and Susan Etlinger, whose credentials include training at L'Auberge de Sedona, Four Seasons in Boston, and culinary school in Milan, Italy. You might feast on cheese blintzes with a brandied peach and cherry sauce, accompanied by sausage and fresh fruit with homemade scones. Or you might enjoy eggs Florentine, Canadian bacon, baked apples with cream, and fresh banana-nut bread—the mouthwatering possibilites are endless.

HOW TO GET THERE: From Highway 89A in Sedona, go through the Uptown (shopping) area, turn onto Apple Street (Oaxaca Restaurant on the corner), and continue on to Jordan Road. Turn right on Jordan and follow the gravel drive past the APPLE ORCHARD sign on your right. The inn is up the slight hill.

Saddle Rock Ranch
Sedona, Arizona 86336

INNKEEPERS: Fran and Dan Bruno

ADDRESS/TELEPHONE: 255 Rock Ridge Drive; (520) 282–7640; fax (520) 282–6829

ROOMS: 3; all with private bath and cable TV with remote. No smoking inn.

RATES: $120 to $150, double; $20 extra person; $5 less single; EPB and afternoon snacks. Two-night minimum stay; extended stay specials.

OPEN: All year.

FACILITIES AND ACTIVITIES: Swimming pool and spa, concierge service, Sedona airport transportation. Nearby: restaurants, shops, hiking, fishing, horseback riding, Hopi Mesa tours.

his luxurious home is not what you would expect from a place that calls itself a ranch. Today the historic homestead, built in 1926, is on the edge of a residential area. But it sits on three acres of hillside overlooking Sedona, and it has starred in many Old West films.

"I just saw a late-night thirties movie, *Angel and the Bad Man*," Dan said, "and there was our whole house! It was a dude ranch back then, and the wife of the owner always played an Indian princess in the films," he added with a laugh.

Fran and Dan, who met while both were employed at a prestigious California hotel, are experts in providing special attention to guests. What we found was the same VIP treatment that they gave to many of the "rich and famous." And before that Dan had a rather adventurous career: My companion recognized his name, because he played football for the Pittsburgh Steelers.

"He's lived every man's fantasy," Fran said. "He also raced with Mario Andretti on the Indy circuit." They moved to Sedona for the climate, and now Dan and Fran are having an adventurous time innkeeping. "Our guests are wonderful, outstanding, and we want them to have the same total experience throughout their visit. It's a point of pride to us that our guests get the best of not only what we have to offer, but also what Sedona has to offer as well," Dan said, and we reveled in full concierge service with restaurant reservations at Sedona's finest—concerts, theater, tours, and anything else we could think of.

Guest rooms are elegantly comfortable, as is the living room. Large Saddle Rock Suite has a country French canopied bed and a rock fireplace; furniture in the Rose Garden Room was Fran's great-great-grandfather's, and the room has its own private, walled rose garden. The Cottage in back, with wood-paneled walls, is surrounded by panoramic vistas as well as having its own private

patio. Robes, nightly turndown, chocolates, bottled water, afternoon snacks, guest refrigerator, and microwave oven—we made ourselves right at home in this just-about-perfect inn.

There are cuddly teddy bears everywhere, and it's Dan who collects them! "I was born at home, and the doctor brought a bear when he delivered me—I still have it," he said. It lives in retirement with other teddy bears on a daybed that belonged to his great-great-grandfather.

Breakfast is served in the large and sunny dining room, and specialties are heart-shaped peach waffles and individual Dutch babies (pancakes) filled with apples and vanilla ice cream or yogurt. "I like to use our local Sedona apples, peaches, and pears," Fran said. Orange juice is always fresh-squeezed, and if you prefer tea to coffee, there are sixteen different ones to choose from.

At the rear of the property, a national forest shelters wildlife; deer come to the salt lick, and quail abound. The inn has tamer specimens in Diana and Fergie, miniature schnauzers. "But guest quarters are off-limits to them," Fran said, "unless you particularly request some puppy love!"

HOW TO GET THERE: Take Highway 89A (Airport Drive) to Valley View; go south 1 block to Rock Ridge Drive, left to Forest Circle, and right to Rock Ridge Circle; continue beyond Rock Ridge Drive and take the gravel road on the left up the hill to Saddle Rock.

The Suncatcher
Tucson, Arizona 85748

INNKEEPER: Shirley Ranieri

ADDRESS/TELEPHONE: 105 North Avenida Javelina; (520) 885–0883 or (800) 835–8012

ROOMS: 4; all with private bath, phone, TV, and VCR; wheelchair accessible. No smoking inn.

RATES: $140 to $165, double; $25 extra person; EPB.

OPEN: All year.

FACILITIES AND ACTIVITIES: Heated pool and spa, bicycle. Nearby: restaurants, tennis and health club, hiking, horseback riding, Saguaro National Monument; fifteen minutes to downtown Tucson.

*H*ere's a really romantic retreat, out in the wide open spaces under the sun and the warmth of the desert. Yet there's elegance here, too.

"The Suncatcher has tried to take all the qualities of a first-class hotel and put in the charm of a bed-and-breakfast," Shirley said of her luxurious inn. "I've kept everything just about the same as it was with the previous owner, David Williams." A sure clue is each guest room's name, that of one of the world's prestigious hotels. There's the Connaught, the Four Seasons, the Regent, and the Oriental; staying here is almost like taking a romantic trip around the world.

One guest room opens off the huge airy and spacious common area, two have French doors opening off the pool, and the fourth is around the corner with its own entrance.

The Connaught (London) is furnished with Chippendale-style furniture in gleaming dark mahogany; the Four Seasons with a formal canopied bed; the Regent (Hong Kong) has lovely original Oriental scrolls, and the Oriental (Bangkok), the largest, has its own Jacuzzi among its other splendors. We chose the Oriental—oh, that Jacuzzi!—but all have at least one comfortable chair, writing desks, original artwork, and fresh flowers.

Shirley has kept the inn emblem, little terra-cotta faces that are on the walls and elsewhere. "The inn was named for the desert attractions—the sun, the dry heat, the desert—and I want to keep it as a retreat, a getaway, a place to catch the sun."

She had a restaurant in New Jersey for fourteen years, "and I was ready for a change," she said. "I began thinking about other things I could do." She'd always come west for vacations, and when she began to look for a house, with plans to open another restaurant, she came across The Suncatcher for sale. With the inn, she says she has the best of both worlds: a home and looking after people. (And, she confided, she's finding innkeeping much less work than a restaurant!)

The huge common area (70 feet square), with its soaring ceiling, has several focal points. In one corner there's a large copper-hooded fireplace; in another, a mirrored mesquite bar. Display cases show off treasures from Shirley's travels to Thailand and Hong Kong, and she has also collected interesting Southwestern pieces. The entire area—sitting, dining, kitchen—is open, and you can watch the chef prepare breakfast. It's a full hot meal, with Southwestern eggs, or maybe an omelette, mushroom, perhaps, or ham and mozzarella cheese—accompanied by corn muffins, blueberry muffins, cheese pastries, and bagels.

"People can mingle; they hang out in the main house now, since I leave the door open all the time. We sit around and talk and laugh; people talk about things in their lives. It's nice. My pleasure is sitting down and speaking with my guests."

HOW TO GET THERE: The inn is on the edge of Saguaro National Monument. From I-10 and downtown Tucson, take Broadway east, crossing, as a last landmark, Houghton. Continue on to Avenida Javelina, bearing in mind that Avenida Javelina is beyond the dead-end sign on Broadway. Turn north on Javelina, and the inn is on the left in the middle of the block.

Terry Ranch Inn
Williams, Arizona 86046

INNKEEPERS: Sheryl and Del Terry

ADDRESS/TELEPHONE: 701 Quarterhorse; (520) 635-4171

ROOMS: 4; all with private bath, with wheelchair access. No smoking inn.

RATES: $60 to $125, double, seasonally; $15 extra persons; EPB.

OPEN: All year.

FACILITIES AND ACTIVITIES: Nearby: quaint small town with walking map of shops and restaurants; Grand Canyon, Grand Canyon Railway, Grand Canyon Helicopter tours, nine-hole golf course, hiking, hunting, fishing, skiing

There's a romantic reason why this inn calls itself a ranch, and it's not because it really is a working ranch. There has been a Terry Ranch in the Terry family since the 1650s, although back then the locale was Bucks County, Pennsylvania.

"Family tradition dictated that only the eldest son could inherit the family spread, so younger sons went off and created their own Terry Ranch," Del Terry said.

Sheryl said she always wanted a bed-and- breakfast inn, all the while they were raising Brangus cattle (still are).

"I knew I could build it (the inn). I knew I could decorate—but I wasn't certain I could run it," she confessed with a laugh. "I'm a shy person basically. But I was inspired by another Arizona innkeeper, and I've learned how wonderful it is to meet new people."

So Del and Sheryl built the inn from scratch—literally. "We built it ourselves, log by log," Sheryl said as she lovingly stroked one of the smooth wood logs that make up the walls of Terry Ranch Inn.

"We try to offer the same hospitality that Terry Ranches have provided since 1670," the innkeepers said.

Guest rooms and baths are exceptionally roomy. The guest rooms are named for the brides who lived at Terry Ranch during the 1800s, a lovely, romantic theme. A portrait of each bride hangs in her room, and each is decorated in her favorite colors.

Mary Ann's Room is named for the first Utah bride, who helped build the Utah ranch, first living in a dugout, then a stone fort.

Eliza Jane, the second bride, was the youngest—sixteen. She came west as a "child bride." Hannah Louisa's Room is named for the third bride, who, "at twenty-three, was the oldest," Del said.

Charlotte Malinda helped her husband establish the town of Enterprise, Utah, just south of the Terry Ranch there. She liked baby blue and white, and on the wall of her room hangs a quilt made by Sheryl.

The large dining room table easily seats twelve, and it's covered with a lovely lace cloth made by Del's mother. In the shelves on each side of the fireplace repose grandmother's wedding china. But pretty as it is, it has to share space with Sheryl's collection of twelve individual place settings that she serves breakfast on. Each one has a story.

Speaking of breakfast, the Terrys serve a real hearty ranch breakfast—what else? Begin with fruit topped with yogurt, cream, and sweet crumb sprinkles; then English Floddies, which are grated potato, egg, onion, and crumbled bacon pancakes; along with Amish friendship bread muffins.

The Amish friendship bread has a history, too—Sheryl makes it from a starter she's had since the late seventies!

HOW TO GET THERE: Take Fourth Street north to Railroad Avenue. Turn right (east) and follow it around to Rodeo Drive. Turn left and go a short way to Quarterhorse; the inn is on the corner of Rodeo and Quarterhorse.

Casa del Granjero
Albuquerque, New Mexico 87114

INNKEEPERS: Victoria and Charles (Butch) Farmer

ADDRESS/TELEPHONE: 414 C de Baca Lane Northwest; (505) 897–4144 or (800) 701–4144; fax (505) 897–9788

ROOMS: 6; all with private bath; wheelchair accessible. No smoking inn.

RATES: $79 to $159, double; $20 extra person; EPB, complimentary beverages and snacks.

OPEN: All year.

FACILITIES AND ACTIVITIES: Lunch and dinner by arrangement; hot tub, pool, bicycles, exercise equipment, rose garden, lily pond and waterfall, gazebo, horses (to pet), pygmy goats. Nearby: hiking trails, Albuquerque Old Town Plaza, Historic San Felipe Church, Museum of Natural History, Albuquerque Museum, skiing.

*T*he name of this inn (pronounced "gran-hair-o") means "the farmer's house." When Victoria and Butch found this wonderful adobe hacienda nestled in the historic North Valley of Albuquerque, "we knew we were home." More to the point for the likes of us, right from the beginning they were encouraged to open their home to guests. "Everyone told us that this is the kind of romantic place everyone wants to see and explore," Victoria said happily. She immediately set to work furnishing and decorating the home in a manner worthy of its size and history. The main house was 110 years old when they arrived, with beams from an 1860s bakery and bricks from the roadbed of famous old Route 66 (acquired when the highway was paved).

The first surprise at Casa del Granjero is opening the front door and walking into the huge common area, with Mexican tiles and a pool sunk in the middle of the room. It's surrounded by soft pink brick walls, a corner fireplace, and cushy white sofas, cactus, clay pots of other green plants, a huge Oriental rug in tones of soft reds and blues—and overhead, glass clerestory windows add even more dimension. For Victoria the inn has many happy memories of Butch's grandmother, now deceased. "Granny didn't know what a bed-and-breakfast was. When we told her she said, 'Oh. I can maybe make quilts!' She came across the country in a covered wagon when she was five; she died at eighty-seven," Victoria says. "She was my best buddy." Her name was Lilla Farmer, and she regaled guests with stories of old Taos (north of Albuquerque and Santa Fe).

Victoria likes to take guests out on the patio. "Those are Granny's wind chimes. There are days when there is no wind . . . yet we hear the chimes . . . "

In the dining room the long Spanish mission–style table and chairs rest

on another huge Oriental rug, while two breakfronts display an assortment of glass and objets d'art. The dark-brown wood beams overhead are older than the house.

In Quarto del Rey (King's Room) the old radio actually works, handcrafted Mexican tiles accent the kiva fireplace, and the view is of not only the courtyard but also the mountains and trees. Quarto de Flores (Flowers Room) boasts great-grandmother's flower needlepoint as well as Granny's colorful quilts. French doors lead to the patio and the portale that winds around to the main courtyard. The Allegre Room presents an old-fashioned romantic air: Butch made the four-poster that is hung with white satin and Battenburg lace.

Breakfast is a wonderful concoction of blue-corn pancakes with sour cream and a caramelized apple topping, cool apricot-pear-pineapple frappe, a molded rice custard (a variation of the Mexican flan, with rice instead of eggs but still with the traditional, delicious baked-on caramelized sugar sauce), and crisp bacon. "I find that people don't always like breakfast meats, so I often serve chicken instead," Victoria said.

HOW TO GET THERE: From I–40 north take Alameda Boulevard west to Fourth Street. Turn left at C de Baca, then take a right to the inn, which is on the left.

Casa de Patron
Lincoln, New Mexico 88338

INNKEEPERS: Cleis and Jeremy Jordan

ADDRESS/TELEPHONE: P.O. Box 27; (505) 653–4676

ROOMS: 3, plus 2 two-room casitas; 3 rooms with private bath; casitas with private bath, hide-a-bed, and kitchen; no air-conditioning (elevation 5,700 feet). No smoking inn.

RATES: $89, double; $13 extra person, single deduct $10; EPB for main house, continental for casitas; afternoon drinks and snacks.

OPEN: All year.

FACILITIES AND ACTIVITIES: Dinner by advance reservation. VCR, special entertainment such as German Evenings and musical Salon Evenings. Nearby: Billy the Kid country with state monuments and Heritage Trust museums; Lincoln National Forest, hiking, skiing; horse races at Ruidoso Downs; soap-making and quilting workshops.

nnkeepers Cleis (pronounced "Cliss") and Jeremy used to camp in nearby Lincoln National Forest, and she fell in love with the little town of Lincoln. We did, too, and could understand when she told us. "I told Jerry I *had* to live here," Cleis said with a laugh. "He thought I was bananas; this house was a wreck. But it had great charm, and after it was fixed, we decided to share it with others."

The historic nineteenth-century house was the home of Juan Patron, born in 1855. The Jordans decided to name the inn after his family, who lived in the house and kept a store there during the mid-1800s. Young Juan lost his father in an 1873 raid on Lincoln, forerunner of the Lincoln County Wars. Billy the Kid, Sheriff Pat Garrett, murders, and rival mercantile establishments—these are the ingredients of the bloody Lincoln County Wars. We could hardly wait to visit the museums and hear the story; it was pretty wild in Lincoln back then.

But we found plenty of peace and tranquil-lity in the beautiful forested country, the calm broken only by the festivals and pageants in the tiny town and in nearby Capitan (home of Smokey Bear) and Ruidoso.

Each guest room in the spanking white adobe-and-viga house is decorated with collectibles and antiques such as the 1800s spinning wheel from Jerry's family back in Deerfield, Illinois. The number 1 Southwestern Room has twin beds and a full bath; number 2 Southwest-ern Room has a queen-sized bed and washbasin and private bath around the corner; the Old Store has a queen-sized bed, private bath, and outside entry to a patio. We loved the complete privacy of the casitas, and the Jordans are understandably proud of the fact that they built them from scratch. Casa Bonita has a cathedral ceiling in the living area and a spiral staircase winding up to the loft bedroom.

For our breakfast we had Cleis's baked egg soufflé, strawberry-walnut muffins, home-fried potatoes, and fresh fruit—in the clear mountain air, appetites are hearty. The huge kitchen has a wonderful collection of wash-boards, those old-fashioned thingamajigs for scrubbing clothes. Our refresh-ing evening drinks were enhanced by music, with Cleis at the baby grand in the parlor or at the pipe organ in the dining room. The music was professional—Cleis has a master's degree in organ music.

As for dinner, you can drive to La Lorraine in Ruidoso, Chango in Capitan, or Tinnie's Silver Dollar in Tinnie; but, said Cleis with a laugh, "that's one of the reasons we went into the dinner business (by prior arrangement only): People said, 'What, you mean we have to get in the car and drive 12 miles?'"

A Salon Evening might be a night of ragtime and American cuisine, or Ger-man specialties accompanied by suitable music if you're feeling sociable. We went for a walk in the cool mountain air.

HOW TO GET THERE: Casa de Patron is located at the east end of Lincoln on the south side of Highway 380, which runs between Roswell and I–25. The highway is the main and only road through the tiny town.

Eaton House
Socorro, New Mexico 87801

INNKEEPERS: Anna Appleby and Tom Harper

ADDRESS/TELEPHONE: 403 Eaton Avenue; (505) 835–1067 or
(800) 383–CRANE

E-MAIL: crane@eatonhouse.com

WEB SITE: www.eatonhouse.com

ROOMS: 7; 3 plus 4 casitas; all with private bath. No smoking inn.

RATES: $85 to $135, September 1 through May 1; $70 to $110, June 1
through August 31; $20 extra person; continental breakfast or Birding
Basket for bird-watchers.

OPEN: All year.

FACILITIES AND ACTIVITIES: Nearby: historic town walking tour, Mineral Museum, New Mexico Tech Golf Course, petroglyphs, observatory,
Bosque del Apache Wildlife Refuge, Alamo Indian Reservation.

*T*he inn, on the New Mexico Historical Register, was built in 1881
and is a cross between eastern Victorian and New Mexican Terri-
torial—there's even a widow's walk on the roof! It was built by
Colonel Ethan W. Eaton, who was an important figure in the $30-million
Magdalene Kelly Mine back in the 1880s. The area is rich in silver, lead, zinc,
and copper as well as ancient points of cultural interest, such as the Piro
Indian petroglyphs in nearby San Acacia.

Socorro in Spanish means "aid" or "help," and it got its name back in 1598
when Spanish explorers received aid from the Piro Indians, who are believed
to have been the area's first inhabitants. The climate, typical of high desert,
is a great bird-watching area, and many Eaton House guests have come for
just that. "We have hundreds of hummingbirds from April to September, as
well as dozens of other species," Anna said.

Guest rooms, bright and comfortable, contain Southwestern furniture,
much of it made by a local artisan. In spacious Colonel Eaton's Room,
though, there's a four-poster from Santa Fe and an antique 1859 desk and
old liquor cabinet.

The *trastero* (combined bench and armoire) in the Vigilante Room is an
interesting piece. Handmade quilts, antiques complemented by furniture
made by local artisans, lace, needlework, and wicker and wood combine with

push-button switches, rim locks, and octagonal tile to create a comfortable feeling of the past as well as present elegance. There's sybaritic luxury in the European goose-down comforters and the huge bath sheets.

The iron bars in the windows of the hallway are a reminder of a 1906 earthquake—that's when the colonel put them in. The only thing changed from the original house are the portales added so that each room could have its own secluded entrance.

Walk hand in hand through the herb garden and the fruit orchard, where native plants were chosen for an environmentally sound landscape. Enjoy the compound, planted for birds, butterflies—and people. Indoors, the East Room is the place to plan a day filled with birding, hiking, exploring, or just relaxing in the gardens or the shade of the brick portal, where it's always warm in the winter and cool in the summer. Hummingbirds hover and fly through the portal from April to September.

HOW TO GET THERE: From I-25 in Socorro take Manzanares west to California. Turn south on California for 2 blocks to Church, west on Church 4 blocks to Eaton Avenue, south on Eaton to 403.

Adobe & Pines Inn
Taos, New Mexico 87557

INNKEEPERS: Charil and Chuck Fulkerson

ADDRESS/TELEPHONE: P.O. Box 837, Rancho de Taos, 87557; (800) 723-8267; fax (505) 758-8423

E-MAIL: adobepines@taos.newmex.com

WEB SITE: www.taosnet.com/adobepines

ROOMS: 8; all with private bath; 2 with TV. No smoking inn.

RATES: $95 to $185, double; $20 extra person; EPB.

OPEN: All year.

FACILITIES AND ACTIVITIES: Jet tub. Nearby: historic St. Francis de Assisi Church; shopping; art galleries; seven minutes from Taos with its historic Plaza, galleries, shops, and restaurants; historic Taos Pueblo; Kit Carson Home and Museum; Rio Grande Gorge; Taos Ski Valley.

*E*ven the innkeepers admit that if you're not watching for the orange, blue, and turquoise poles that mark the road to the inn, you'll miss the turnoff to this romantic hideaway. But, like me, you can always turn around and look again. And once you find it, you'll get a friendly welcome from Rascal, the cocker-terrier, who, said Charil, "along with our horse, Desi, requests no other pets at the inn."

And what an inn; it's full of beauty, beginning with the lovely mural at the end of the 80-foot-long portale, a 1950s scene of the famous Taos Pueblo. "We didn't come into this blind," Charil said. "We even hired a consultant who told us what to expect from innkeeping." She laughed. "We've had our eyes opened even more since."

Like so many happy innkeepers, they were looking for a lifestyle different from their hectic one in San Diego. They sold everything they owned and traveled in Europe for a year. "We didn't know we were doing our homework," Chuck said. They landed in Taos because Chuck had a birthday and romantic Charil surprised him with tickets to the balloon festival in Albuquerque. While there they chanced to look at an advertisement on business opportunities. "Taos was not a plan, but we fell in love and made an offer."

"Then we had three-and-a-half months of intense renovation," Chuck says ruefully of the 150-year-old adobe home on four acres of fruit and pine trees. He brightened up. "But it's all Charil's decor. She does a dynamite gourmet breakfast, too!"

This was true. It was so gorgeous that guests left the table to get cameras for photos before we destroyed the 4-inch-tall puff pastry hiding banana yogurt and the German pancakes smothered with fresh raspberries and golden raisins. Chuck is no slouch, either, when it comes to muffins. Lemon poppyseed, apple cinnamon . . . "Guests dub them Chuck's killer muffins," Charil said. They've had so many requests for recipes that Chuck has compiled their own Southwest cookbook.

Adobe & Pine Inn, Ranche de Taos NM

Rooms are beautiful, too. Two open off the portale: Puerta Azul, a blue room with an antique writing desk and a hand-painted kiva fireplace; and Puerta Verde, with green and rust colors and a romantic canopy bed and sitting area by the fireplace. "We utilized the one-hundred-year-old 'Dutch' doors," Charil said. They open at the top for a view outside without opening the entire door.

Puerta Rosa, off the courtyard, conceals a surprise under vaulted ceilings: an oversize, sunken bathroom with Mexican tiles surrounding a large cedar sauna (and a separate shower). There's a fireplace to warm the room and another in the bedroom by the sitting area. Puerta Turquesa, a separate guest cottage off the courtyard, has a jet whirlpool bath as well as two fireplaces. There's a kitchen here, too, if you want to stay awhile and make yourself at home.

HOW TO GET THERE: The inn is off Highway 68, 4 miles south of Taos. The turnoff to the inn, which is on the east side of the road, is marked by orange, blue, and turquoise poles ³⁄₁₀ mile south of St. Francis Plaza and 4 miles north of the Stakeout Grill and Bar. Both landmarks are on the east side of the road.

Casa Europa
Taos, New Mexico 87571

INNKEEPERS: Marcia and Rudi Zwicker

ADDRESS/TELEPHONE: 157 Upper Ranchitos Road; (505) 758–9798

ROOMS: 6; all with private bath; several with built-in bancos that convert to twin beds; no air-conditioning (elevation 7,000 feet). No smoking inn.

RATES: $95 to $165, double; $20 extra person; EPB and afternoon tea.

OPEN: All year.

FACILITIES AND ACTIVITIES: Swedish sauna, hot tub, three private courtyards. Nearby: historic Taos Plaza with restaurants, shops, and art galleries; hiking, horseback riding, and winter skiing; Taos Indian Pueblo and museums.

*T*here's nothing like majestic mountains to bring out the romance in us. Casa Europa, two miles out of town, offers beautiful mountain views in a peaceful country setting. Birds sing, horses graze nearby, silence reigns supreme, and our hosts Rudi and Marcia are very hospitable: Both are used to the public and enjoy entertaining. Before coming to Taos, they were proprietors of a fine restaurant in Boulder, Colorado, for many years.

"But," Rudi said, "I needed to do something with people again."

"He needs to work about eighteen hours a day," Marcia added with a fond laugh.

"Well, we get our guests started, we introduce them, and then they are fine," Rudi explained. We certainly were fine, our only problem being one of indecision at teatime; should we choose the chocolate mousse–filled meringue or the raspberry Bavarian? Or perhaps the Black Forest torte or one of the fresh fruit tarts? (I really wanted one of each, all made by chef Rudi, who was trained at the Grand Hotel in Nuremberg, Germany.)

Breakfast is another such feast prepared by chef Rudi. We had fresh fruit salad, a mushroom-and-asparagus quiche, lean bacon edged in black pepper, home-fried potatoes, and fresh homemade Danish that absolutely melted in my mouth.

The house itself is a treasure, with fourteen skylights and a circular staircase to the gallery above the main salon, displaying the paintings, pottery, and sculpture of local artists, as well as wonderful Navajo rugs. The inn appears deceptively small from the outside; inside, the large common rooms (but very uncommon!), both upstairs and down, lead to six exceptionally spacious and elegant guest rooms. The new large suite in the west wing has five rooms: kitchen, dining room, sitting room, bedroom, and bath, as well as a private hot-tub room and private phone. It's also very comfortable. The wood floors are graced with Oriental rugs; the white stucco walls are hung with original art. The front courtyard is bright with flowers around the Spanish fountain; the European garden in back offers quiet relaxation. The English Room is a departure, with fine antique English furniture. "It goes into a place where people can see it," Marcia said.

Outdoors, there are numerous cats and dogs, and "two horses for petting," said Rudi. "But only outdoors!"

HOW TO GET THERE: Driving into Taos from the south on Highway 68, take Lower Ranchitos Road left at the blinking-light intersection just north of McDonald's and south of Taos Plaza. Go 1½ miles southwest to the intersection of Upper Ranchitos Road, which will be on your right. There's an upper ranchitos road sign there now, so you'll know it when you see the sign.

Hôtel St. Germain
Dallas, Texas 75201

INNKEEPER: Claire Heymann

ADDRESS/TELEPHONE: 2516 Maple Avenue; (214) 871–2516; fax (214) 871–0740

ROOMS: 7; all with private bath, TV, and radio. Smoking permitted except in diningroom.

RATES: $245 to $600, double; continental breakfast.

OPEN: All year.

FACILITIES AND ACTIVITIES: Dinner by reservation only; bar service, room service, valet parking; guest privileges at the Centrum Health Club. Nearby: downtown Dallas, with Dallas Museum of Art, Kennedy Memorial, Old City Park, Reunion Tower, West End Historic District, Farmer's Market, more.

For sheer luxury, unabashed, unashamed sybaritic living, the small and elegant Hôtel St. Germain takes the prize. Well, it's already taken several prizes, like the *Inn Business Review*'s naming the St. Germain "one of the outstanding inns of 1992."

The inn, a beautiful residence built in 1906, is architecturally imposing. The white, three-story structure has two balconies on the left and two curved porches on the right, with black wrought-iron railings, which also frame two sets of stairs to the curved driveway in front. French doors lead out, and in the stairwell, a huge twenty-four-paned window is crowned with a glass arch.

With its impressive foyer, 14-foot ceilings, sumptuous parlor, stately library, and lavish suites, it takes all the adjectives in *Roget's Thesaurus* to describe this inn adequately. The antique pieces alone are a feast for the eyes.

"My mom was an antiques dealer," Claire said, pointing out the Aubusson carpets, the Mallard beds, and huge armoires. "We serve on antique Limoges—my grandmother's heavy gold china—Waterford crystal, and sterling." She alternates eight different sets of china; they're stored in the china cabinet in the small dining room.

The large dining room has bay windows of decorative glass, topped with an extravagant valence over Austrian shades. The crystal chandelier is palatial. Beyond is a romantic New Orleans–style walled courtyard. Breakfast here took on another dimension: The chive and cheese quiche and blueberry muffins tasted like nectar and ambrosia.

Soft classical music played in the library, and there is a grand buffet piano for more personalized music. The original wallpaper is charming, and we enjoyed looking at the before-and-after-renovation photographs in the hall.

Suite One, a huge room decorated in rose and gray, has a rose spread and a high canopy over the bed. Suite Three has what appears to be a larger-than-life king-sized bed, which can be divided into two twins. The sitting room has a lovely antique Belgian sofa, and there's a separate dressing room. Suite Four boasts a Jacuzzi as well as a Mallard bed, a huge armoire, and a sitting area with a sofa and fireplace.

The Dangerous Liaison Suite is 600 square feet of blue, green, and gold. Beside the bed, there's a bed-lounge in the wall, a cheval mirror, and antique Mallard furniture. In the sitting area are a fireplace and a sparkling chandelier.

The Smith Suite, on the third floor, overlooks downtown Dallas. The Napoleon sleigh bed has a crown canopy, and there is a Victorian sitting area, complete with fireplace. The padded cloth walls are another example of sheer luxury, an atmosphere that the Jacuzzi in the bath does nothing to dispel.

Hôtel St. Germain is really a taste of another world!

HOW TO GET THERE: From Central Expressway exit at Hall Street; turn right to Cole. At Cole turn left onto Cedar Springs, take a left onto Maple Avenue and go half a block. From North Dallas Toll Road, heading south, pass the Wycliff exit and veer to the left as you curve around to the first traffic light, which is Wolf Street. Turn left for 2½ blocks to Maple, turn right, crossing Cedar Springs to the inn, the large white mansion with a curved driveway.

Sunset Heights Inn
El Paso, Texas 79902

INNKEEPERS: Consuelo "Grandma" Martinez

ADDRESS/TELEPHONE: 717 West Yandell; (915) 544–1743

ROOMS: 3; all with private bath, phone, and TV; wheelchair accessible (electric chair lift from first to second floor). No smoking inn.

RATES: $75 to $150, double; EPB.

OPEN: All year.

FACILITIES AND ACTIVITIES: Dinner for a minimum of six people; pool and Jacuzzi. Nearby: many museums and historic fort, old Spanish missions, Tigua Indian Reservation, zoo, scenic drive, Ciudad Juárez in Mexico just across the Rio Grande.

uilt in 1905 up in the high-and-mighty area of El Paso overlooking downtown, this inn on the National Register of Historic Homes is a three-story corner house of dark-yellow brick surrounded by an iron fence. Tall palm trees wave over it, and the large grounds of nearly an acre are graced by roses blooming much of the year.

Authentic Tex-Mex food is now the specialty of the inn, says "Grandma" Consuelo Martinez, who has taken over the innkeeping reins from earlier innkeepers Richard Barnett and her daughter, Roni Martinez. "I am truly a Tex-Mex cook," she said. "I have people coming from all over, from Europe and the East Coast, and they don't want gourmet food, they don't want Mexican. No, they want Tex-Mex, our regional cuisine," she said emphatically.

So for breakfast you'll get huevos rancheros, frijoles with salsa, and omelette-stuffed tortillas. "I even offer vegetable omelettes for my vegetarian guests, with spinach, cheese, mushrooms, and all sorts of vegetables. I put them on a tortilla, splash them with cheese, and put them in the oven." Once her guests get their fill, off they go for the day, hiking and sightseeing.

The inn is a decorator's dream, with beautifully coordinated fabrics and wall coverings, mirrored doors, and sybaritic bathrooms. The Oriental Room has a beautiful coromandel screen, Chinese tables, and a cabinet in ivory and black. The bathroom, with elegant fixtures and a huge bathtub, is on what was once a porch. But not to worry: All the windows are now one-way mirrors.

"Roni displayed great talent in the decorating of the inn," said her mother with pride. "She did most of the pleasing color selections, while much of the furnishings are antiques from Richard's family." The parlor has a Victrola dating from 1919, and it still plays. Although the old table radio is a replica, the kerosene lamp is one Richard studied by when he was a boy on a farm in Oklahoma. "The farm didn't have electricity," Grandma Consuelo said. "That old lamp got him through school."

I reminded her that when Richard and Roni were in charge, they were noted for gourmet meals. She smiled. "I put in my little two-cents worth. I know what my guests like!"

HOW TO GET THERE: From I–10 West take Porfiro Diaz exit and turn right for 2 blocks to Yandell. Turn right for 6 blocks (count the ones on the right, not the left) to Randolph, and the inn is on the far corner to the left.

The Veranda Country Inn
Fort Davis, Texas 79734

INNKEEPERS: Kathie and Paul Woods

ADDRESS/TELEPHONE: 210 Court Avenue (mailing address: P. O. Box 1238); (915) 426–2233

ROOMS: 8 in the main house and the Carriage House just behind the main building; all with private bath, plus three "extra" for guest use. No smoking inn.

RATES: $60 to $70, double; $10 extra person; EPB.

OPEN: All year.

FACILITIES AND ACTIVITIES: Courtyards, walled garden, orchards, rocking chairs on the verandas. Nearby: restaurants in the Limpia Hotel and The Drug Store, Fort Davis National Historic Site, Overland Trail Museum, Neill Doll Museum, Davis Mountain State Park, McDonald Observatory, Big Bend National Park.

*I*f you're really serious about getting away, this Texas outpost is the perfect place. Fort Davis is set in the Davis Mountains of far west Texas, and the Wild West ruins of Fort Davis are there to haunt you—in a nice way, of course, by reminding you of more simple times gone by (but more dangerous, too!).

"We find we're sort of a refuge," Kathie Woods said of the very small town. "Professionals from the hectic life actually 'tear up' when they tell us what a pleasant weekend they've had! Many of them work sixteen hours a day, and they really need a place to relax and rest."

The inn was called the Lempert Hotel back in 1883 when it was built by W. S. Lempert, who was a mail guard and scout for the Overland Trail.

"By 1880 the area was considered free of the Indian menace," Kathie said. Evidently so, since in 1884 the new hotel hosted Quannah Parker, son of Comanche Chief Peta Nocona and white captive Cynthia Ann Parker (one of the romantic and colorful episodes in Texas history).

Kathie and Paul have restored many of the features of the old adobe building, preserving the pine floors, the 14-foot-high ceilings, and the transom windows of the original hotel. The adobe walls are 2 feet thick, making air-conditioning in the cool mountain air totally unnecessary.

The Veranda of the inn's name is the place to relax. We spent hours out there in the cool of the evening, rocking away and watching the stars. "Our sky here is famous," Kathie said.

But there are also two secluded walled courtyards, with large shade trees, lilac bushes, and irises. The entire grounds take up a city block, and there are roses and other flowering plants, as well as an herb and a vegetable garden.

There's even an orchard, with apples and figs, peaches and apricots, as well as grape and blackberry vines.

Much of this good gardening turns up at breakfast. A favorite are Scotch eggs—hardboiled and wrapped in sausage, rolled in breadcrumbs and then browned. Kathie's special German farmer's omelette, which won Kathie a first prize at the Alpine Fair, is served at the inn with homemade biscuits and sour-cream coffee cake.

There's always fresh fruit—remember the orchard!— yogurt, and both dry and hot cereal for lighter eaters.

Rooms are roomy, and although baths are private to each room, many had to be built across the hall because of the building's age. But thick, soft Egyptian cotton robes are provided for those whose bath is not attached to the room. Half the baths have large "soaking tubs"; the rest have showers, so take your pick. Linens are hung outside to dry in the fresh mountain air— think how deliciously fragrant that makes them!

HOW TO GET THERE: One block west of the Courthouse. (Kathie says, "We do not describe our location in terms of the Overland Trail, because all streets in Fort Davis are unmarked, and people cannot readily locate the Overland Trail.")

The Texas White House
Fort Worth, Texas 76104

INNKEEPERS: Jamie and Grover McMains

ADDRESS/TELEPHONE: 1417 Eighth Avenue; (817) 923-3597 or (800) 279-6491; fax (817) 923-0410

ROOMS: 3; all with private bath, TV, and radio. No smoking inn.

RATES: $80 to $115, double; $15 extra person; continental breakfast on weekdays, EPB on weekends.

OPEN: All year.

FACILITIES AND ACTIVITIES: Membership in health club. Nearby: Texas Christian University, bocce ball, horseshoes, zoo, four museums, Botanic Gardens, Water Gardens, Trinity Park, golf. And there's always the romance of the Fort Worth Historic Stockyards District, where the police are mounted and the motto is "Where the West begins."

What could be more romantic than staying in an inn called The Texas White House? (Well, the *real* Texas White House is down at the LBJ Ranch in Stonewall, but then, it's not an inn!) This White House has been collecting awards such as the Historic Preservation Council Pedestal Award and the City of Fort Worth Historic Landmark.

Decorated in elegant country style, the downstairs has both a parlor and a living room with fireplace as well as a formal dining room and a half bath for convenience of guests. The large wraparound porch invites guests to enjoy lazy afternoons and romantic evenings.

Just think, you can have early-morning coffee service if you wake early but want to laze in bed. You can, depending on how much seclusion and privacy you want, have television and telephone, and check-in and checkout times are flexible.

Upstairs the Land of Contrast Room has a brass bed; Lone Star is brown and gold, and Tejas provides a drop-leaf desk. Soaps, lotions, bubble bath, thick plush towels, your choice of pillows—even a feather bed (upon request)—add to guests' comfort, as do afternoon snacks and beverages.

Guests say things like "Thanks for putting the romance that's so often forgotten back into life" and "My husband and I found our 'smiles' again" or "Breakfast is for visiting royalty."

Depending on how romantic you're feeling, you can have breakfast privately in your room or join the gang in the dining room. Either way, you're in for a treat of a baked fruit compote and baked egg casserole served with homemade breads and muffins. This is served on antique china with sterling silver and crystal, and is offered anytime during the morning. "Vegetarian? Diabetic? Food restrictions? Just let us know," said these innkeepers, "and we'll meet your needs."

HOW TO GET THERE: From I–30 take the Summit exit and turn left (south) at the Ballinger stop sign. Ballinger dead-ends at Pennsylvania; turn right. Go 2 blocks west and turn left (south) on Eight Avenue. The inn is 1½ blocks pass the fourth light (Magnolia).

The Gilded Thistle
Galveston, Texas 77550

INNKEEPERS: Helen and Pat Hanemann

ADDRESS/TELEPHONE: 1805 Broadway; (409) 763–0194 or
(800) 654–9380

ROOMS: 3; 1 with private bath; all with TV and TTD for hearing
impaired. No smoking inn.

RATES: $135 to $165, per room; EPB and snack tray in evening.

OPEN: All year.

FACILITIES AND ACTIVITIES: Discounted tickets to Galveston Racquetball Club for exercise, tennis, and golf. Nearby: historic Ashton Villa and
the Bishop's Palace; the historic Strand, with Galveston Art Center,
Galveston County Historical Museum, Railroad Museum, shops and
restaurants; the Seawall and Gulf Coast beaches, Moody Gardens Rain-
forest Pyramid, Texas Seaport Museum.

We asked innkeeper Helen Hanemann to explain The Gilded
Thistle's name, because it seemed to be a contradiction.
Helen, very much into the island's history, said that like native
thistle, sturdy Texas pioneer stock sank deep and lasting roots into the
sandy island soil, building a Galveston that flowered into a gilded age of
culture and wealth.

Her home was part of those people and their times—in the late 1800s
Galveston's Strand was known as "the Wall Street of the West"—and The
Gilded Thistle is a lovely memorial to Galveston's past.

The beautiful antiques throughout
the house make it an exceptionally elegant place to stay, but the atmosphere is
so homey that our awe melted away to
pure admiration. Helen is on duty at all
times, and we joined the other guests in
her kitchen, watching her arrange the
fresh flowers that fill the rooms.

It wasn't hard to get used to being
served on fine china, with coffee or tea
from a family silver service. Breakfast,
Helen said, is "whenever you want," so we
could sleep late and then eat lazily on the

L-shaped screened porch around the dining room, especially enjoying Helen's specialty, "nut chewies," and her crispy waffles. Guests might also have Pat's fulsome scrambled eggs, country sausage, spicy baked potatoes, and homemade biscuits. "That'll take them through lunch," he said.

Tea and coffee are available at all times, and we loved it when our morning began with orange juice and a pot of boiling water for coffee or tea at our bedroom door.

The evening snack tray could almost take the place of dinner; there are strawberries and grapes and other fruit in season, ham and cheese and roast beef sandwiches, at least four kinds of cheese, and wine. And if after that you don't feel like going out, Pat will rustle up something gourmet, such as a bowl of his seafood gumbo with special rice and French bread, compliments of the house.

The Gilded Thistle has been gilded horticulturally: In recent years the inn's landscaping has won two prizes, the Springtime Broadway Beauty Contest and an award for a business in a historic building. And now there's a lovely new gazebo. But the climate never makes it easy and has given rise to the Texas saying (borrowed from Mark Twain) that if you don't like the weather, wait a minute, it'll change. "A few years ago we had that bitter winter," Helen said. "Now we've put in lawn sprinklers and wouldn't you know—too much rain."

In the evening we took a leisurely stroll down Broadway, admiring the oleander lining the esplanade, a Galveston landmark.

HOW TO GET THERE: Stay on Highway 45 south, which becomes Broadway as soon as you cross the causeway onto Galveston Island. The inn is just beyond Eighteenth Street, on the right.

La Colombe d'Or
Houston, Texas 77006

INNKEEPER: Steve Zimmerman

ADDRESS/TELEPHONE: 3410 Montrose Boulevard; (713) 524–7999

ROOMS: 6 suites; all with private bath; wheelchair accessible.

RATES: $195 to $575, per suite; EP.

OPEN: All year.

FACILITIES AND ACTIVITIES: Restaurant, bar. Nearby: within five minutes, Houston central business district, Houston Museum of Fine Arts, Rice University, and Menil Art Foundation; the Astrodome.

We didn't have to go to France for romance; this very special inn is patterned after one of the same name in St. Paul de Vence, France, where many famous French painters traded their work for lodging. Houston's La Colombe d'Or ("the golden dove") is hung with fine art, too, and each suite has a name I certainly recognized.

We stayed in the Van Gogh Suite, named for one of our favorite Impressionist painters. Others are named for Degas, Cézanne, Monet, and Renoir; the largest suite, up at the top, is called simply The Penthouse. The suites

are decorated with fine art, although there are no original works of their namesakes.

But we hardly miss them, so swathed in beauty and luxury were we in this prince of an inn. On our coffee table we found fruit, Perrier water, and wine glasses waiting to be filled from our complimentary bottle of the inn's own imported French wine.

Owner Steve Zimmerman has succeeded in bringing to the La Colombe d'Or the casual elegance of the French Riviera. European and American antiques, as well as his own collection of prominent artists' works, are set in the luxurious house that was once the home of Exxon founder Walter Fondren and his family.

The twenty-one-room mansion, built in 1923, is divided into suites. Each consists of a huge bedroom with a sitting area and a glass-enclosed dining room where Queen Anne furniture, china plates, linen napkins, and cutlery are in readiness for breakfast. As soon as we rang in the morning, a waiter arrived with a tea cart from which he served a very French-style plate of sliced kiwi fruit, raspberries, and strawberries; orange juice; coffee; and croissants with butter and jam. We ate this artistic offering surrounded by the green leafy boughs waving outside our glass room.

You may have luncheon or dinner served in your room, too, but we feasted downstairs on meunière of shrimp and lobster, cream of potato and leek soup, the inn's Caesar salad, and capon Daniel; and as if that weren't enough, we ended with crème brûlée!

If you long to visit France, you may decide you don't have to once you've visited La Colombe d'Or. The inn is a member of *Relais et Châteaux,* a French organization that guarantees excellence, and we absolutely soaked up the hospitality, tranquillity, and luxury.

HOW TO GET THERE: 3410 Montrose is between Westheimer and Alabama, both Houston thoroughfares.

Gruene Mansion
New Braunfels, Texas 78130

INNKEEPERS: Sharon and Bill McCaskell

ADDRESS/TELEPHONE: 1275 Gruene Road; (210) 629–2641 or 629–8372; fax (210) 629–7375

ROOMS: 25, in assorted cottages on the river; all with private bath and TV. No smoking inn.

RATES: $85 to $200, double; $10 extra person; breakfast $5 extra. No credit cards.

OPEN: All year.

FACILITIES AND ACTIVITIES: Restaurant and bar overlooking the river. Nearby: Grist Mill Restaurant; Gruene Dance Hall; antiques; museums: Hummel, Sophienburg, Handmade Furniture, and Children's; Schlitterbahn Water Park; rafting, tubing, and swimming on Guadalupe and Comal rivers; bicycling; horseback riding; golf; tennis; Natural Bridge Caverns and Wildlife Ranch; Canyon Lake, with fishing, boating, swimming, and waterskiing; discount shopping malls.

*S*haron and Bill not only wanted a resort, they wanted one with history. They found it in the Gruene Mansion, set on a historic cotton plantation on the banks of the Guadalupe River.

The inn is located within the Gruene (pronounced "green") Historic District on the northern edge of New Braunfels's city limits. "Bill and I really like the history of Gruene Mansion," Sharon said. "We feel as if we're caretakers of the property, and we try to carry on the tradition of *gemutlich* begun by Henry Gruene back in the mid-1800s."

Gruene Dance Hall, just down the street, is the oldest dance hall in Texas. Sharon spoke of the original owner as though she knew him. "Henry built the hall for the closeness and warmness of his friends. He also had a little house where travelers could come and stay; they just had to replace the logs for the fire. He was kind to strangers, and we wanted to live that way. It's the best way to meet people."

Curious, we wandered down to Gruene Dance Hall for a beer and some Texas two-stepping. We were thrilled to find live music. We dined next door at the Grist Mill Restaurant, housed in the ruins of a hundred-year-old cotton gin beneath a water tower on the banks of the Guadalupe River, with its pretty little rapids and its happy whitewater rafters, many floating down from Canyon River when the water's right.

Cottages with little porches overhang the river, and they are furnished with antiques and handmade quilts; each room is different. Sharon had a great time decorating—imagine having seventeen rooms to design!

We loved Fireside Lodge #2 with its slanted ceiling, papered with a pretty flowered wallpaper of pink and blue flowers on a black background. You can imagine the interesting contrast that makes with the rough wood paneling, made from both poplar and yellow pine. The fireplace wall is white stone; the brass bed has a colorful patchwork quilt and a crocheted afghan laid across the foot. (Feet can get chilly on cool Hill Country nights.)

But tempting, too, was Bluebonnet Lodge, with huge bluebonnets painted on the walls, both bedroom and bath. The shower curtain in the bath is an old quilt (protected by a liner, of course) and dolled up with a pointed lace valance—Sharon has many original ideas. Walls in the Grand River Lodge are painted bright blue between the wood strips and stenciled with red and yellow stylized tulips.

New is the "Sunday Haus" with eight rooms decorated in Victorian rustic elegance. King-sized beds, fireplaces, old Victorian bathtubs, and antiques make the *haus* (German for house) a great addition to the inn.

HOW TO GET THERE: From I–35 take exit 191 (Canyon Lake) and go west on Highway 306 for 1½ miles, following the Gruene Historical signs. Turn left into Gruene and go to the end of the road. The inn is on the right as you turn left onto Gruene Road.

The Ogé House
San Antonio, Texas 78204

INNKEEPERS: Sharrie and Patrick Magatagan

ADDRESS/TELEPHONE: 209 Washington; (210) 223–2353 or (800) 242–2770; fax (210) 226–5812

ROOMS: 10; all with private bath and TV. No smoking inn.

RATES: $135 to $195, double; deluxe continental breakfast.

OPEN: All year.

FACILITIES AND ACTIVITIES: Parking. Nearby: Downtown San Antonio, with The Alamo, La Villita, Convention Center, museums, RiverCenter Mall, El Mercado.

*I*f you're looking for a proper mansion, you have found it. A tall, three-story building squared off by a set of porches top and bottom, the Ogé House looms ahead at the end of the street, looking almost like a misplaced plantation house. But not too misplaced, because it's set on large, lovely grounds ending only at San Antonio's famous river.

The Ogé House (pronounced "oh-jhay"—it's French) is one of the most magnificent homes to be found in San Antonio's historic King William District of fine homes. It was built in 1857 for Louis Ogé, a pioneer cattle rancher and a Texas Ranger.

Like many old beauties, the home had become an apartment house, but it was just waiting for Sharrie and Patrick to find it. They had been looking, driving up the East Coast for six weeks, before they realized that this was where they wanted to be.

"I used to redo old houses back East," Sharrie said. "And we'd been collecting antiques for ten, twelve years." Visiting her father here, they heard that the old house might be available.

The house is huge, with two guest rooms opening off the majestic lobby, which is actually the second floor, since you climb eleven steps up to the front door. Once there you'll admire the antique French set of two settees and two chairs. "They're from a private suite in the Waldorf Astoria in New York," Patrick said.

The Library, at the rear of the house, is relaxing, with soft-yellow walls, white woodwork, satin-striped sofas, and books (although "there are books all over the house," as Sharrie says). The brass bucket in The Library is filled with menus from the city's many fine eating places.

Upstairs (third floor) the Giles and Mathis suites both open onto the porch across the front of the house, while Riverview, off the landing by the

back stairs, is intensely private, with its own porch and view of the river.

Down below, on the main level, the Mitchell Suite has a platform canopy bed. The Bluebonnet Room is done in Texas antiques, with a four-poster rolling-pin bed and the desk of an old Texas judge. But that's all we found of Texas.

"We're not a Texas country inn," Sharrie said. "We have more of the flavor of a small European hotel or an English country manor house."

Sharrie's "Deluxe Continental Breakfast" begins with poached pears and goes on to such delicacies as pecan log roll, apple torte, cherry cheese cake, and fruit pasties.

You can join everyone for breakfast in the dining room, take it out on the front veranda, or go out on the grounds and sit overlooking the river. "We're on one and a half acres, and when all the trees leaf out in the summer, you can't see any of the neighbors. We couldn't believe we were in downtown San Antonio!"

HOW TO GET THERE: From I–35 take 281 south and exit at Durango. Turn right and go through three traffic lights to St. Mary's. Take the first left to Pancoast; the inn is head-on at the end of the street.

Mulberry Manor
Sweetwater, Texas 79556

INNKEEPERS: Beverly and Raymond Stone

ADDRESS/TELEPHONE: 1400 Sam Houston Street; (915) 235–3811 or (800) 235–3811

ROOMS: 6; all with private bath; 2 with TV; wheelchair accessible. Pets welcome.

RATES: $70 to $225, double; $7.50 extra person; EPB and afternoon snacks.

OPEN: All year.

FACILITIES AND ACTIVITIES: Lunch and dinner by reservation, hot tub. Nearby: horseback riding; golf; Pioneer City–County Museum; lakes Sweetwater, Trammell, and Oak Creek Reservoir with fishing, boating, and water sports; World's Largest Rattlesnake Roundup (March).

*I*t's a surprise to discover a mansion like Mulberry Manor in a town the size of Sweetwater (about 12,000 population). It was built in 1913 for banker, businessman, and rancher Thomas Trammell—and the architect was John Young, father of movie star Loretta Young.

Which may account for the Hollywood glamor of this showplace. The focal point of the mansion is a glass-domed atrium, filled with green plants and sunshine, in the center of the house. A white, slatted fence encloses this, the heart of the house, and the inn's rooms surround it. The formal French parlor to the right of the entry is furnished in authentic Louis Quinze; the tailored parlor on the left also contains lovely pieces, garnered from all over.

"Just about everything is from estate sales and antiques shops," Beverly said. "We bought everything in this house on weekends." This gave them something to do while the house was being restored.

The house had a checkered life after the Trammells were gone. To give you some idea of the scale, in 1923 it became Sweetwater and Nolan County's only hospital. Then, like many old homes, the 9,800-square-foot house was divided into apartments. Eventually, it somehow became part of the estate of the brother of General Clair Chennault of the famous Flying Tigers.

The house has three downstairs guest rooms plus a vast suite upstairs. The separate barroom has an oversized television screen and a sitting area.

The formal dining room is impressive, but so is the so-called breakfast room, with its brocaded French chairs, a beautiful mirrored sideboard, and an Oriental rug on the polished wood floor.

But most exotic is the upstairs suite, which Beverly described as "neoclassical." To give you an idea of the size, originally it was a ballroom. "It was an apartment, and it was horrible," Beverly shuddered. Now, on the huge expanse of white carpet, the furniture is gold and black, with green plants (there's even a fern behind the king headboard). A statuary group, busts of classical figures, occupies a corner. The adjoining bath is suitably sybaritic.

Breakfast is as opulent as the manor: fresh fruit compote, eggs Benedict or quiche, hashed browns, sausage or ham, biscuits and gravy, cinnamon raisin biscuits, strawberry cream cheese on croissants. And afternoons there's a big snack tray with the beverage of your choice; our snack was cream puffs filled with ham salad. Who does all this? "Me. I'm the cook!" Beverly said.

Her dinners are spectacular seven-course meals, too.

And to cap it all off, Raymond takes guests for a fun ride in that shiny 1929 Model A Ford out front.

HOW TO GET THERE: Take exit 244 off I–20 and go north 4 blocks to Sam Houston Street and number 1400. There's a sign on the model A Ford out in front.

Charnwood Hill Inn
Tyler, Texas 75701

INNKEEPERS: Kim Demetri and Don Walker

ADDRESS/TELEPHONE: 223 East Charnwood; (903) 597–3980;
fax (903) 592–6473

ROOMS: 7, including 1 suite; all with private bath; 5 with TV.
No smoking inn.

RATES: $95 to $270, double; $15 extra person, single $15 less; EPB
weekends; a lighter meal is served on weekdays.

OPEN: All year.

FACILITIES AND ACTIVITIES: Tea and dinner by reservation, elevator,
gift shop. Nearby: Municipal Rose Garden & Museum, Brookshire's
World of Wildlife Museum and Country Store, Hudnall Planetarium,
Caldwell Zoo, Azalea Trail, Texas Rose Festival, East Texas State Fair.

We found it pretty romantic to experience the style of living enjoyed
by an old-time Texas oilman. Charnwood Hill Inn was built
around 1860 by a Professor Hand, who was headmaster of a
school for girls. The mansion passed through several hands until it was purchased by H. L. Hunt in the early 1930s.

"The Hunt family extensively remodeled and redecorated," Don said as we
wandered through the tall-ceilinged rooms full of opulent furniture.

We weren't sure what sort of furnishings the Hunts had when this gorgeous mansion was their home, but it would have to be something to equal
Patsy and Don's collection. "We spent seventeen years collecting and didn't
want to get rid of it," Don said. They needed to find a place worthy of such
beautiful antiques, and Charnwood Hill shows them off to perfection. Patsy
and Don bought the home in 1978.

We were in a mansion, all right.
Common areas of the inn include
the formal living room, library, television room, the Great Hall on the
first floor and the Lodge on the second floor, the Garden Room, the
Gathering Hall, the front and east
balconies, screened swing porch,
front porches, the arbor, and the

beautiful east and west gardens. "Tyler's famous Azalea Trail starts right outside this house," Don said.

Tyler considers itself "Rose Capital of the World," and the annual Texas Rose Festival is an important local event. Margaret Hunt was Rose Queen in 1935; and JoAnne Miller, daughter of the then-owner of the home, was Rose Queen in 1954. Both times the Queen's Tea was held in the gardens.

A pair of curved steps leads up to the white-columned entrance. The large foyer and living room are stately. The dining room is impressive, with a handmade table and ten chairs of solid pecan, a Chinoiserie breakfront displaying antique Meissen china, an Oriental rug, and a delicate chandelier. It makes a contrast to the bright breakfast room, although even that, in its way, is formal, with its glass tables, chairs covered with summery floral fabric, bricked floor, and branched chandelier.

The 1,500-square-foot Art Deco Suite on the third floor was constructed for the two Hunt daughters; the gray carpet makes a perfect foil for the Chinoiserie pieces and the print fabric on a black background. The second-floor sleeping porch and one bedroom were converted into what is now called The Lodge, which has a bar, television, and lots of room for meetings.

Breakfast on weekends is a full gourmet feast. Eggs Benedict is served with an inn specialty—a tasty breakfast potato casserole—and a mélange of mixed fruits, and juices, coffee, and tea. If you wish, at 4:00 P.M. Patsy will serve a Lemon Tea of cheesecake with fresh fruit.

Dinners are as you like, also, with Texas steak a specialty.

HOW TO GET THERE: From I-20 take Highway 69 south to North Broadway, which becomes South Broadway at Tyler Square. Continue south 4 blocks to Charnwood and turn left. The inn is on the right, and there's a sign.

The Inn Above Onion Creek
Wimberley, Texas 78676

INNKEEPERS: Janie Orr

ADDRESS/TELEPHONE: 4444 Highway 150 West (mailing address: P.O. Box 2230); (512) 268-1617; fax (512) 268-1090

ROOMS: 6; all with private bath, telephone, and TV; 1 with wheelchair access. No smoking inn.

RATES: $150 to $250, double; $30 extra person; EPB.

OPEN: All year.

FACILITIES AND ACTIVITIES: Lunch and dinner; meeting room; swimming pool; 5 miles of trails in the Hill Country leading to an overlook of Onion Creek; cooking, art class, and musical weekends. Nearby: San Marcos, with outlet shopping mall; canoeing, tubing, and swimming on the San Marcos River; galleries, restaurants and shops in Wimberley and Gruene.

This inn is a true retreat, set on 500 acres of the Texas Hill Country, 5 miles from the nearest town: tiny Kyle, once the home of novelist Katherine Ann Porter.

Janie knew exactly what she wanted, but it took longer to find than she expected. "Looking at land was a lot of fun," Janie said. "I wanted to be no more than 30 miles from Austin, yet off a picturesque road that made you feel you were going back in time."

While the setting is rural, the accommodations are not. Each room is large, with room for a sitting area of sofa, love seat, or chaise in front of a stone fireplace. Shelves to put things on are built on one side of each fireplace, and there is room to move around the bed and bedside tables.

And the bathrooms are to rave about. Janie, into major hydrotherapy, said, "Shoot the budget on bathrooms!" The results are stupendous. Four of them have huge Jacuzzis, several have large, two-party showers enclosed in glass bricks, and for light, several have French doors opening onto small wrought-iron balconies.

The exterior is rustic. "We were really trying to find an old ranch house to save, but they turned out to be scarce," Janie said. So she built her own old ranch house out of cedar and Hill Country stone; upstairs porch railings, of rough cedar posts, are very early-homestead evoking!

Breakfast is a delicious torta of venison sausage ("My son is the mighty hunter," Janie said), eggs, parmesan and cheddar cheese, with O'Brien potatoes and homemade biscuits, all prefaced by Rio Star grapefruit, the crème de la crème of the famous Texas Ruby Red.

For dinner—"supper" in these parts—we had chicken *enchiladas suizas,* black beans, corn dip olé, and Oreo cheesecake.

The wide porches in the rear look out over miles and miles of Hill Country, with not a sign of civilization in sight. The Capt. Fergus Kyle Room, downstairs, is both wheelchair accessible and wheelchair prepared, with railings and a wheel-in shower.

The Jack Hayes Room upstairs, in a rust-and-gray color scheme, has a king-sized bed and a chaise lounge in front of its stone fireplace.

Both the Hayes Room and the Michaelis Room next door open onto a porch with a wonderful north view. Convenient, too: There are back stairs leading down to the swimming pool.

The Michaelis Room's accent wall is a medium blue, very pleasant. All rooms have wonderful huge armoires, and I wondered how Janie had found so many. "I haunted antiques and garage sales—and watched the ads like crazy!" She also found an artisan who could build her some of the rustic-looking pieces she wanted, such as the tables and chairs in the large dining room.

HOW TO GET THERE: From I–35 take exit 213 (Kyle) and go west on Kyle's main Center Street to the stop sign at FM 150. Take FM 150 and go $^5/_{10}$ miles to the inn gate on the right—there is a sign. Turn in at the gate and go 1 mile, slowly, on a narrow, curved road until you reach the inn.

Rocky Mountain Region

by Doris Kennedy

In an attempt to select the most romantic inns from the many hundreds I have visited, I first asked myself what I would look for when choosing such an accommodation for my husband and myself. Next I interviewed friends and colleagues, questioning them as to the qualities they would seek in their ideal hideaway for two.

I discovered most of us thought pretty much the same, with the main difference being in the order of preference.

As for me, I would look for a secluded place, private, with soothing sounds in the form of birdsong, the steady chirp of crickets, the rush of a river, or the distant call of coyotes at dusk.

Luxurious or rustic, either would be fine; but if a turret room were available, I would absolutely have to have it, for here we would leisurely sip morning coffee and take turns reading aloud. I would like a fireplace and perhaps a four-poster canopied in ruffles and lace, or one made of rough-hewn logs and covered with billowy quilts.

No phones, please. And if a television must be present, let it be hidden away in an armoire.

Blessed is the innkeeper who is attentive yet discreet. Guests seeking a romantic rendezvous want to be greeted warmly, then graciously left alone. Let the innkeeper spin his or her magic by leaving treats and morning coffee outside the door and, while we are out, a fresh rose on the bed, a pitcher of ice water spiked with floating fresh strawberries, and a love poem or a sachet of potpourri under the pillows.

Flowers, candles, adjustable soft lighting, and a nearby wood or a park for wandering hand in hand would be nice.

Most of all, let it be peaceful, where hushed conversations proceed without interruption, where secrets are shared and promises made, and where cherished memories have their beginnings.

Rocky Mountain Region

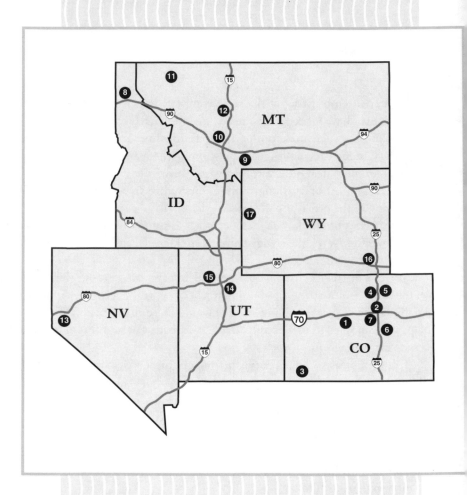

Rocky Mountain Region

Numbers on map refer to towns numbered below.

Sardy House
Aspen, Colorado 81611

INNKEEPER: Kim Stachowski

ADDRESS/TELEPHONE: 128 East Main Street; (970) 920–2525 or (800) 321–3457

E-MAIL: hotlsard@rof.net

WEB SITE: www.aspen.com/sardylenado

ROOMS: 20, including 6 suites; all with private bath and TV, most with whirlpool bath, suites with VCR, stereo, and dry bar. Air-conditioning in some rooms (elevation 7,908 feet).

RATES: $90 to $750, single or double, depending on choice of room and season; full breakfast.

OPEN: All year.

FACILITIES AND ACTIVITIES: Dining room open to public for breakfast, dinner, and Sunday brunch. Concierge service, room service. Bar, heated outdoor pool, sauna, Jacuzzi. Nearby: restaurants, shopping, art galleries, free ski shuttle, all within walking distance; summer music festivals, hiking, fly-fishing, river rafting, downhill skiing (Aspen Mountain, Snowmass, Aspen Highlands, and Buttermilk), cross-country skiing, ice skating.

RECOMMENDED COUNTRY INNS® TRAVELERS' CLUB BENEFIT: 10 percent discount, Monday to Thursday.

*I*f your ideal romantic getaway leans toward turreted, Victorian mansions, perhaps this is the inn for you: a red-brick masterpiece with original oak staircases and sliding parlor doors, round reading rooms tucked away in a turret, gourmet breakfast set upon pearl-gray linen centered with fresh flowers, and fine dining in the evenings as well.

Soft plum carpeting with pale pink roses, made in Ireland especially for the Sardy, is used throughout the building, and wallpaper of subdued gray cloaks the walls. The guest rooms have thick terry his and her robes, heated towel racks, down comforters with Laura Ashley duvets, and televisions hidden in walls or armoires. Except for two units with antique tubs, all have whirlpool baths.

We have a thing about carriage houses, and that is where we chose to stay, in a beautifully appointed complement to the main mansion. Our room had a vaulted, many-angled ceiling; natural wicker table, chairs, and writing desk; a cherry-wood, high-off-the-floor bed with feather-filled comforter and five fluffy pillows; and a bay window that looked out on Aspen Mountain and the ski slopes. The almond-scented lotion, shampoo, and bath gel were another nice touch. If you add just a few drops of bath gel to your whirlpool bath, you'll both disappear into boundless bubbles!

Our breakfast was a Sardy Frittata, with eggs, Brie cheese, scallions, and *pico de gallo;* a garnish of fresh fruit; coffee; and orange juice.

For dinner we chose an appetizer of lobster crabcakes with red pepper chili aoili; a warm spinach salad with mushrooms, onion, eggs, and applewood-smoked bacon dressing; and grilled Rocky Mountain rainbow trout stuffed with shiitake mushrooms, leeks, and fresh chives. Alas, despite the wonderful dessert selections, I sadly had to decline.

For those who prefer the privacy of their room, the Sardy House will serve either breakfast or dinner or both in your guest room.

The Sardy House is a popular place for small weddings, receptions, and private dinners. It has been awarded the Mobil four-star rating: "Outstanding . . . worth a special trip."

HOW TO GET THERE: Sardy House is on the corner of Main and Aspen Streets in downtown Aspen.

Castle Marne
Denver, Colorado 80206

INNKEEPERS: Jim and Diane Peiker

ADDRESS/TELEPHONE: 1572 Race Street; (303) 331–0621

E-MAIL: themarne@ix.netcom.com

WEB SITES: www.castlemarne.com
www.bedandbreakfastinns.org/castle

ROOMS: 10; all with private bath and phone; 3 with jetted whirlpool tubs for two on private balconies. Air-conditioning in some rooms but seldom needed (walls are 20 inches of solid stone); No smoking inn.

RATES: $70 to $220, single; $85 to $220, double; full breakfast, Victorian tea.

OPEN: All year.

FACILITIES AND ACTIVITIES: Concierge service; Victorian luncheons and candlelight dinners available with prior arrangement; game room with pool table and exercise equipment; gift shop. Nearby: Elitch Gardens Amusement Park, Coors Field, Bronco Stadium, McNichols Arena, business and financial districts, Colorado State Capitol, U.S. Mint, Center for the Performing Arts, restaurants, convention center, museums, recreation centers, shopping facilities, professional sporting events, golf, tennis, hiking, fishing, biking; downhill and cross-country skiing approximately 50 miles away.

RECOMMENDED COUNTRY INNS® TRAVELERS' CLUB BENEFIT: 5 percent discount, Sunday to Thursday. Please mention when making reservation.

*F*or those of us not lucky enough to grow up in a castle amidst opulence and grandeur, the Castle Marne provides a wee glimpse of what we missed. The exterior is stunning. For years, passersby have paused to admire the medieval-looking rusticated stone structure. Now they come to spend the night.

Inside, one can't help but marvel at the glowing woodwork, original fireplaces, and exquisitely decorated rooms. The parlor, blessed with a baby grand piano and treasured family antiques, lends itself nicely to the intimate Victorian tea served each afternoon on heirloom porcelain china and silver.

There's something hopelessly romantic about climbing the stately oak staircase, past the resplendent beveled-crystal and stained-glass Peacock Window, to your guest room. Our favorite chamber is the Presidential Suite, an elegant affair featuring a king-sized brass and white-iron tester bed with rose bed cover peeping through ecru lace. This room is further enhanced by a tiny fireplace, an antique gentleman's dresser, and a cozy turret room surrounded by five lace-paneled windows. French doors lead to a private solarium with a large whirlpool tub and a balcony overlooking downtown Denver.

The Conservatory also caught our fancy. This light and airy room has a queen-sized bed, a wicker armoire and love seat, and creamy walls sprinkled with cabbage roses.

Imagine a private candlelight dinner in the Castle Marne's formal dining room amid the gracious ambience of days long past. Soft music accompanies your conversation, and you scarcely notice the striking of the wall clock as you dine on chilled marinated shrimp and Cornish game hen with apricot glaze and fruit-and-nut stuffing, followed by chocolate mousse and café au lait. Later you climb that wonderful oak staircase, soak in the oversized Jacuzzi with balcony doors open to the stars and, eventually, sip a cup of wine or tea in your own tiny turret hideaway. Every couple should have such an evening at least once in their lifetime. Hopefully, many, many times.

Extraordinarily good breakfasts come from Jim and Diane's kitchen, too. A fresh fruit plate is followed by wonderful homemade breads, muffins, and cinnamon sticky buns. Perhaps you will choose one of their many waffle varieties with real maple syrup, an innovative quiche, or a hot-from-the-oven breakfast casserole.

HOW TO GET THERE: From East Colfax Avenue, turn north onto Race Street. Proceed for almost 1 block. Inn is on southeast corner of Race Street and Sixteenth Avenue.

Queen Anne Bed & Breakfast Inn
Denver, Colorado 80205

INNKEEPERS: Tom, Chris, and Dave King

ADDRESS/TELEPHONE: 2147-51 Tremont Place; (303) 296–6666 for information; (800) 432–INNS for reservations; fax (303) 296–2151

E-MAIL: queenanne@worldnet.att.net

WEB SITE: www.bedandbreakfastinns.org/queenanne

ROOMS: 14; all with private bath, phone, air-conditioning, and stereo chamber music. No smoking inn.

RATES: $75 to $175; full breakfast and evening wine and cider. Special rates for travel agents, entertainers, and members of AAA. Inquire about rates for Romance Package.

OPEN: All year.

FACILITIES AND ACTIVITIES: Innkeeper will arrange horse-and-carriage rides, catered candlelight dinners, musicians for private serenading, tours of Denver and Colorado, reservations for restaurants and other inns, and just about anything else your imagination can come up with. Nearby: Colorado State Capitol, U.S. Mint, Center for the Performing

Arts, Elitch Gardens Amusement Park, Coors Field, Bronco Stadium, McNichols Arena, museums, shopping, restaurants (several five-star), all within walking distance; hiking, fishing, biking; downhill and cross-country skiing approximately 50 miles away.

The two side-by-side Victorians that make up the exceptionally romantic Queen Anne Inn reign amid a row of lovely old homes in downtown Denver's Clements Historic District. While you relax in the beautifully appointed parlor, you are apt to witness a breathless couple arriving by horse and carriage, she still in her long, white wedding dress, he nervously trying to avoid stepping on same. Or the newest arrivals might be a middle-aged pair, with bottle of champagne in hand, bent on escaping their lawn-mowing, car-polishing neighbors for a romantic weekend getaway. They've come to the right place.

Every guest room is different, and each one is special in its own way. The Fountain Room, overlooking Benedict Fountain Park, boasts a four-poster with frilly, white-ruffled arched canopy, soft peach walls, a blue-and-peach love seat, and a black-tiled sunken tub tucked away in one corner. A more romantic room would be hard to find.

While the Tower Room, with European carved king-sized bed and bay window love seat, is exceptionally inviting, the Aspen Room is definitely the most unusual. Located in the turret, it features a hand-painted, wraparound mural of an aspen grove. If you lie on the bed and look up at the ceiling, you will gradually see the forest come alive until the aspen leaves seem to quake in the alpenglow.

The grounds are positively lovely. A series of latticework arbors leads to an enclosed backyard garden bordered by brick and flagstone planters filled with flowers and greenery. Ornate, white iron tables and chairs and a center fountain beckon couples to linger awhile.

According to Tom, "This inn is known for providing 'White Lace Romance.' The Queen Anne hosts an average of two honeymoon couples, two anniversary couples and three couples on a 'getaway' per week." When I asked him what he thinks makes his inn so romantic, he replied, "The fresh flowers, chamber music, champagne upon arrival, candlelight dinners, antique brass beds and canopied four posters, claw-footed tubs and soaker tubs-for-two, lights on dimmer switches, direct-dial phones to call friends with happy news, and late checkout. And then there's the private garden, perfect for a secluded breakfast or evening glass of wine."

Numerous publications, including *Bride's* magazine, *Romantic Hideaways, Bridal Guide, Country Inns, Travel Holiday,* and *Vacations* agree. All have raved about the Queen Anne's romantic qualities.

HOW TO GET THERE: From East Colfax Avenue, take Logan Street north to 20th Avenue. Turn left onto 20th Avenue and then immediately right onto Tremont Place.

Apple Orchard Inn
Durango, Colorado 81301

INNKEEPERS: John and Celeste Gardiner

ADDRESS/TELEPHONE: 7758 County Road 203; (970) 247–0751 or (800) 426–0751

E-MAIL: apple@frontier.net

WEB SITE: www.appleorchardinn.com

ROOMS: 10, including 6 cottages; all with private bath and TV; 4 with private patio, Jacuzzi tub, and fireplace; 3 with refrigerator. No smoking inn.

RATES: $85 to $150 per couple; full breakfast. Dinner available, with prior reservations, at an additional charge.

OPEN: All year.

FACILITIES AND ACTIVITIES: Outdoor hot tub, award-winning landscaped grounds. Nearby: restaurants, shopping, Trimble Hot Springs, Durango & Silverton Narrow Gauge Railroad, Mesa Verde National Park, Anasazi Heritage Center, Crow Canyon Archaeological Center, Hovenweep National Monument; gold-mine tours, hiking, biking, fishing, soaring, golfing, whitewater rafting, kayaking, horseback

riding; cross-country skiing and downhill skiing at Purgatory-
Durango Ski Area.

his luxurious, award-winning farmhouse-style inn keeps beckon-
ing us to come back and once more stroll the beautifully landscaped grounds and relax in one of four guest rooms in the main
house or one of the six charming cottages.

All the bed chambers are inviting, but our favorite remains the enchanting cottage called Liberty, where we spent the night on our first visit. Here we
found a love seat set before the gas-log fireplace, a gigantic mirrored armoire,
and a lovely queen-sized sleigh bed. Our chamber was further enhanced by a
vaulted ceiling, television, minirefrigerator, whirlpool bathtub, and private
patio with a white-iron table and chairs.

After indulging in one of Celeste's outstanding gourmet dinners, we
enjoyed a restful slumber and awoke to lilting birdsong and the cry of indus-
trious crows. As we sipped our early-morning coffee in the wooden swing on
our private porch, we watched the inn's pet ducks merrily glide across the
miniature mirrorlike lake and planned our activities for the day.

Should be rent mountain bikes to embark on one of a number of close-
by trails, arrange for a rafting trip down the scenic Animas River, or spend
the day lolling about at the nearby
hot springs? Then, again, we
would be perfectly content to stay
right here at the inn where,
engulfed by the surrounding
serenity, we could read on our private patio, soak in the outdoor hot
tub, or laze the day away on the
large shared patio that looks out
upon the inn's spacious lawns,
gardens, trout pond, and meandering stream.

Day trips might include exploration of Mesa Verde National Park—a
52,000-acre World Heritage Site containing spectacular cliff dwellings once
occupied by the Ancient Pueblo People—or a captivating ride aboard the
coal-fired, steam-operated Durango and Silverton Narrow Gauge Railroad
from Durango to Silverton and return.

Celeste studied the culinary arts in Italy, France, and Belgium, so you can
count on the morning repast to be memorable. Your entree might be a Mexican dish called *migas*—made with scrambled eggs, cheddar cheese, onions,
fresh tomatoes, green chilies, and jalapeños—or Belgian waffles garnished

with fresh raspberries, blueberries, and strawberries and dusted with powdered sugar. Accompaniments include fresh-baked breads, crisp bacon, orange juice, and flavored coffees.

HOW TO GET THERE: From Durango, take U.S. Highway 550 north for 6 miles to Trimble Lane. Turn left onto Trimble Lane to County Road 203. Turn right onto County Road 203 for 1^4/$_{10}$ miles. Inn is on the right-hand side of the road.

River Song Inn
Estes Park, Colorado 80517

INNKEEPERS: Gary and Sue Mansfield

MAILING ADDRESS/TELEPHONE: P.O. Box 1910; (970) 586–4666

E-MAIL: riversng@frii.com

WEB SITE: www.romanticriversong.com

ROOMS: 4 in main inn, 1 carriage house suite, 4 deluxe cottages; all with private bath; 3 with whirlpool tubs; 3 with wheelchair access. No air-conditioning (elevation 7,522 feet). No smoking inn.

RATES: $135 to $225; double, EPB. Inquire about rates for three-night Elopement Package.

OPEN: All year.

FACILITIES AND ACTIVITIES: Candlelight dinner and box lunches by reservation. In-room picnics for fireside dining available. Wedding performed on-site by RiverSong's own "Marrying Sam." Romance, honeymoon and elopement packages available. Located on twenty-seven acres of land with easy hiking trails. Nearby: Rocky Mountain National Park, restaurants, shopping, hiking, fishing, sailing, mountain climbing, golf, tennis, wildlife seminars, cross-country skiing, snowshoeing.

*I*f planning a formal wedding is not to your liking, you may want to check out the River Song's three-night Elopement Package. Included are a full breakfast each morning, one therapeutic massage per person, a gourmet picnic lunch, and a candlelight dinner for two. The bride and groom can take their vows, performed by innkeeper Gary Mansfield, either at the inn or, during winter, on snowshoes among breathtakingly beautiful surroundings in Rocky Mountain National Park.

The River Song recently added a wonderfully secluded two-unit cottage, with guest quarters separated by a foot-and-a-half-thick wall to ensure privacy. Named "Wood Nymph" and "Meadow Bright," the two chambers are nestled on the mountainside (easily accessible) near a rushing stream and tranquil, trout-filled pond, with a spectacular view of the snow-capped peaks of Rocky Mountain National Park. Both have fireplaces, canopied beds (Wood Nymph's is handmade of river birches, and Meadow Bright's is a massive hand-hewn log affair), decks, and radiant-heated floors. Wood Nymph has a Jacuzzi whirlpool tub, and Meadow Bright features a fireside jetted tub, and a waterfall shower. Both rooms have wheelchair access.

But if you are looking for something unique and also romantic, you really should ask for the River Song's most requested accommodation: Indian Paintbrush. A charming cottage sequestered among tall pine trees, it is tastefully done in Southwestern decor and features a love seat, handwoven Navajo wall hangings, an oversized bathtub, and, best of all, a swinging queen-sized bed suspended from the ceiling by heavy white chains in front of a rose-tiled fireplace.

Sue is an excellent cook and makes many delectables such as apple pandowdy, blueberry cobbler served with vanilla yogurt, and corn fritters topped with genuine Vermont maple syrup.

Elegant candlelight dinners, served in style with heirloom silver, crystal, and china, are available with prior notice. A typical repast might begin with Avocado RiverSong, followed by Oriental soup with shrimp and shiitake mushrooms, basil chicken, rice pilaf, Japanese eggplant, and amaretto torte.

A wall of windows in the luxurious living room reveals a magnificent view of tall pines and mountains. Two other walls are lined with books, a warm fire crackles in the fireplace, and the grandfather clock periodically chimes the hour. All's well at River Song.

HOW TO GET THERE: Going west on Elkhorn Avenue, Estes Park's main street, turn left onto Moraine Avenue and proceed 4 blocks. At first stop sign, turn right onto Highway 36. At stoplight (1²/₁₀ miles) turn left onto Mary's Lake Road. Watch for River Song Inn mailbox just across bridge. Turn right and proceed for ⁸/₁₀ mile. The road ends at River Song.

The Lovelander Bed & Breakfast Inn
Loveland, Colorado 80537

INNKEEPERS: Lauren and Gary Smith

ADDRESS/TELEPHONE: 217 West Fourth Street; (970) 669-0798

E-MAIL: love@ezlink.com

WEB SITE: www.bbonline.com/co/lovelander/

ROOMS: 11; all with private bath, air-conditioning, and phone; some with whirlpool bath. No smoking inn.

RATES: $100 to $150 per couple; full breakfast and evening dessert.

OPEN: All year.

FACILITIES AND ACTIVITIES: Meeting and reception center. Nearby: restaurants, shopping, art galleries, museums, concerts, performing arts, lectures, theater, outdoor and indoor swimming pools, outdoor and indoor Jacuzzis, golf, tennis, hiking, biking, fishing, boating, cross-country skiing, llama farm, Rocky Mountain National Park.

RECOMMENDED COUNTRY INNS® TRAVELERS' CLUB BENEFIT: Stay two nights and get third night free.

*L*oveland, Colorado, is known nationwide as the Sweetheart City, where one can send his or her valentines to be postmarked by hand and mailed from "Loveland." What better way to impress that special someone?

The Lovelander Bed & Breakfast Inn fits right into the scheme. Its Victorian elegance definitely lends itself to romance. Here guests whisper sweet promises in the garden, sip sherry on the porch, and take a tea tray to the privacy of their room. Want more? How about a soak in an antique footed tub filled to the brim with passion fruit–scented bubbles?

A wide veranda wraps around the front and one side of this lovely circa-1902 inn; inside, gleaming woodwork, an ornate organ from the late 1800s, a corner fireplace, and plush overstuffed furniture add to the inviting glow of the parlor.

Lace-curtained bay windows spread soft light into the dining room, where one can always find coffee or tea and genuine homemade Victorian vinegar cookies on the sideboard. Breakfast is served either at tables set for two or at the large oval dining room table.

And the two of you are in for a treat when you come down to breakfast. Baked eggs Florentine, cinnamon-raisin breakfast pudding, stuffed French toast with fruit sauce, almond scones, banana-oatmeal pancakes, gingered melon with honey, and strawberry-banana smoothies are only a few of the specialties cooked up in the kitchen.

The private and secluded guest rooms are tucked away in downstairs corners and upstairs gables. Sloped ceilings and lots of nooks and crannies, along with antique writing desks, armoires, carved walnut and oak and brass and iron beds, and claw-footed bathtubs, add to the charm of these chambers.

Our favorite is the Columbine, with king-sized bed and elegant bath with 6-foot whirlpool tub.

The Lovelander dedicates the entire month of February to romance. The chef creates gourmet candlelight breakfasts, and lovers receive commemorative valentines and complimentary boxes of chocolates.

HOW TO GET THERE: From I–25, turn west onto Highway 34 to Garfield Avenue. Turn left onto Garfield to West Fourth Street. Turn right onto West Fourth Street. Inn is on the right.

Rockledge Country Inn
Manitou Springs, Colorado 80829

INNKEEPERS: Hartman and Nancy Smith

ADDRESS/TELEPHONE: 328 El Paso Boulevard; (719) 685–4515 or (888) 685–4515; fax (719) 685–1031

E-MAIL: rockinn@webcom.com

WEB SITE: www.rockledgeinn.com

ROOMS: 4 suites, all with TV, VCR, and private bath; 3 with jetted tubs; 1 with wood-burning fireplace. No smoking inn.

RATES: $195 to $250 per couple; full gourmet breakfast and late-afternoon and evening refreshments. Fruit and candy always available. Dinner available, with prior notice, at additional charge.

OPEN: All year.

FACILITIES AND ACTIVITIES: Outdoor spa, landscaped grounds, concierge services, library, dinners available with prior reservations. Nearby: Pikes Peak, Seven Falls, Cave of the Winds, Garden of the Gods, Pikes Peak Cog Railway, U.S. Olympic Training Complex, U.S. Air Force Academy; restaurants, shopping, hiking, biking, fishing, golf, horseback riding.

One of Colorado's newest and most romantic country inns, the Rockledge Country Inn was built in 1912. The Tudor-style masterpiece is graced by flower gardens, a patio hot tub, and stone terraces—all within view of scenic Pikes Peak.

Upon entering the grand foyer, you will find a two-story copper-hooded stone fireplace and sitting area. To the left, a circa-1875 rosewood Steinway grand piano holds court in the living room, further enhanced by an Italian-marble fireplace and tan leather couches. An antique sled serves as a coffee table, and against one wall resides a walnut Civil War–era desk and hutch.

The twenty-room mansion embraces four exquisitely furnished suites, three with king-sized featherbeds, 32-inch stereo televisions, VCRs, separate sitting areas, and private baths with European bidets. The Carriage House Suite boasts two queen-sized featherbeds, a two-person jetted tub, a separate shower, a 45-inch stereo television, a full kitchen, and a private courtyard entry.

Our choice of guest room at this fine inn is Spindle Top, named for the Texas oil field that helped the original owner of the house progress from a field worker to one of the country's wealthiest businessmen and benefactors. This outstanding chamber boasts a golden marble wood-burning fireplace and a pillar-adorned jetted tub-for-two with overhead duo shower spigots and a

whimsical swan waterspout. The king-sized bed abides in a cozy alcove where guests awaken to a captivating view of magnificent Pikes Peak.

Innkeepers Hartman and Nancy Smith serve delightful gourmet breakfasts in the formal dining room. Entrees include cobbled chicken with veloute sauce topped with a poached egg, Rocky Mountain trout quiche seasoned with leeks and dill, and basil strata with proscuitto. Accompaniments might be oven-crisped potato wedges with fresh Parmesan or potatoes gratin. Add to this such specialties as banana-pecan bread, fresh peach cobbler, or old-fashioned apple dumplings served with heavy cream, and you might want to consider an after-breakfast hike to the top of Pikes Peak.

With advance reservations, the Smiths will indulge you with a candlelit gourmet dinner for two. A typical meal would consist of a shrimp bisque, peach-chutney pepper steak, potatoes, tomatoes Florentine, and a truffle torte with raspberry coulis. Colorado wines accompany the epicurean feast.

HOW TO GET THERE: From I–25 at Colorado Springs, take exit 141 onto Highway 24. Go west on Highway 24 toward Manitou Springs. Take Manitou Springs Business exit, turn right onto Manitou Avenue, and proceed under the overpass. Turn right onto Garden of the Gods Place; at the top of the hill, turn left onto El Paso Boulevard to inn.

Meadow Creek Bed & Breakfast Inn
Pine, Colorado 80470

INNKEEPERS: Pat and Dennis Carnahan

ADDRESS/TELEPHONE: 13438 U.S. Highway 285 (Berry Hill Lane at Douglas Ranch); (303) 838–4167 or (303) 838–4899

ROOMS: 7, including 1 luxury cottage; all with private bath; 3 with private hot tub, gas-log fireplace, and king-size bed, 4 share outdoor hot tub and sauna. Air-conditioning in Grandma's Attic and Room in the Meadow; ceiling fans in 4 rooms (elevation 8,200 feet).

RATES: $95 to $180 per couple; full breakfast. Two-night minimum stay on weekends preferred.

OPEN: All year.

FACILITIES AND ACTIVITIES: Dinner available, with twenty-four-hour advance reservation, Friday and Saturday evenings, $18 per person. Outdoor hot tub, sauna, gazebo, gift shop, picnic table, fire pit in old brick silo for marshmallow roasts; thirty-five acres of woods to roam, toboggan hill. Nearby: restaurants, mountain towns, shopping, hiking, fishing, golf, cross-country skiing, one hour to downhill skiing.

Our idea of a perfect couple of days would be to hide away in this inn's Room in the Meadow, a delightful cottage set in a grassy meadow and blessed with a fireplace, Jacuzzi for two, brass king-sized bed, private deck, microwave, and fridge. We would spend time outdoors, too, wandering through the woods in search of wildflowers and forest critters; listening to the wind rustle through the aspen, fir, and pine; and having afternoon lemonade in the gazebo—all the while absorbing the peace and quiet of the countryside.

Or your choice might be the new Colorado Sunshine Suite, a dream-come-true love nest with a king-sized bed, see-through double-hearthed fireplace, private hot tub, sauna, and patio. From above, skylights spread moonbeams and stardust over all.

This inn was once the summer home of a prince, and in my opinion it's still fit for a king and queen. The two-and-a-half-story stone structure was built in 1929 for Prince Balthasar Gialma Odescalchi, a descendant of nobility from the Holy Roman Empire. When the prince left Colorado in 1947, the residence was absorbed into a 250-acre ranch; more recently it has been transformed into a lovely country inn.

Among other guest accommodations are the Wild Rose Room, where a lop-eared cousin of Flopsy, Mopsy, and Cottontail, dressed in pink taffeta, sits on a queen-sized bed covered with white lace, and the cheery Sun Room, featuring a white wicker bed and love seat.

I recommend that you make dinner reservations at the time you book your room. The night we were there, the fare was marinated grilled chicken with mandarin orange sauce, homemade bread, tossed green salad, pecan pie, ice cream turtle pie, and an inn specialty, Mountain Mud Slide: a cookie crust filled with layers of cream cheese and chocolate mousse, whipped cream, and chocolate bits.

A full breakfast is provided at the inn, or a couple may take a continental-style repast of homemade pastries, fruit, and juice to their room the night before if they don't care to come down to the inn for breakfast in the morning.

HOW TO GET THERE: Take Highway 285 (Hampden Avenue) south from Denver to Conifer. From the traffic light at Conifer, continue on Highway 285 for exactly 5³⁄₁₀ miles. Turn left, follow road past school and take next left onto Douglas Drive at Douglas Ranch. Turn right onto Berry Hill Lane and continue to inn.

The Blackwell House Bed & Breakfast
Coeur d'Alene, Idaho 83814

INNKEEPERS: Kathleen Sims and Margaret Hoy

ADDRESS/TELEPHONE: 820 Sherman Avenue; (208) 664–0656 or (800) 899–0656

ROOMS: 8, including 3 suites; 6 with private bath.

RATES: $75 to $140 per couple; full breakfast and late-afternoon refreshments; champagne in room for special occasions.

OPEN: All year.

FACILITIES AND ACTIVITIES: Catered luncheons and dinners for six or more guests; weddings, and receptions. Minister on staff. Music room with grand piano, large yard with gazebo and barbecue, within walking distance to downtown. Nearby: Lake Coeur d'Alene, "World's Longest Floating Boardwalk," Tubb's Hill nature trails; shopping, restaurants, hiking, fishing, boating, bicycling, downhill and cross-country skiing, snowmobiling.

*P*eople passing by with no intention of spending the night cannot resist ringing the doorbell and asking if they can see the interior of this stately mansion. From the attractively appointed parlor to the music room with its antique grand piano, from the sweeping staircase to the upper floors of absolutely picture-perfect guest rooms, this inn is a designer's showcase—the perfect place for a wedding. And wouldn't you just know—there's a minister on call to perform the ceremony!

Built by F. A. Blackwell in 1904 as a wedding gift for his son, this magnificent three-story structure was allowed to deteriorate over the years to the point that when Kathleen bought it in 1982, it took nine months, one hundred gallons of paint remover, 282 rolls of wallpaper, nineteen tons of sod, and unmeasured amounts of laughter and tears to help bring it around to the masterpiece it is today.

The morning repast is served in the Breakfast Room, where French doors open out onto the patio and spacious lawns. A fire in the fireplace removes the early-morning chill, fresh-ground Irish cream coffee warms the tummy, bowls of fruit center the round cloth-covered tables, and baskets of huckleberry muffins soon appear hot from the oven.

The second-floor Blackwell Suite is a pink-and-white dream with oak-spool bed; white wicker settee, table, and chairs; white ruffled curtains with pink tiebacks; white eyelet-trimmed comforter and bed ruffle; pink floral wallpaper; dusty rose carpet; and claw-footed bathtub sequestered in its own little alcove.

But before you decide on this one, you must also see the former servants' quarters and children's playroom on the third floor. Smaller but ever so cozy, the three rooms share a sitting area with love seat, and they, like the others, are exquisitely decorated.

The hospitality here even extends to your friends, who are welcome to join you for late-afternoon tea and cookies or wine and munchies. If you haven't yet tried staying at country inns, The Blackwell House would be a great place to start.

HOW TO GET THERE: From city center, go east on Sherman Avenue (main street) for approximately 5 blocks. Inn is on the right.

Gregory's McFarland House
Coeur d'Alene, Idaho 83814

INNKEEPERS: Winifred, Carol, and Stephen Gregory

ADDRESS/TELEPHONE: 601 Foster Avenue; (208) 667–1232 or (800) 335–1232

E-MAIL: mcfarland@nidlink.com

WEB SITE: www.bbhost.com/mcfarlandhouse

ROOMS: 5; all with private bath and air-conditioning. No smoking inn.

RATES: $85 to $150 per couple; full breakfast and complimentary afternoon wine, tea, coffee, and cookies. Reduced off-season rates available. Special packages available for skiers and wedding parties.

OPEN: All year.

FACILITIES AND ACTIVITIES: Landscaped grounds, piano. Private entrance and area for weddings; minister and photographer on staff. Nearby: Lake Coeur d'Alene, "World's Longest Floating Boardwalk," Tubb's Hill nature trails; restaurants, shopping, hiking, fishing, horseback riding, golf, swimming, waterskiing, sailing, snowmobiling, downhill and cross-country skiing.

RECOMMENDED COUNTRY INNS® TRAVELERS' CLUB BENEFIT: Stay two nights and get third night free, October 15 through April 15, excluding all holidays and holiday weekends.

This inn hosts many weddings and receptions, due to its lovely facilities and attentive innkeepers. Warm and hospitable, Win and Stephen clearly enjoy seeing to it that brides and grooms have a memorable wedding day. Year after year, many couples return to celebrate their anniversaries.

The McFarland House just keeps getting better and better, with the addition of more and more quality antiques. Guests have the use of all the common areas, including the more casual family room with its regulation oak-wood pool table, television, VCR, and stereo.

And then there's the pretty-as-a-wedding-cake conservatory. Looking out onto the beautifully landscaped backyard, it features pink wicker chairs padded with pink floral cushions; pink tablecloths, place mats, and napkins; and pots and pots of pink geraniums. I am convinced that even on a cloudy day, this room must glow with cheerfulness.

The conservatory is where we had breakfast, and it was gourmet to the last crumb. A frothy fruit drink made of blended fresh fruits and skim milk and served in stemmed glassware began the affair. Next came a fresh fruit cup, muffin, and Irish cream coffee. A light and fluffy egg dish garnished with spears of fresh asparagus and slices of wheat toast completed this extraordinarily delicious meal.

Many of the antiques throughout the inn are from Win's family. Our room had a circa-1860 bed with a pink-on-white bed cover, ecru eyelet ruffled skirt, and piles of eyelet-trimmed pillows. Later, when we returned from dinner, Win had left a mint surprise, Stephen brought ice water to our room, the ceiling fan circulated the cool evening air filtering through the imported lace curtains, and the floral-upholstered love seat beckoned. It feels very good here.

I have another reason for especially liking this inn. The Gregorys' three cats, Sweet Boy, Valentino, and Lil Darlin', gave me my "cat fix" for the day. It surely helped for the moment, but three days later I was happy as usual to get home to my own cream Persian, Murphy, my bluepoint Himalyan, Frosty, and my calico, Garfy the Wonder Cat.

HOW TO GET THERE: Located 7 blocks from Coeur d'Alene Lake. From midtown, go east on Sherman (Coeur d'Alene's main street) to Sixth Street. Go north on Sixth Street to Foster. Inn is on the northeast corner.

The Voss Inn
Bozeman, Montana 59715

INNKEEPERS: Bruce and Frankee Muller

ADDRESS/TELEPHONE: 319 South Willson; (406) 587–0982; fax (406) 585–2964

E-MAIL: vossinn@imt.net

WEB SITE: www.wtp.net/go/vossinn

ROOMS: 6; all with private bath; some with air-conditioning; fans available for others.

RATES: $85 to $95 per couple; full breakfast, a traditional English tea, and a nightcap.

OPEN: All year.

FACILITIES AND ACTIVITIES: During winter, transportation to ski slopes for nominal charge. Nearby: Lewis and Clark Caverns, Museum of the Rockies, Bridger Bowl and Big Sky ski areas; restaurants, shopping, hiking, fishing in blue-ribbon trout stream, downhill and cross-country skiing; personalized daytrips into Yellowstone National Park and other points of interest, including gourmet breakfast and picnic lunch.

RECOMMENDED COUNTRY INNS® TRAVELERS' CLUB BENEFIT: Stay two nights and get third night free.

*O*ften referred to as one of Montana's most romantic bed-and-breakfasts, The Voss Inn is located in Bozeman's historic district. Many a couple, bent on a blissful weekend, walks hand in hand through this inn's English cottage perennial garden, up the steps, past Victorian wicker furniture on a porch ablaze with geraniums, and into the lovely parlor. And it only gets better from here.

As meticulously scrubbed, starched, pressed, and polished as an Easter-morning Sunday School class, The Voss Inn exudes perfection. Antique beds, private sitting areas, breakfast nooks, and bay windows all add to the charm of this stalwart red-brick Victorian. Every room we peeked into was captivating. The Sartain Room on the main floor features a provocative tub and bathing alcove; the front parlor is graced with an ornate etched-glass chandelier. The Chisholm Room, a favorite with honeymooners, boasts a magnificent 9-foot brass headboard with an antique brass lamp hanging from it, a claw-footed bathtub, and an antique gas fireplace.

Flowered wallpaper banks the staircase leading to the immaculate upstairs guest rooms. We entered our favorite, Robert's Roost, by descending three steps into a bright and cheerful garden of white wicker, deep green walls sprinkled with tiny white blossoms, white ruffled curtains, and a private balcony. The bed, brass and iron, has a white eyelet spread and is embellished with dark green, rose-flowered pillows. A miniature bottle of liqueur and two small glasses waited on the bedside table.

Frankee tiptoes upstairs and leaves early morning coffee and tea in the hallway. Then, a little later, she brings fresh fruit, orange juice, homemade cinnamon rolls and muffins, and wonderful egg-soufflé dishes to the hall buffet. Breakfast is taken to tiny tables in the guest rooms, and that's a definite plus because you'll want to spend as much time as possible in your new-found hideaway.

If you prefer, you can enjoy the morning repast in the company of other guests in the parlor, where breakfast is served on hand-crocheted tablecloths from Zimbabwe, accented with heirloom silver and fine china.

According to Frankee, "We endeavor to provide personal service without disturbing our guests' privacy. They may join the other guests for tea and conversation if they like, or they can choose to have no interaction at all. The choice is entirely theirs." If you are celebrating a honeymoon or anniversary, let her know in advance so that she can have champagne or wine in your room awaiting your arrival.

Bruce and Frankee's courtship is proof that love will find a way. While Frankee was on a photo safari in Africa, she met Bruce in Botswana, where he was working at the time. He visited her in Los Angeles, and she later revisited him in Botswana. They subsequently married and tried to live in L.A. but eventually decided that Bozeman, Montana, near Yellowstone National Park, was where they wanted to operate a bed-and-breakfast and raise their family. Another "happily ever after" story.

HOW TO GET THERE: From I–90, take exit 306 into Bozeman. Turn south onto North Seventh Avenue, left onto Main Street, and proceed to South Willson. Go south on Willson for approximately 3½ blocks to the inn.

Copper King Mansion
Bed & Breakfast
Butte, Montana 59701

INNKEEPERS: John Thompson and Erin and Pat Sigl

ADDRESS/TELEPHONE: 219 West Granite Street; (406) 782–7580

ROOMS: 4; 2 with private bath; 1 with TV. Pets allowed with prior approval. No air-conditioning (elevation 5,280 feet).

RATES: $60 to $95 per couple; full breakfast, wine or beer, and tour of the mansion.

OPEN: All year. Mansion tours for public occur between 9:00 A.M. and 5:00 P.M., May through October. During this season, bed-and-breakfast guests check in between 5:00 and 9:00 P.M. and must check out by 9:00 A.M.

FACILITIES AND ACTIVITIES: Robes for shared bath, bottled water. Nearby: World Museum of Mining, Arts Chateau Gallery, historic walking tour, ghost towns; hiking, fishing, horseback riding, snowmobiling, downhill and cross-country skiing.

"A mile high, a mile deep, and always on the level," was the motto in Butte, Montana (elevation 5,280 feet), when its nineteenth-century copper mines burrowed an equal depth underground. The man most noted for the extraction of ore from the region was William Andrews Clark, better known as the "Copper King," who later became a U.S. senator.

Clark built this mansion in 1884 at a cost of $250,000—a mere half day's wages at the height of his earnings (estimated at $17 million a month). He spared no expense to procure the best craftsmanship and quality. German woodcarvers chiseled ornate figures in the Philippine mahogany fireplace. Rosewood, cherry, and oak are among the nine different woods that adorn the house, including the hand-carved central staircase and parquet floors. Frescoed ceilings and jeweled Tiffany stained-glass windows are part of the opulent decor.

While the building attests to Clark's wealth and taste, the preservation and renovation of the home reflect the resourcefulness of two women, the grandmother and mother of the current innkeepers. They acquired the building, stripped of its appointments, in 1953 and filled it with period pieces dating from 1880 to 1930, the era when the copper magnate and U.S. senator called Butte home. Today twenty original items from the Clark family are among the priceless furnishings.

Guests seeking a romantic interlude can pamper themselves regally with a stay in the Master Suite, with adjoining sitting room and private bath. A carved headboard stands sentinel over the satin and hand-crocheted bed covers. Overhead, a fresco of nudes has been restored—a group of nuns, former occupants, had discreetly painted over it. Perfume bottles and an ivory manicure-and-comb set leave the impression that Clark and his wife still use this room.

No matter which quarters one chooses, there's no need to fear missing anything at this inn. Overnight lodging includes a tour of the mansion as well as a delicious breakfast of French toast, quiche, or omelette served on Limoges china with silver service. Tasteful elegance reigns in the dining room under a gold-embossed leather ceiling hung with a crystal chandelier.

HOW TO GET THERE: From I–90, take Montana Street exit. Turn left onto Montana and proceed to West Granite Street. Turn left onto West Granite and go 1 block to Idaho Street. Inn is on the corner of West Granite and Idaho Streets.

Izaak Walton Inn
Essex, Montana 59916

INNKEEPERS: Larry and Lynda Vielleux

ADDRESS/TELEPHONE: Off Highway 2 (mailing address: P.O. Box 653); (406) 888–5700, fax (406) 888–5200

E-MAIL: izaakw@digisys

WEB SITE: www.vtown.com/izaakw

ROOMS: 31, plus 2 suites and 4 cabooses; all with private bath; 1 with gas fireplace. No air-conditioning (elevation 3,860 feet).

RATES: $98 to $150 per couple. Cabooses: $475 for three nights; $850 for seven nights. Breakfast not included. Three-, five- and seven-day packages, including meals, available. Personal checks preferred.

OPEN: All year.

FACILITIES AND ACTIVITIES: Full-service dining room, bar, sauna, laundromat, ski shop, gift shop with Montana-made items; Amtrak flag stop # E.S.M., train activity, train memorabilia; mountain bike rentals and tours, antique "jammer" bus tours over the "Going-to-the-Sun Highway" in Glacier Park, cross-country ski rentals, snowshoe rentals, guided cross-country ski tours into Glacier National Park, guided snowshoe treks. Nearby: Glacier National Park and Bob Marshall Wilderness Area, constituting more than a million acres of wilderness; fishing, hiking, horseback riding, rafting, wildlife viewing, photography, cross-country skiing.

For couples seeking seclusion and total privacy, a stay in one of this inn's cozy "little red cabooses" would be a great choice. Genuine Great Northern cabooses, now resting on the hillside overlooking the inn, have been totally remodeled with pine interior and accented with blue-and-white pinstripe bedding and red pillows and include a minikitchen, private bath, and deck. If you prefer complete isolation, you can forego the meals offered in the inn's dining room by requesting, in advance and for an additional fee, that your tiny cupboard and fridge be stocked in anticipation of your arrival.

I recommend that you, on at least one of your nights here, first pamper yourselves in the Finnish-style sauna and later indulge in a moonlit dinner on your caboose's private deck. As Larry and Lynda proclaim, "At our inn, time stands still and lets you catch up." Allow a couple extra days here, and there even will be time to "catch up" on a little old-fashioned courting.

Built in 1939 to accommodate service crews for the Great Northern Railway, whose enormous task it was to keep the mountain track open during winter, the inn is still very much involved in the railroad business. It is here that "helper" engines hook onto lengthy freight trains and help push them over the Continental Divide. The inn is also a designated flag stop, with Amtrak passing through daily. If you decide to arrive via Amtrak, inn personnel will meet you at the platform to help with luggage.

Fifteen to twenty freight trains pass by the front door of the inn each day; and whether resting in one of the charming guest rooms, playing volleyball in the playfield, or downing a few in the Flag Stop Bar, one is hard-pressed to keep from running outdoors like a kid to watch as the massive trains chug by.

The Izaak Walton is packed with signal lanterns, vintage photographs, and all sorts of train memorabilia. In the Dining Car Restaurant, you may be seated next to a striped-capped engineer from the train waiting out on the tracks or sharing a meal and spirited conversation with members of an international rail fan club.

Highlights of our stay at the Izaak Walton: lovely accommodations, light and fluffy breakfast crepes filled to overflowing with huckleberries; a dinner of honey-glazed chicken sautéed with orange slices and onions; the sighting of whole families of shaggy, beautiful mountain goats zigzagging their way down the hillside to a salt lick; and spotting a yearling bear cub peacefully munching his way along the side of the road.

Wildlife photographers can have the time of their lives here: black bears, mountain lions, mountain goats, spawning salmon, and, from early October to early November, a sometimes large migration of bald eagles.

HOW TO GET THERE: Inn is ½ mile off Highway 2, on southern rim of Glacier National Park between East and West Glacier. Watch for sign for Essex turnoff.

The Sanders-Helena's Bed & Breakfast

Helena, Montana 59601

INNKEEPERS: Bobbi Uecker and Rock Ringling

ADDRESS/TELEPHONE: 328 North Ewing; (406) 442–3309

ROOMS: 7; all with private bath, phone, TV, and air-conditioning. No smoking inn.

RATES: $90 to $110 per couple; full breakfast, snacks, and beverages.

OPEN: All year.

FACILITIES AND ACTIVITIES: On National Register of Historic Places, flower gardens. Nearby: St. Helena's Cathedral, Holter Museum, Myrna Loy Theater, historic governor's mansion, state capitol building, Historical Museum, cultural center; fishing, downhill and cross-country skiing.

Montana Senator Wilbur Sanders and his wife, Harriet, built this Queen Anne home in 1875, at the beginning of his political career. An important figure in Helena, Sanders also founded the Montana Historical Society and was its president for twenty-six years.

Innkeepers Bobbi Uecker and Rock Ringling realized the importance of preserving as much of this landmark structure as possible when they under-

took the restoration of the mansion. A museum in its own right, the inn still houses most of the original furnishings belonging to its first family. Today, as then, rich wooden paneling, gleaming oak floors, and priceless antiques add elegance throughout the inn.

The luxurious Colonel's Room features the Sanderses' 8-foot-high headboard of bird's-eye maple, matching dressers (one with a marble top), and a bay window. Modern amenities are tastefully hidden away in armoires and dressers.

The sleep chamber called Teddy's Buckaroo, named in honor of Bobbi's cattleman father, appeals to honeymooners. A four-poster brass bed, draped with a canopy of mosquito netting, dominates this room. The adjoining bathroom, however, is the drawing card. A 5-by-5-foot tile enclosure with dual shower heads invites guests to linger amid lush potted plants.

Lest the inn showcase only the Sanderses' past, some items modestly pay homage to Rock's family. A portrait of his great-grandfather, Alf T. Ringling, one of the five brothers who began the famed Ringling Bros. Circus, hangs prominently in the Colonel's Room. Above the upper stairway is a bust of "Chili Bean," a roping steer who performed at Madison Square Garden and spent his old age at the Ringling Ranch.

Come morning, both Bobbi and Rock appear in chef's hats. Bobbi's concoction of orange soufflé and the Sanderses' recipe for cream cheese–filled French toast delight guests. The huckleberry pancakes, mushroom crepes, and Grand Marnier French toast also receive raves from visitors.

HOW TO GET THERE: From I–90, take the Capitol Area exit and follow Prospect Street west to Montana Street. Turn left onto Montana Street and proceed to Sixth Avenue. Turn right onto Sixth Avenue and right again onto North Ewing. Inn is on the left.

Gold Hill Hotel
Gold Hill, Nevada 89440

INNKEEPERS: Carol and Bill Fain

ADDRESS/TELEPHONE: Highway 342 (mailing address: P.O. Box 304, Virginia City, NV 89440); (702) 847–0111

E-MAIL: gldhilhotl@aol.com

ROOMS: 12, plus 2 guest houses; 10 rooms and both guest houses with private bath, second-floor guest rooms with wheelchair access.

RATES: $45 to $150 per couple; rate depends on choice of room and season; continental breakfast.

OPEN: All year except two weeks in January.

FACILITIES AND ACTIVITIES: Full-service dining room with wheelchair access, limited menu on Mondays and Tuesdays; Great Room lounge; saloon, lectures by local historians on most Tuesday evenings. Nearby: restaurants, gambling casinos, excursion train, mine tours, hiking, fishing, exploring; downhill and cross-country skiing at Lake Tahoe, approximately 35 miles away.

*N*ot many years ago, this luxurious country inn was nothing more than a decaying six-room, one-bath hotel and bar. Built during the gold rush to the Comstock Lode in 1859, the hotel served a bustling community that received as many as fifty scheduled trains a day, hauling commodities in and ore out. The stone section of the building still stands, and a new wooden addition has been added to replace that which disappeared sometime before 1890. It is the oldest operating hotel in Nevada.

A walk through this comfortably elegant hotel reveals quality antiques and a genteel ambience unexpected in this rather remote section of Nevada.

The guest rooms boast period furnishings and lovely decor, but our choice, and often that of newlyweds, was Room 6, with a private balcony, stone fireplace, beautiful circa-1850 half-tester bed, marble-topped dresser and bedside tables, wet bar, fine-print blue wallpaper, and an extra-large bath. The pink-draped corner windows look out to the Sierra Nevada mountain range.

In the hotel's Crown Point Restaurant, the tables are clad with white linen and set with crystal stemware and fine china. Soft rose drapes and upholstered chairs, sea-green carpet, and an antique sideboard contribute to the elegance of this room. Chef Herb Richardson serves a wide range of French and Continental cuisine. Although the dining room exudes elegance, casual dress in keeping with Nevada's informality is most acceptable.

The cozy stone-walled bar has a large corner fireplace and is home to an extensive wine list, an astonishing number of old whiskies from Scotland and Ireland, imported cognacs and brandies, and more than fifty imported and domestic bottled beers.

The former mining metropolis of Gold Hill is now a small village surrounded by historic sites and adjacent to the rollicking former mining town of Virginia City. Area hiking includes trails along old mining roads and abandoned rail lines.

For a glimpse into the Old West, browse the Gold Hill Hotel's bookstore and gift shop to see more than 2,000 titles describing the history of the western United States. Upon request, you may view a videotape of more than 200 historical photos dating from the 1860s to the present.

HOW TO GET THERE: From Reno, take Highway 395 south to Highway 341 turnoff to Virginia City. At Virginia City, continue south for 1 mile to Gold Hill. Hotel is on the right.

Angel House Inn
Park City, Utah 84060

INNKEEPERS: Jan and Joe Fisher-Rush and Axel Rose the Cat

ADDRESS/TELEPHONE: 713 Norfolk Avenue (mailing address: P.O. Box 159); (435) 647–0338 or (800) 264–3501

E-MAIL: jrush@ditell.com

WEB SITE: www.parkcityus.com/~jrush

ROOMS: 9; all with private bath; 3 with TV. No smoking inn.

RATES: $85 to $285 per couple, depending on room chosen and season; full gourmet breakfast and afternoon refreshments. Picnic baskets available at additional charge. Dinner, spa, and accommodation packages available during spring, summer, and fall.

OPEN: All year.

FACILITIES AND ACTIVITIES: Outdoor hot tub. Located only 100 yards from Town Lift ticket office. Nearby: Park City Historic District, restaurants, shopping, art galleries, theater, mine tours. Golfing, indoor and outdoor tennis, hiking, fishing, alpine slide, gondola rides, swimming, horseback riding, cross-country skiing, snowmobiling, and downhill skiing at Park City Ski Area, Deer Valley Ski Resort, and The Canyons Ski Area.

A more romantic inn would be difficult to find. With an abundance of angels, cherubs, cupids, roses, pearls, ribbons, and lace, the essence of romance is everywhere at the Angel House Inn. Built in 1889 for Ephraim D. Sutton, the house was the finest in all of Park City at the time.

The lovely parlor has a fireplace, a wall of books and collectibles, and a bay window sheathed with white lace curtains. A violet-hued carpet hugs the floor, pink cabbage roses embrace the settee and armchairs, and a magnificent chandelier with etched-glass globes and dangling teardrops glistens overhead.

All the guest rooms are named for angels, and every one is a gem. The room called Gabriel and Hope (the angelic messengers) has an antique queen-sized wrought-iron bed and a claw-footed bathtub. Uriel and Aurora (angels of peace) features a queen-sized four-poster, an antique armoire and dresser, and will soon have its very own "Secret Garden."

Victoria (angel of freedom) boasts an ornate queen-sized antique burled-wood French bed, period armoire with French inlay, and a beautiful stained-glass panel that fills the center section of the bay window.

Ah, but you must come into *our* room, Chamael and Amora (angels of love). It features a king-sized white-iron and brass bed adorned with a soft

mauve-and-white crocheted coverlet and a lace canopy with gossamer draping. Two wicker chairs sit beside a round table graced with a cut-glass lamp with matching shade, and wispy white curtains and Battenburg lace draperies frame the bay window. Pale pink walls, chaste-white woodwork, and a velvety sea-green carpet add to the pastel splendor.

The huge bathroom features a gray-marble floor trimmed with pink and white tiles accented by floral hearts. A vanity resides against one wall, and an alcove holds an extra large claw-footed bathtub curtained in lace.

Breakfast is truly gourmet. The morning we dined here, we were served a fruit plate of cantaloupe and banana slices garnished with strawberries, blueberries, and sweet orange-flavored yogurt. Next came a warm and flakey puff pastry filled with raspberries. The final course brought eggs scrambled with garlic and fresh asparagus, wrapped in a crepe shell and enhanced by a sprinkling of grated Parmesan cheese.

HOW TO GET THERE: From I–80 east, take Highway 224 south to Park City; 224 turns into Park Avenue at Park City. At Town Lift, turn right onto Eighth Street. Proceed for 2 blocks to Norfolk Avenue; turn left. Inn is on the right.

Washington School Inn
Park City, Utah 84060

INNKEEPERS: Nancy Beaufait and Delphine Covington

ADDRESS/TELEPHONE: 543 Park Avenue (mailing address: P.O. Box 536); (435) 649–3800 or (800) 824–1672

ROOMS: 15, including 3 suites; all with private bath. Wheelchair access; no air-conditioning (elevation 7,000 feet).

RATES: $89 to $300, depending on season; full breakfast and afternoon refreshments. Seniors, 65 and over, 10 percent discount.

OPEN: All year.

FACILITIES AND ACTIVITIES: Lunch for groups of ten or more. Hot tub, Jacuzzi, sauna, exercise equipment, concierge services. Nearby: restaurants, golf, tennis, hiking, fishing, horseback riding, sailboarding, sailing, waterskiing; Park City Ski Area, The Canyons Ski Area, Deer Valley Ski Resort, downhill and cross-country skiing.

Although the perfect hideaway for grown-up childhood sweethearts, there's no more "readin', 'ritin', and 'rithmetic" at the old Washington School. The three R's now more accurately stand for "romance," "rendezvous," and "resplendent." Built in 1889, the structure served as a public school for forty-two years, became a social hall during the '30s, and lay vacant from the '50s until 1984. The hammered-limestone exterior, bell tower, dormer and classroom windows, and curved entry porticos have been retained, thus qualifying the inn for the National Register of Historic Places.

The entry hall still has the feeling of an old-fashioned schoolhouse, with exposed original timbers supporting the three-story bell tower. A library/mezzanine overlooks the elegant living room, where complimentary beverages await your arrival and refreshments are served during the afternoons.

Each morning an antique sideboard in the formal dining room is lavishly spread with breakfast items such as eggs Florentine or cheese strata served with bacon, ham, or sausage; fresh fruit and lemon-nut bread; homestead pumpkin bread; Grandma Anderson's brown bread; or, perhaps, Utah beer bread.

During winter, après-ski refreshments bring crabcakes, fondues, or baked Brie with raspberries, along with hot cider and wine. Afternoon tea, with fresh-baked cookies or chocolate-dipped strawberries, is served in the summertime.

All guest rooms are elaborately custom decorated and bear the names of former school teachers. Miss Thatcher has a brick fireplace, king-sized bed, rose carpet, and, heavens to mercy, a pink-flowered love seat and a wet bar. Miss Thompson has a green iron-and-brass bed, fireplace with round windows on either side, and a love seat and wet bar. Our favorite room was Miss Urie. Bright and sunny, it has pink and blue flowers sprinkled on yellow wallpaper, a chatting corner, a writing alcove, and a four-poster pine bed. An antique book acts as a doorstop.

Couples especially enjoy the lower level of the inn, which features a wine cellar and a luxurious whirlpool spa with stone floor, bent-willow furniture, dry sauna, and steam showers. Wouldn't the Misses Thatcher, Thompson, and Urie have loved this as their "Teacher's Room"?

Some comments I gleaned from the guest book that I would like to share with you: "Long live our marriage, thanks to our first night at the Washington School Inn." "A wonderful honeymoon retreat." "Just like another honeymoon." "Great place for newlyweds." "Beautiful, charming place to spend a romantic weekend."

HOW TO GET THERE: From I–80, take Highway 224 south to Park City; 224 turns into Park Avenue at Park City. Inn is on the right side of street.

Pinecrest Bed & Breakfast Inn
Salt Lake City, Utah 84108

INNKEEPERS: Phil and Donnetta Davis

ADDRESS/TELEPHONE: 6211 Emigration Canyon Road; (801) 583–6663 or (800) 359–6663

E-MAIL: pdj27@aol.com

WEB SITE: www.pinecrest-utah.com

ROOMS: 6 in inn, plus 1 guest house; all with private bath; 3 with fireplace and Jacuzzi.

RATES: $85 to $195 per couple; full breakfast.

OPEN: All year.

FACILITIES AND ACTIVITIES: Sauna; six acres of formal gardens, land-scaped and natural grounds. Nearby: Temple Square, Great Salt Lake State Park, state capitol, University of Utah, LDS Genealogical Library, museums, restaurants; shopping, hiking, fishing, swimming, downhill and cross-country skiing.

RECOMMENDED COUNTRY INNS® TRAVELERS' CLUB BENEFIT: 10 percent discount, Monday to Thursday.

*J*ust 6 miles up Emigration Canyon, the same canyon from which Brigham Young and his followers first entered what was to become Salt Lake City, the Pinecrest Bed & Breakfast Inn stands sedately amid acres of tall pines and blue spruce, wildflowers and forest paths, and meticulously landscaped formal gardens. The large iron gates leading to the inn were installed in the '30s by David Henderson, a Hollywood actor who owned the estate at the time and who bought the gates from Paramount Studios.

The spacious living and dining area features rich cherry-wood paneling and woodwork, a large stone fireplace, red-wine velvet couches, and a splendid grand piano. A wall of windows looks out onto the garden area.

Guest rooms are exceptionally well situated to ensure privacy. The Jamaican Jacuzzi Room is accessed by a wrought-iron circular staircase that leads to the lower level from one corner of the living room. This very private chamber has a king-size bed, a sauna, and a sunken Jacuzzi. The Library is on the main floor and features a king-size bed and a 1930s radio that Phil has rigged to play Glenn Miller and George Burns and Gracie Allen tapes, in addition to many other old-time favorites. The Oriental  Suite takes the entire upper story and has a king-sized bed, private balcony, Jacuzzi, Ming silk couches, and an exquisite coromandel screen from mainland China. Phil and Donnetta have added a lovely new room with Southwestern decor and a fireplace and Jacuzzi.

The guest house is comfortably rustic and has had as guests the likes of Robert Redford.

Phil prepares a delicious breakfast of, perhaps, sour cream–banana pancakes, Mexican eggs, French toast, or fresh-raspberry crepes, fruit coffee cake; juice, and coffee or tea. There are several good restaurants close by. Phil recommends the Santa Fe Restaurant or Ruth's Diner for lunch, dinner, or Sunday brunch. He also tells me that Crompton's, a favorite with locals, probably makes the best hamburgers and sandwiches in all of Salt Lake City.

This is a restful place with plenty of room to wander about outdoors, breathe the good fresh air, and listen to the birds sing. There's even a chance you might see raccoons, porcupines, squirrels, and three gigantic moose that live in the canyon. Keep your camera handy.

HOW TO GET THERE: Go east on 800 south, past Research Park on your left and the zoo on your right, to Emigration Canyon Road. Proceed on Emigration Canyon Road for approximately 6 miles past zoo. Inn is on your left.

Nagel Warren Mansion
Cheyenne, Wyoming 82001

INNKEEPER: Jim Osterfoss

ADDRESS/TELEPHONE: 222 East Seventeenth Street; (307) 637–3333 or (800) 811–2610

ROOMS: 12; all with private bath, TV, phone, and air-conditioning; 6 with gas-log fireplaces; 1 specifically designed for exceptionally challenged individuals. No smoking inn.

RATES: $85 to $135 per couple; full breakfast and refreshments.

OPEN: All year.

FACILITIES AND ACTIVITIES: Outdoor hot tub, therapeutic massage room, exercise room, conference/party rooms. Nearby: restaurants, shopping, State Capitol, Frontier Stadium and Park where "Cheyenne Frontier Days" and "The Daddy of 'Em All Rodeo" are held the last full week in July each year, F. E. Warren U.S. Air Force Base, Curt Gowdy State Park, Granite Reservoir, Medicine Bow National Forest.

*S*tep into this opulent mansion and the two of you will be immediately carried back to the late 1800s. So convincing is the impeccable restoration and refurbishing of this Western Victorian showplace that as my husband and I sipped iced tea in the third-floor turret sitting room, I found myself silently wishing for a long skirt, ruffled blouse, and high-topped shoes to replace my khaki pants and Nikes.

Built in 1888 for successful merchant Erasmus Nagel, the palatial residence became the home of Wyoming Governor Francis E. Warren in 1910.

The elegant parlor features large oil paintings, original to the house, a marble-topped antique sideboard, and a splendid bronze fireplace crowned by an ornately framed mirror. A chandelier extends from the ceiling, and on either side of the fireplace hang gaslight fixtures, also original to the building.

The Music Room boasts an 1879 Weber grand piano and a second bronze fireplace. The Library has a tile-faced fireplace, a stained-glass window, and a antique "hooded" chair, said to be a sanctuary for husbands whose wives were a bit too chatty (or the other way around, perhaps?).

A grand staircase leads from the entry hallway to four guest rooms on the second floor and two on the third. Six additional bed chambers abide in the Carriage House. Any one of the rooms would be an excellent choice for spending the night, but our favorite remains Barbara Sullivan, named for one of the previous owners who began the structure's restoration. This chamber boasts an iron four-poster draped with a cream lace canopy, a marble-topped antique dresser and washstand, a mirrored armoire, dainty pink frosted-glass bedside lamps, and, in an alcove by the window, an irresistible circa-1884 fainting couch upholstered with pink roses.

Breakfast, beautifully presented in the formal dining room, might be eggs Benedict, Swedish waffles, or a baked egg dish, accompanied by fresh fruit, homemade breads, juice, yogurt, and beverages. Complimentary homemade cookies, coffee, soft drinks, and juices always are available.

At this fine inn, you and your companion can work out in the exercise room, soak your cares away in the outdoor hot tub, and arrange for therapeutic massages in the massage room.

HOW TO GET THERE: At the corner of Central Avenue and Seventeenth Street in midtown Cheyenne, turn left onto Seventeenth Street. Proceed for 2 blocks to the inn.

Rainsford Inn
Cheyenne, Wyoming 82001

INNKEEPER: Nancy Drege

ADDRESS/TELEPHONE: 219 East Eighteenth Street; (307) 638–2337;
fax (307) 634–4506

E-MAIL: ToBEDS@aol.com

ROOMS: 7; 5 with private bath, cable TV, phone jack with private line, and
air-conditioning; 4 with whirlpool tub. Wheelchair accessible; 1 room with
roll-in shower designed for handicapped. No smoking inn.

RATES: $95 per couple; full breakfast, snacks, and beverages.

OPEN: All year.

FACILITIES AND ACTIVITIES: Player piano, sunporch, patio. Nearby:
restaurants, microbrewery, antiques shops, state museum, Old West
Museum, Vedauwoo Park, Terry Basin Ranch, with horseback riding;
Curt Gowdy State Park, Cheyenne Frontier Days, Wyoming–Colorado
Railroad excursions (45 miles, at Laramie), rock climbing, fishing.

RECOMMENDED COUNTRY INNS® TRAVELERS' CLUB BENEFIT: 10 percent discount, not valid during Cheyenne Frontier Days, last full week
in July.

The hospitality here is first class, with a friendly greeting upon arrival
and, quite possibly, a bear hug when you leave. This outstanding
turn-of-the-century inn sits in a quiet, tree-shaded neighborhood
within walking distance of downtown Cheyenne. A gracious ambience greets
guests as they enter the antiques-filled parlor. Here lace curtains filter the afternoon sunlight, wood floors gleam, a player piano awaits would-be musicians,
and a vintage rocking chair begs travelers to come sit awhile.

From the entryway, an oak staircase leads to four guest rooms on the second and third floors. The School Room is particularly enticing with its red,
navy, and cream–colored patchwork quilt displaying old-fashioned school-
houses. Here, tiny classroom chairs, rag dolls on an antique bench, a framed
"Teacher's Rules," and a braided rug present a nostalgic glimpse of long-ago
school days.

While any one of the lovely, individually decorated rooms is sure to invite
special moments, perhaps the most romantic of all is the Moonlight and Roses
Suite. Blessed with lace-covered bow windows, an ornate antique bed with
matching armoire and marble-topped dresser, oak floors, ceiling fans,

whirlpool tub, sitting corner, with Victorian couch and balloon-back chairs, and gas fireplace, this chamber is just as popular with not-so-newlyweds as it is with newlyweds. A small table set in the bay window alcove allows for a romantic, private breakfast for two.

The first-floor guest room is designed for those with special needs. Light

and airy with a bay window, it features a heart motif quilt on the queen-size antique bed, a matching dresser, and roll-in shower with bench, handrails, and hand-held shower head.

In addition to homemade breads, jams, and granola, breakfast might include sausage-and-cheese casserole or waffles and bacon. For the health-minded, Nancy will prepare poached eggs and dry toast or an entree using egg substitute. Whatever your needs or wants might be, you won't go away hungry.

One more thing: Be sure to ask Nancy to show you the hidden staircase she discovered during the renovation of the house.

HOW TO GET THERE: Located in Cheyenne on the corner of 18th and House Streets in the Rainsford Historic District, east of downtown area.

Davy Jackson Inn
Jackson, Wyoming 83001

INNKEEPERS: Kay and Gordon Minns

ADDRESS/TELEPHONE: 85 Perry Avenue (mailing address: P.O. Box 20147); (307) 739–2294 or (800) 584–0532, fax (307) 733–9704

E-MAIL: davyjackson@wyoming.com

WEB SITE: www.davyjackson.com

ROOMS: 11; all with private bath, cable TV, and direct-dial phone; 3 with fireplace; 3 with Jacuzzi tub and steam shower. One room especially designed for physically challenged persons. Rooms available for nonsmokers.

RATES: Summer: $179 to $219 per couple; winter, $129 to $179 per couple; low season (spring and late fall) $129 tpo $149 per couple; full breakfast and afternoon tea year-round. Christmas dinner at additional charge. No charge for Christmas Eve and New Year's Eve buffets.

OPEN: All year.

FACILITIES AND ACTIVITIES: Outdoor hot tub, turndown service. Nearby: Snow King Ski Resort, Yellowstone National Park, Grand Teton National Park, National Elk Refuge, Jackson Hole Ski Resort; restaurants, shopping, art galleries, wildlife viewing, hiking, fishing, downhill and cross-country skiing.

RECOMMENDED COUNTRY INNS® TRAVELERS' CLUB BENEFIT: 10 percent discount.

*T*his lovely Victorian-style inn, a masterpiece in design, invites guests to read before the fireplace, wander the hallways to admire the antiques, and sit down at the grand piano in the parlor. (Go ahead and play, even if you are not an accomplished pianist. Good-natured Kay is quick to assure you that she herself plays the radio better than she can play the piano.)

Located in a quiet neighborhood, only a few blocks from the Town Square, this inn has twelve guest rooms, each one impeccably furnished.

Among my favorite chambers is the Tower Room (Number 302), with a king-size four-poster bed enhanced by a dainty hand-tied cotton-thread canopy, an antique Victorian fainting couch, a whirlpool tub, a steam shower, and a gas-log fireplace.

Room 303 is another of my favorites. A king-size four-poster and a white-wicker love seat, chair, lamp, and table enhance this chamber. A steam shower and Jacuzzi await in the bathroom, and the private balcony provides the perfect place for an early morning cup of coffee.

All chambers have down comforters and solid maple beds, nightstands, and armoires made by the renowned Hitchcock Chair Company.

More than twenty years ago, while driving across the country, Kay and Gordon fell in love with the small town of Jackson, Wyoming, and the massive mountains that surround it. Years passed, during which time they owned and operated a bed-and-breakfast in Suffield, Connecticut, before finally opting to move west. Connecticut's loss is Wyoming's gain.

Kay's breakfasts begin with fresh-squeezed orange juice, fruit, and her grandmother's recipe for homemade cinnamon rolls. Or perhaps she will have baked her sour-cream coffee cake or apple dumplings for this morning's repast. Special sourdough pancakes might follow or, maybe, potato pancakes, eggs, and sausage.

For guests staying over during Christmas, Kay prepares a traditional family-style feast of turkey, ham, mashed potatoes and gravy, sweet potatoes, and pumpkin pie. She also serves a buffet on Christmas Eve and New Year's Eve.

Each afternoon a formal tea of cookies, cakes, or scones and wee sandwiches is available in the formal dining room. Under a crystal teardrop chandelier, on tables sheathed with cutwork-linen tablecloths, tea is poured from a silver service into antique teacups. Alas, the elegance of days long past.

HOW TO GET THERE: From the Town Square go north on North Cache Street to Perry Avenue. Turn left onto Perry Avenue. Inn is on the right.

The Wildflower Inn
Jackson, Wyoming 83002

INNKEEPERS: Sherrie, Ken, and Jessica Jern

ADDRESS/TELEPHONE: 3725 Teton Village Road (mailing address: P.O. Box 11000); (307) 733–4710, fax (307) 739–0914

E-MAIL: wildflowerinn@compuserve.com

WEB SITE: www.Jacksonholenet.com/JH/Lodging/SBB.Wi.htm

ROOMS: 5; all with private bath and TV; no air-conditioning (elevation 6,200 feet). No smoking inn.

RATES: $140 to $275 per couple, depending on choice of room and season; full breakfast. Inquire about off-season rates.

OPEN: All year.

FACILITIES AND ACTIVITIES: Solarium, hot tub, deck. Nearby: Yellowstone National Park, Grand Teton National Park, National Elk Refuge; restaurants, art galleries, artist studios, museums; Old West Days, Mountain Man Rendezvous, Jackson Hole Arts Festival, Grand Teton Music Festival, Dancers Workshop, summer theater, acting workshops; rodeo, chuckwagon dinner shows, stagecoach rides, covered wagon trips; photography, wildlife viewing, hiking, fishing, biking, golf, tennis, climbing, horseback riding, llama treks, rafting, ice skating, sleigh rides, snowmobiling, dogsledding; downhill, helicopter, Snow Cat, and cross-country skiing.

*S*herrie confided to us that she and Ken dream of one day saving an evening just for themselves. They plan to choose their favorite guest room, pack the well-used champagne bucket with ice, take along the crystal glasses etched with wildflowers, gaze at the stars from the private deck, and hear nothing but the melancholy vocalizing of happy frogs. Now how could you go wrong with romantic innkeepers like these?

Made of glowing lodgepole pine inside and out, with balconies, gables, and, everywhere, wildflowers, this inn is at once both elegant and country. In the expansive sitting room, Native American rugs hang on log walls, a freestanding wood stove stands before a massive river-rock wall, and the polished wood floor is centered with a colorful braided rug. This room, along with the solarium and dining room, looks out onto a wooded three acres of aspen and cottonwood trees, a creek-fed pond, and a meadow where horses graze. Just the day before we visited, a mama duck and her baby ducklings had paddled into the pond, lingered a while, and then ventured on downstream.

The guest rooms have a secluded feeling, and all five are beautifully decorated. Indian Paintbrush has a cathedral ceiling and private deck. The queen-

sized hand-hewn pine-log bed, made by Ken, sports a bed ruffle made of black-and-white ticking and a red print down comforter. Red-and-white checked curtains flank the windows, and red plaid Ralph Lauren towels brighten the private bath.

Sherrie is a master of spontaneous, creative cooking and serves a full outdoorsman's breakfast, including homemade granola, fresh fruit, oatmeal muffins, and either buttermilk pancakes, French toast, or an egg dish. She will see to it that you don't leave hungry.

Besides appealing to romantics, this inn is popular with outdoor enthusiasts. Ken is a ski instructor and climbing guide, and both he and Sherrie are authorities on the many interesting things to do in the Jackson Hole area.

After a day of hiking or skiing, put your sports gear in the separate storage area, pile into the hot tub, relax, and watch the day fade to twilight over misty fields and distant mountains.

HOW TO GET THERE: From Jackson, go west on Highway 22 toward Wilson. Before the town of Wilson, turn right onto Teton Village Road. Turn left onto Shooting Star Lane. Inn is at end of roadway.

West Coast

by Julianne Belote

I once facetiously told a friend that the secret of my forty-plus years of marriage to the same man was never to have a meaningful conversation. I now concede there is another factor: frequent visits to romantic country inns.

Who can deny the spell cast by precisely the right ambience? Some couples will be delighted with a heart-shaped Jacuzzi tub and champagne breakfast in bed. Others prefer romantic weekends in elegant surroundings with sophisticated food and glamourous big-city attractions. I can go for that.

The West Coast has plenty of inns where you can indulge those yens. But it is our dramatic 2,000-mile-long coastline that offers some of the most beguiling lodgings. It's hard to beat walks above a windswept surf and intimate candlelight dinners in a cozy's inn's dining room.

This collection reflects a range of lodging from simple to splendid. If you claim even a faint ember of romance still glowing, *something* in these selections will fan it. That old Rogers and Hart song says, "My romance doesn't need a castle rising in Spain." Right. I don't need a castle either. But you do have to have a companion for a romantic idyll. And just to encourage a perhaps reluctant partner, it is worth noting that these West Coast inns are undoubtedly a lot more comfortable than most castles. If Jacuzzis, great food, or crashing waves don't pique a partner's interest, promises of comfort just may win the day.

West Coast

West Coast

Numbers on map refer to towns numbered below.

Imperial Hotel
Amador City, California 95601

INNKEEPERS: Bruce Sherrill and Dale Martin

ADDRESS/TELEPHONE: Highway 49 (mailing address: P.O. Box 195); (800) 242–5594 or (209) 267–9172; fax (209) 267–9249

E-MAIL: host@imperialamador.com

WEB SITE: www.imperialamador.com

ROOMS: 6; all with private bath, air-conditioning; two with balcony. No smoking in rooms.

RATES: $75 to $105, double occupancy, full breakfast. Two-night minimum when Saturday is involved, lower midweek rates. Singles deduct $5.

OPEN: All year.

FACILITIES AND ACTIVITIES: Full bar, restaurant; serves dinner every night and Sunday brunch. Wheelchair access to dining room. Nearby: antiques and specialty shops in town; attractive opportunities for photographers in town and nearby mines; many wineries; seasonal events include fall Miwok Big Time Days at Indian Grinding Rock State Park, Daffodil Hill's spring blooms, Amador City's Calico Christmas.

RECOMMENDED COUNTRY INNS® TRAVELERS' CLUB BENEFIT: Receive 10 percent discount each night, Monday through Thursday; excludes holidays, subject to availability.

I am smitten with this addition to gold country lodgings. The 1879 red-brick building with a painted white balcony stretching across the top story sits at the end of the main street running through tiny Amador City, population about 179 citizens. The scene awakens gold rush nostalgia; it's old, authentic, and redolent of romance.

The outside of this venerable hotel is thoroughly old-fashioned, but inside you'll find it has been stylishly renovated with all the modern amenities and a first-class restaurant. First stop should be the beautiful, old full-bar, not a reproduction but the real McCoy. In addition to the usual spirits, they stock a large selection of beers and California wines. The low-key, friendly service here is one aspect of a romantic atmosphere throughout the inn.

The dining room has a certain touch of elegance, with high ceilings, white tablecloths, and fresh flowers, yet it is welcoming and casual. The intimate room (seats fifty-five) has a changing display of local artwork that stands out beautifully against white walls. Dine in your traveling clothes, by all means, but you won't feel out of place if you want to dress for a special occasion, either.

The dinner chefs offer a menu that is both Continental and California fresh. The appetizers are so good that it takes careful planning to save room for the entree. Roasted garlic with Brie and polenta crostini topped with prosciutto were the two we chose. The main event was a roast pork loin in prune sauce followed by an excellent salad with a house dressing I wish I could duplicate. The pastry chef had several hard-to-pass offerings and, after all her work, how could we skip a poppy-seed butter-cream tart with fresh raspberries? Eating it seemed the only kind thing to do.

Six bedrooms upstairs are not large, but they are unexpectedly comfortable and whimsically decorated. One has an Art Deco feeling with Maxfield Parrish prints and a ceiling fan. One has a vivid hand-painted headboard over the king bed and bright folk art on the walls. Rooms One and Two are slightly larger than the others and open onto the front balcony. (The traffic going by does fade away by 10:30 or 11:00 P.M.) Each room has a radio and a sparkling white tile bathroom that sports a hair dryer and heated towel bar.

Two balconies are upstairs, one at the back and one at the front of the hotel. A small library is at one end of the hall, with a desk, telephone, and door opening out to the balcony.

In the morning the innkeepers place coffee and newspapers in the hallway outside the guest rooms for early risers. Breakfast is a full, fresh meal prepared with the same skill as the dinner menu. Guests have the option of eating in their rooms, on the second-floor balcony, or downstairs in the dining room.

HOW TO GET THERE: Amador City is two and a half hours from San Francisco on Highway 49.

Ventana Inn
Big Sur, California 93920

INNKEEPER: Sal Abaunza, General Manager

ADDRESS/TELEPHONE: Big Sur; (408) 667–2331 or (800) 628–6500

ROOMS: 60; all with private bath and TV; most with fireplace; some with private hot tub on deck.

RATES: $195 to $260 for standard guest rooms; $475 to $970 for suites with fireplace and hot tub; double occupancy; continental breakfast and afternoon wine-and-cheese buffet.

OPEN: All year.

FACILITIES AND ACTIVITIES: Restaurant serves lunch and dinner; cocktail lounge; The Ventana Store. Hot tubs, saunas, swimming pool. Guided nature walks, massages, and facials available. Nearby: hiking, picnicking, shopping, galleries, restaurants in Carmel.

The Big Sur coast has always welcomed the offbeat, and even this sybaritic paradise was designed as a "different" kind of place: no tennis, no golf, no conventions, no Muzak, no disco delights.

What it does offer is a window (*ventana* means "window" in Spanish) toward both the Santa Lucia Mountains and the Pacific Ocean from a redwood and cedar lodge on a magnificent slope. This is the ultimate hideaway, a tasteful, expensive world of its own harmonizing with the wilderness surrounding it. For activity there are two 75-foot pools (heated all year) and two separate bathhouses with luxurious Japanese hot tubs, one of them with saunas. And there are walks over grassy slopes, through the woods, or on the beach. From every point your eyes go to the spectacular Big Sur coast, where boulders send white foam spraying into the air.

Some rooms in the cottages clustered around the lodge look down into a canyon of trees; others face the ocean. Their uncluttered blend of natural fabric and design makes each room seem to be the best one. Every detail—folk baskets holding kindling, window seats, quilts handmade in Nova Scotia, private terraces—has been carefully conceived.

A gravel path leads to the Mobil four-star restaurant, with the opportunity of seeing native wildflowers and an occasional deer or bobcat on the way. The food is colorful California cuisine: fresh fish, veal, chicken, creative pastas, and a good wine list. The place to be at lunch is the expansive terrace with its 50-mile view of the coast. Dinner inside is a candlelight-and-linen affair. If you've

walked over the hills enough, indulge in one of the many desserts from the in-house bakery.

A continental breakfast buffet, accompanied by baroque music, is spread in the lodge lobby by the rock fireplace: platters of melons, papayas, strawberries—whatever is fresh—pastries and breads baked in the Ventana kitchen, honey and preserves, yogurt and homemade granola. An afternoon wine-and-cheese buffet has an incredible array of domestic and imported cheeses.

The Ventana Store near the restaurant (books, baskets, original-design clothing, handmade knives, bird whistles) is as intriguing as its staff—all of whom seemed to be bilingual and have fascinating histories.

If "trickle-down economics" has dropped a little gold your way, this is the place to liberate your plastic for a romantic splash.

HOW TO GET THERE: On State Highway One, Ventana is 311 miles (about a six-and-a-half-hour drive) north of Los Angeles. The inn's sign is on the right. From San Francisco, the inn is 152 miles, 28 miles south of Carmel.

Blue Lantern Inn
Dana Point, California 92629

INNKEEPER: Lin McMahon

ADDRESS/TELEPHONE: 34343 Street of the Blue Lantern; (714) 661–1304 or (800) 950–1236

ROOMS: 29; all with private bath, Jacuzzi tub, wet bar, telephone, color television, and fireplace; most with panoramic ocean views. Handicapped facilities.

RATES: $140 to $500, double occupancy, buffet breakfast and afternoon tea, wine, and hors d'oeuvres. Special celebration packages.

OPEN: All year.

FACILITIES AND ACTIVITIES: Library, exercise room, facilities for weddings and private events. Nearby: Dana Point Yacht Harbor; shops, galleries, and cafes of Dana Point and neighboring Laguna Beach.

RECOMMENDED COUNTRY INNS® TRAVELERS' CLUB BENEFIT: 25 percent discount, Monday through Thursday, September through January, excluding holidays and special events, subject to availability, not combinable with other discounts.

*D*ana Point is one of those picturesque little beach towns that epitomize the glamour of Southern California's coast—except that it's even better than most of them. Not as crowded as Newport and Balboa, not as rowdy as Santa Monica and Venice, not as nose-in-the-air exclusive as Malibu.

Blue Lantern Inn has a prime location atop Dana Point bluffs. When he stopped along this coast in 1834, Richard Henry Dana wrote in his journal, which was to become *Two Years Before the Mast,* "High table-land running boldly to the shore, and breaking off in a steep hill, at the foot of which the waters of the Pacific are constantly dashing."

Sound romantic? You bet it is—and gorgeous, too. Ask for a balcony room so that in the morning you can look down on a sparkling harbor, a 121-foot replica of Dana's brigantine, *Pilgrim.* Beyond the harbor breakwall, on a clear day, you'll catch a view of the curve of Catalina Island.

For an inn so splendidly situated, the Blue Lantern more than lives up to its promise of comfort. Looking rather Cape Cod in style, the ambience inside is serene, understated, and luxurious. The lobby/sitting room has overstuffed couches and a massive stone fireplace that blazes a welcome at the slightest hint of a chill. A lavish and beautiful breakfast buffet is served at one end of this area, where you help yourself and sit at tables for two or four. On our visit breakfast included juices, melon slices, strawberries, blueberries, granola, cheese quiche, and muffins. The friendly help kept coffee cups filled and tables cleared.

An adjacent library features bleached oak paneling and more comfortable, cushy chairs. Afternoon tea and wine, with fresh fruit, cheese, and raw vegetable platter, are served here.

Our room had a fireplace, a small balcony large enough to sit on, and a huge bathroom featuring a separate shower and Jacuzzi tub-for-two, with a shutter door to fold back and watch the living room fire while you soak.

Every guest room is spacious, and some, like the Tower Suite, are downright lavish. Soft, muted colors like seafoam, lavender, periwinkle blue, and beige; traditional furniture; original art, and printed wall coverings combine for a romantic setting. Refrigerators and terry-cloth robes are just part of the scene.

The most unexpected aspect of your stay may be the warmth of your welcome and the genuine hospitality of the staff. It may sound cynical, but at an upscale Orange County beach inn, I almost expected a certain amount of slickness. How pleasant to be surprised.

HOW TO GET THERE: From Los Angeles, take 405 Freeway south to the 5 Freeway south. Exit at Pacific Coast Highway and veer to the right. Continue on PCH for 2½ miles to Street of the Blue Lantern. Turn left; inn is on the right.

Harbor House
Elk, California 95432

INNKEEPERS: Elle and Sam Haynes

ADDRESS/TELEPHONE: 5600 South Highway One (mailing address: Box 369); (707) 877-3203 or (800) 720-7474

ROOMS: 10, including 4 cottages; all with private bath; 5 with private deck; 9 with fireplace.

RATES: $185 to $285, double occupancy; breakfast and dinner included; lower winter rates. No credit cards.

OPEN: All year.

FACILITIES AND ACTIVITIES: Dinner by reservation. Private beach, fishing, ocean kayaking with guide. Nearby: Mendocino shops, galleries, restaurants; forest walks, local wineries; golf, tennis, horseback riding.

The windswept solitude of this stretch of Northern California's shore is one of nature's tens. And for an inn on the bluffs above the rocky coast, Harbor House has it all: a dramatic location, unique architecture, fresh decor, and fine food.

The house was built in 1916 entirely of virgin redwood by the Goodyear Redwood Lumber Company as a place to lodge and entertain its executives and guests. In the 1930s the house was converted to an inn, and it then variously faded and flourished over the years. Anyone who has ever stayed here knows what a spell this inn can cast.

The large living room, completely paneled in redwood with a high-beamed open ceiling, sets the tone: quiet and unpretentious. Comfortable sofas and a piano are grouped on a rich Persian rug before a huge fireplace, with books and a stereo nearby. (Christmas here sounds wonderful—the redwood room glowing in firelight, a giant tree, roasting chestnuts, festive dinners, and music by local musicians.) Bedrooms and cottages are freshly decorated, many with pastel watercolor prints by a local artist of flowers and birds indigenous to the area.

Ocean views from the dining room are breathtaking. On blustery North Coast days, some guests choose to spend the day in this redwood-paneled room watching the churning surf. It's comforting to know that you don't have to leave this warm atmosphere to find a restaurant; wonderful food is in store for you here. Plan on candlelight and wine and long romantic dinners.

The innkeepers subscribe to that old verity of California cooking: Use only the freshest, best ingredients possible, and keep it simple. Many ingredients are plucked right from the inn's own garden. What they don't grow, they purchase from the finest local sources, like baby potatoes and locally raised lamb. Fresh fish is often featured, prepared with Harbor House nuances. All the breads and breakfast pastries are homemade. Desserts also tend to reflect whatever is fresh. Typical are poached pears with raspberry sauce, or a sweet flaky pastry stuffed with apricots and cream. A fine California wine list and a good selection of beers are offered. Dinner is a fixed menu, changing every night, but with advance notice, they'll try to accommodate any special dietary needs.

Mendocino's attractions are only twenty minutes farther north, but I'm all for staying right here. Walking on the beach, discovering the secluded patios and paths—one leads to a waterfall and grotto—these are the quiet seductions of the inn. If you're in during the day, a bottle of local wine and a cheese platter from the kitchen are available to hold body and soul together until dinner.

HOW TO GET THERE: From the Bay Area, take Highway 101 to Cloverdale, then Highway 128 west to Highway One. The inn is 6 miles south on the ocean side of Highway One.

Hotel Carter
Eureka, California 95501

INNKEEPERS: Mark and Christi Carter

ADDRESS/TELEPHONE: 301 L Street; (707) 444–8062 or (800) 404–1390

WEB SITE: www.humboldt1.com/~carter52/Welcome.html

ROOMS: 19 rooms, 4 suites; all with private bath, TV, telephone; 8 with whirlpool baths; suites with fireplace. Smoking in lobby only.

RATES: $89 to $300; full breakfast, evening wine and hors d'oeuvres.

OPEN: All year.

FACILITIES AND ACTIVITIES: Restaurant serves dinner every night. Lobby and dining room showcase of contemporary art. Tours of exceptional kitchen gardens available. Nearby: walk along brick pathway bordering marina, through restored Old Town with specialty shops, restaurants; hundreds of restored Victorian homes, many art galleries in town.

In the charmingly restored Old Town district of Eureka, the Hotel Carter brings an old Rodgers and Hart song to my mind—"There's a Small Hotel." I've always thought of that song, and small hotels, as the quintessence of sophisticated romance. More cosmopolitan than a homespun B&B, more warmly inviting than a sleek grand hotel, the Hotel Carter is everything you could want in the romantic lodging category. It's the perfect rendezvous—intimate, glamorous, and serving some of the best food and wines available north of San Francisco.

Most first-time visitors assume that Mark Carter restored the yellow Victorian-style building, but it is newly constructed, modeled after a nineteenth-century Eureka hotel. It blends the exterior look and ambience of the past era with today's luxurious conveniences, all done with Carter's impeccable taste in detailings and furnishings. (He also built from scratch the magnificent Victorian-style B&B across the street.)

You may very well fall in love with the hotel the minute you step into the lobby. Despite the Old World elegance of 14-foot-high ceilings here and in the adjoining dining room, even casually dressed travelers will feel at home in an atmosphere both chic and inviting. Plump sofas and chairs are grouped around the room and the work of local Humboldt County potters and painters is showcased brilliantly against the salmon-colored walls. Regional wine and hors d'oeuvres are set out in front of the lobby's marble fireplace in the late afternoon.

You may enjoy a look at the hotel's wine shop (The 301 Wine Shop) with its excellent selection of rare and hard-to-find wines for sale. The restaurant's list won a "Best of Awards of Excellence" from the *Wine Spectator* in 1995.

Guest rooms are decorated in pale earth colors, with peach and white linens. They are furnished with handsome antique pine furniture combined with appointments we appreciate—reading lights, telephones, remote-controlled televisions hiding in wardrobes, and whirlpool tubs. Our suite on the second floor, with a fireplace and a window-seat view of Humboldt Bay, was a spot we would love to return to often.

Breakfast and dinner in the intimate dining room bring some outstanding taste treats. Since the days when Christi Carter, while also managing two babies, cooked at their B&B across the street what came to be known as the famous Carter Breakfast, she has taken the lead in searching for the best chefs, the finest ingredients, and true cutting-edge cuisine. The Hotel Carter has become the right place to see that concern for excellent cooking come to fruition.

Our dinner one night began with baby greens dressed with a strawberry vinaigrette, fresh grilled swordfish with lemon butter, three perfect vegetables grown in the Carters' garden, a new small grain (something akin to couscous), and crusty baguettes. A local Chardonnay and a Pinot Noir *had* to be sampled. A scrumptious apple-walnut tart served with homemade ice cream and coffee saw us off to our room impressed with the quiet service and fine food.

If it weren't that the Carters are such nice people, I'd say, "Keep this delightful hideaway a secret."

Gaige House Inn
Glen Ellen, California 95442

INNKEEPERS: Ken Burnet, Jr., and Greg Nemrow

ADDRESS/TELEPHONE: 13540 Arnold Drive; (707) 935-0237 or (800) 935-0237; fax (707) 935-6411

ROOMS: 11, all with private bath, robes, telephone, and air-conditioning; some with fireplace. Television available on request. No smoking inn.

RATES: $125 to $255, double occupancy; full breakfast and afternoon wine and cheese.

OPEN: All year.

FACILITIES AND ACTIVITIES: Swimming pool, beautiful grounds and decks. Accommodates weddings and special events. Concierge services. Nearby: Jack London State Historic Park; wineries in Glen Ellen, Kenwood.

The Sonoma California wine region is an idyllic destination I return to over and over. Its shady country roads and rolling hills of lush vineyards are two never-fail ingredients for a romantic getaway. All you need is the perfect inn.

This 1890 Italianate Victorian called Gaige House Inn is an appealing answer, a classy addition to wine country accommodations. It has been restored with the finest appointments while keeping a romantic ambience. Guest rooms are of unsurpassed comfort: down comforters and bed linens of Egypt-

ian cotton (I heard that one full-time person is employed to do nothing but iron them); huge tiled bathrooms and first-class lighting; fresh floral bouquets; and inviting, cushy furniture.

The entire mansion is filled with fine furniture and riveting art that the innkeepers have collected from around the world. Despite the elegance of polished oak floors and rich colorful rugs, and red velour sofas, the inns ambience is warm and inviting, a decor the innkeepers have dubbed "plantation/ Asia."

Each of the nine guest rooms is uniquely decorated. The largest (the Gaige Suite) could be called the "oh, wow!" room, since that's a frequent reaction on first seeing it. A huge four-poster canopy bed, puffy sofa in the sitting area, private deck overlooking the lawn, pool, and wooded hills, and a gorgeous tiled bath with a large Jacuzzi tub make it a favorite honeymoon suite. For a less expensive choice, consider one of the garden rooms facing the pool. They're smaller but still stylish, with queen-sized beds and private entrances.

Breakfast is served in the dining room or on the deck at tables for two or four. It includes fresh-squeezed juices and local seasonal produce (some of which is grown at the inn) and, perhaps, ham and eggs or oatmeal waffles. I realize you don't go to country inns with kitchens on your mind. Nevertheless, take a look at this one. Sensational!

When you've had enough sporting in the 40-foot pool, lounging on the great deck built over Calabezas Creek, strolling around the beautiful grounds, and exploring this elegant house, there is much more in the surrounding countryside to discover. The little hamlet of Glen Ellen that Jack London made famous is one of the most beguiling settings in the Sonoma wine region. Not smothered with tourists, abundantly picturesque, the Sonoma Valley is at the heart of Northern California's history. Historic landmarks and museums are nearby, as well as dozens of premium wineries, fine restaurants, and local galleries. Not to be missed is the museum of London memorabilia and the remains of Wolf House, his private residence, which was claimed by a fire before it was completed.

HOW TO GET THERE: From Highway 101, take the Napa/Vallejo exit (Highway 37) for 7½ miles. Turn left on Highway 121 for 6½ mile, to Highway 116, then to Glen Ellen/Petaluma for 1½ miles. Continue for 8¼ miles straight to Arnold Drive through Glen Ellen to inn on the left.

Applewood Inn and Restaurant
Guerneville, California 95446

INNKEEPERS: Darryl Notter and Jim Caron

ADDRESS/TELEPHONE: 13555 Highway 116; (707) 869–9093; fax (707) 869–9170

E-MAIL: stay@applewoodinn.com

WEB SITE: www.applewoodinn.com

ROOMS: 16 including 7 suites in two buildings; all with private bath, TV, and telephone, some with fireplace, Jacuzzi tub, and private patio. Complete handicapped access. No smoking inn.

RATES: $145 to $295, single or double occupancy; full breakfast and afternoon wine; two-night minimum on weekends.

OPEN: All year.

FACILITIES AND ACTIVITIES: Restaurant open Tuesday through Saturday; reservations recommended. Swimming pool, spa; facilities for private parties, weddings. Nearby: restaurants, golf, tennis, horseback riding; canoeing and other river activities; Guerneville shops; many local wineries; Sonoma Coast beaches. Armstrong Redwood State Reserve.

*A*pplewood, formerly called The Estate, is an unexpected taste of romantic glamour in the forested hills hugging the Russian River. As it twists through the Guerneville area, the river's beautiful natural setting has long been a popular choice for "resorts," cabins, cottages, and campgrounds. But . . . this is something quite different.

Handsome surroundings don't always mean a relaxing atmosphere, but that's not the case in this Mission Revival–style house. It was built as a private residence in 1922, and it remains an inviting country home, more comfortable and attractive than ever. On the main floor a large rock fireplace divides the living room from a many-windowed solarium. Bedrooms are on this floor as well as on the lower level; there they open to another comfortable sitting room.

I call the decor *Architectural Digest*—with warmth. Darryl studied design in San Francisco, and the house shows it. There's no one "look" but, rather, an understated chic. He's designed stylish slipcovers for some of the chairs and smart duvet covers for the beds. There are fine antiques among some just comfortable furniture. Both he and Jim are always looking for interesting pieces, but they admit that as much as they've bought, it seems to disappear in the large house.

Bedrooms are wonderfully romantic, and there's not a Laura Ashley in the lot. Billowing cotton draperies at an expansive bow of casement windows graced Number 4, my room. But every room, from smallest to grandest, has style, comfortable seating, and good reading lights. The luxury you'll find isn't in ostentation, it's in quality, such as down pillows and comforters, fine linen, and fresh bouquets.

Across the courtyard with splashing fountain the owner/innkeepers have added a second building to the property, a handsome Mediterranean villa that amazingly matches the first house. The new "piccola casa" has seven suites over three floors, with the penthouse being a spacious honeymoon suite with rooftop sundeck and stunning views. The other luxury rooms here have private verandas or patios, personally controlled heat and air-conditioning, showers for two, and oversized Egyptian cotton towels.

But it's not just ambience that you're buying at Applewood. The food is quite special. I've breakfasted on a terrace by the pool and dined by the fire. The new fifty-seat restaurant overlooks a redwood grove and also boasts outdoor dining. Exciting menus feature Provençal/California cuisine made with exotic fruits and vegetables fresh-picked from the inn's extensive organic gardens, and you can choose from a wide selection of local wines.

The ultimate romantic country inn experience, in my opinion, is staying in for dinner, as you can here at Applewood. A relaxing day exploring the Sonoma Coast, visiting wineries, or reading and napping at the inn can be capped off with a leisurely, candlelit dinner right here.

The innkeepers have succeeded in making this classic house a class-act inn by applying a simple philosophy: only the best of everything.

HOW TO GET THERE: From 101 north, take River Road/Guerneville exit just past Santa Rosa; go west 14 miles to Guerneville. At the stop sign at Highway 116 and River Road, turn left, and cross the bridge over River Road. The inn is ½ mile farther on the left. Local airport pickup.

Madrona Manor
Healdsburg, California 95448

INNKEEPERS: John and Carol Muir

ADDRESS/TELEPHONE: 1001 Westside Road (mailing address: Box 818); (707) 433–4231 or (800) 258–4003; fax (707) 433–0703

ROOMS: 22 and 5 suites; all but 3 with private bath; all with cable television, VCR, telephone, and air-conditioning; most with fireplace. Wheelchair access.

RATES: $155 to $220 in the Mansion; $220 to $225 for suites; double occupancy; full breakfast. Half-price special rate January, February, March.

OPEN: All year.

FACILITIES AND ACTIVITIES: Dinner nightly, full bar, Sunday brunch. Swimming pool. Nearby: golf, tennis, hiking, canoeing, fishing, winery tours, picnics, bicycling, Redwood State Park.

RECOMMENDED COUNTRY INNS® TRAVELERS' CLUB BENEFIT: 10 percent discount, Monday to Thursday.

Country inns continue to spring up in Northern California faster than yuppies are going out of style, but Madrona Manor stands alone. First, it is a truly dramatic Victorian mansion sitting in the midst of landscaped grounds and eight wooded acres. But even more notable is its outstanding California restaurant, the only one in Sonoma County rated three stars by *Chronicle* food critic Patricia Unterman.

The inn's romantic atmosphere begins even as you approach up the shaded driveway and the Italianate mansion first comes into view. Elegant accommo-

dations await inside: antique furnishings, period wallpapers and rugs, and rooms with original plumbing and lighting fixtures. The third floor has renovated rooms with fireplaces, queen-sized beds, and antique reproduction furniture from Portugal. Less opulent but more modern rooms are in two other outbuildings and the Carriage House. Suite 400 in the Carriage House, just one of five elegant suites, has French contemporary motif with a bath tiled in marble from Greece, a Jacuzzi tub, a fireplace, and a private deck.

Gourmet and *Travel and Leisure* are just two magazines whose critics have raved about the extraordinary food served here. Check out the fabulous kitchen and you'll see a professional staff at work in modern surroundings (contrasting with the rest of the 1881 setting) complete with a mesquite grill and a smokehouse in back that produces smoked trout, chickens, and meats. The gardens produce all the flowers for the dining room and guest rooms as well as herbs and specialty produce for the kitchen.

Don't miss dining here during your stay . . . it's always a culinary treat. The menu lists four- and five-course prix-fixe dinners, at $40 and $50 respectively, at this writing. But smaller appetites are also taken into account. Both of the prix-fixe menus list prices for each course so that one can order à la carte.

My first course of individual goat-cheese soufflé was perfectly crusty on top, with a softly oozing middle. Every element of the meal, down to dessert of amaretto-soaked cake with chocolate-ricotta filling, was meticulously prepared.

The wine list is both extensive and reasonably priced, which, even though this is the heart of the wine country, is not always true up here. Some selections from small local wineries are offered at near-retail prices on a regular basis.

Breakfast for guests is as carefully done as dinner. It includes the wonderful house bread, toasted; a perfectly timed soft-boiled egg; loads of seasonal fruit; oatmeal and granola; ripe, room-temperature cheeses; and house-smoked meats. When the weather allows, take this meal outside on the palm terrace.

What a beautiful place for a special celebration.

HOW TO GET THERE: From San Francisco, drive north on Highway 101, 12 miles north of Santa Rosa; take the Central Healdsburg exit; follow Healdsburg Avenue north to Mill Street, turn left, and it becomes Westside Road. Inn is ¾ mile on the right. From the north, take Westside Road exit from Highway 101; turn right. Inn is ½ mile on the right.

Orchard Hill Country Inn
Julian, California 92036-0425

INNKEEPERS: Darrell and Patricia Straube, owners

ADDRESS/TELEPHONE: P.O. Box 425; (760) 765–1700 or (800) 71–ORCHARD

WEB SITE: www.orchardhill.com

ROOMS: 12 suites in four separate cottages, 10 rooms in main lodge; all with private bath, TV, VCR, telephone; some with whirlpool tub, fireplace, and private patio. Special accommodations for physically challenged. No smoking inn.

RATES: $132 to $155 for lodge rooms midweek; $155 to $185 weekends; Cottage suites $155 to $195 midweek; $185 to $225 weekends; double occupancy; two-night minimum on weekends. Full breakfast; afternoon wine and hors d'oeuvres. Ask about special packages, off-season discounts.

OPEN: All year except brief closing in January.

FACILITIES AND ACTIVITIES: Dinners served (to house guests only) usually three nights a week and additionally by arrangement; wine, beer, bar; large tape library; terraces, gardens, hammocks. Nearby: walk to downtown Julian for museums, restaurants, antiques, horse-drawn carriage ride to countryside; walk to gold mine; dinner theater; unlimited hiking, horse, and bike trails; local seasonal events.

RECOMMENDED COUNTRY INNS® TRAVELERS' CLUB BENEFIT: Stay two consecutive nights, get second night free, Monday to Thursday, excluding holidays and special events, reservations required.

Julian, Calfornia, may not be a romantic destination that leaps to your mind, but I urge you to reconsider. A new inn—architecturally inspiring, luxuriously comfortable, and staffed with well-trained, amiable people—is waiting to welcome you to a special experience.

Julian is high in the pine- and oak-covered hills of San Diego County's rugged backcountry. A well-preserved 1800s gold-mining boomtown, it is 60 miles northeast of San Diego and has about 500 inhabitants.

On a hilltop in Julian, four 1,200-square-foot cottages—each containing three plush suites—and, still higher on the hill, a magnificent lodge with ten more guest rooms, a great room, and the dining room constitute the inn. All the buildings reflect that noble design style so popular in the 1930s called

California Craftsman. Pat Straube has stunningly decorated all the rooms—she's a pro, but that's obvious when you see her work.

The suites are named for local apple varieties. I was in the Cortland, done in a romantic blue toile fabric and wallcovering, with a private patio through French doors and a whirlpool tub. Suites also include fireplaces, sitting rooms with television and VCR, and private wraparound porches. Some, like the Roxbury, are especially spacious and come with a love seat that converts into a twin bed.

Up at the lodge, with its 180-degree view of the town and surrounding hills, the guest rooms are somewhat smaller than cottage suites. They are, therefore, less expensive and, to my eye, just as thoughtfully appointed and beautiful as the suites.

The lodge's common areas are the awesome great room and a dining room. Large sofas and fine upholstered chairs are grouped around the great room and in front of a stone fireplace. Brilliant rugs on the adobe tile floor, elegant antique pieces, and a small wine bar in one corner only begin to define a remarkable space. French doors, from the dining room also, open to a stone terrace enveloping the lodge. Sit out here for breakfast and watch hawks circle in the smog-free sky, or take a glass of wine out for sunset.

Privacy and quiet are here. So clever is the inn's design, it's surprising to gather for breakfast in the lodge and see other guests. But never, never miss a meal at Orchard Hill. Their food will astonish you with its quality and sophistication. I had a dinner that included a rice vegetable soup, fresh salad greens with Gorgonzola cheese and toasted walnuts, a gorgeous pork ragout, and the inn's trademark bread pudding with lemon sauce. This . . . is eating.

HOW TO GET THERE: From Highway 15 east and north of San Diego, exit east on Poway Road; proceed through the towns of Poway and Ramona to Julian. Cross Main Street and continue up the hill; inn is on your left.

The Red Castle Inn
Nevada City, California 95959

INNKEEPERS: Mary Louise and Conley Weaver

ADDRESS/TELEPHONE: 109 Prospect; (916) 265–5135 or (800) 761–4766

ROOMS: 7, including 3 suites; all with private bath. Third- and fourth-floor rooms air-conditioned. No smoking inn.

RATES: $100 to $145, double occupancy; full breakfast and afternoon tea. Two-night minimum Saturdays April 1 to December 31.

OPEN: All year.

FACILITIES AND ACTIVITIES: Prix-fixe dinners served en suite by special arrangement; Saturday morning carriage rides, historical narratives and poetry readings, Victorian Christmas dinner and entertainment, picnic baskets by advance request. Nearby: walking path to downtown shops, restaurants, antiques; local theater, musical events; swimming in mountain creek; cross-country skiing twenty minutes away.

ooking for all the world like the cover background for a Victorian romance novel, The Red Castle has an undeniably romantic appeal. Hanging on a hillside and nestled among dense trees, the inn is an impressive sight from many places around Nevada City. The Gothic Revival mansion is wrapped in rows of white-painted verandas and lavished with gingerbread trim at roofline and gables. From the private parking area, guests walk through an unusual Gothic arbor, past landscaping sprinkled with tiny lights to the front of the house, where you can survey the historic mining town's rooftops and church steeples.

Since it was built in 1857, the castle has had a succession of caring owners who have maintained it without compromising its elegant period character. The Weavers have brought not only their respective professional skills in architecture and design but also some impressive art, including several Bufano sculpture pieces, and fine furniture. Seven guest rooms and suites range over the four floors, each one of them a vibrantly decorated, tasteful delight. Most furnishings are Victorian, but not fragile or frilly. An explosion of color from wallpapers, fabrics, and rugs has an engaging effect in combination with the dramatic architecture. The two-bedroom Garret Suite, on the fourth floor, has a sitting room, bath, and balcony. It was from here that the original owner's son, when the spirit (or spirits) moved him, used to serenade the town with impromptu trumpet concerts.

A cozy sitting room/parlor off the entry hall has gradually taken on a more authentic nineteenth-century form with the addition of a pair of upholstered Bar Harbor wicker armchairs and a handsome John Jelliff settee; Jelliff was a noted designer of parlor furniture of the time. Here, also, is a large and inviting collection of Gold Rush history and art books. We helped ourselves to an elegant tea spread here and took it outside.

Three small terraced gardens, one with a fountain and pond, are idyllic sitting and strolling areas. All the rustic fences, gazebos, and arbors are handcrafted from branches of the incense cedars that make up the small forest surrounding the Castle. A path through shrubs and cascading vines leads down to Nevada City's main street.

Like many Gold Rush towns, Nevada City is a "happening" place with an astonishing number of cultural, historical, and just plain fun events. These innkeepers see that guests have access to whatever is going on. They'll arrange a horse-drawn carriage tour through the town's historic district or a visit and conversation with Mark Twain or Lola Montez, if these famous "guests" appear at teatime. The inn's own Victorian Christmas celebration is a truly memorable feast, one for which you should book well ahead of time.

The lavish breakfast buffet is a splendid sight—all of it homemade. Ours was typical, but the menu varies every day: juice, poached pears, glazed fresh strawberries, a baked-egg curry with pear chutney, cheese croissants, banana bread, jams, Mary Louise's grandmother's bread pudding (what a treat!) with a pitcher of cream, and, of course, great coffee.

HOW TO GET THERE: From Highway 49 at Nevada City, take Sacramento Street exit to the Chevron station; turn right and immediately left onto Prospect Street. The driveway takes you to the back of the house. Walk around the veranda to the front door.

The Estate by the Elderberries
Oakhurst, California 93644

INNKEEPER: Erna Kubin-Clanin, owner

ADDRESS/TELEPHONE: 48688 Victoria Lane (mailing address: P.O. Box 577); (209) 683–6860; fax (209) 683–0800; restaurant reservations (209) 683–6800

ROOMS: 10; all with private bath, wood-burning fireplace, balcony, CD stereo system. TV and telephone available upon request. One room with handicapped access.

RATES: $285 to $435, double occupancy; European-style breakfast and afternoon tea. Inquire for Château exclusive (up to twenty persons).

OPEN: All year.

FACILITIES AND ACTIVITIES: Swimming pool, walking paths, small chapel; restaurant serves a six-course prix-fixe menu ($38.50 to $40.00 without wine) Wednesday through Monday and Sunday brunch; will arrange weddings and other special celebrations. Nearby: Yosemite National Park, Badger Pass ski area, boating and skiing on Bass Lake.

*D*oes a fairy-tale castle in wooded mountain foothills, holding beautiful treasures and every luxury you can desire, sound promising as a romantic idyll? I can tell you about such a place; *you* must provide an appropriate companion.

A ten-room castle/hotel called Château du Sureau (translates to "Castle by the Elderberry") and an extraordinary restaurant called Erna's Elderberry House comprise this remarkable inn. There is simply nothing else like it on the West Coast inn scene.

Both of the white-stucco, turreted, and red-tile-roofed buildings are the result of Erna Kubin-Clanin's dream to create an outstanding restaurant and then a small, very personal auberge in the California mountains. The astounding thing is that this uncommonly elegant lodging and sophisticated restaurant are in Oakhurst, a nondescript little town nestling in the rocky foothills of the Sierra Nevada, 20 miles from the south entrance of Yosemite National Park.

Plenty of people (especially her bankers) called her mad, but Erna opened her restaurant, Elderberry House, in 1984. Remote it may be, but Craig Claiborne of the *New York Times* found it, was captivated by the food, and stayed three days—sometimes helping Erna in the kitchen. Rave reviews in *Gourmet* and other publications followed, and Elderberry House was on the map.

Erna next turned her sights to building an accommodation as splendid as was required by guests who made their way to Oakhurst for her food. Château du Sureau opened in 1991, a $2-million, ten–guest room inn reminiscent of Erna's native Austria or a luxurious hillside estate in Provence. Don't give a thought to feeling ill at ease in an atmosphere this elegant. Just the opposite is true. I've rarely seen service of this caliber combined with such genuine warmth and hospitality.

On arrival, tour the castle from the tiny chapel to the kitchen. Everything you see speaks of luxury and comfort: antique tiles, Oriental rugs, tapestries, magnificent furniture, fresh flowers, and sumptuous bathrooms. The Grand Salon soars to an 18-foot beamed ceiling, with an 1870 piano from Paris the focus of attention two steps up in the circular Music Tower. We were still trying to absorb the splendor of our guest room surroundings when a chambermaid tapped at our door with a beautifully presented tea tray and gourmet snacks.

That evening we walked through the lighted garden to Elderberry House for a leisurely paced, magnificent six-course dinner. We agreed with our waiter's selection of three wines for the dinner, though you can choose from a large list. After returning to the Château, we lounged before the fire with some fine port, and so to bed.

I hope you won't just look at the rates and turn the page. Long after you've forgotten how much it cost, you'll remember dining and staying at Château du Sureau, this castle by the elderberries.

HOW TO GET THERE: Drive north on Highway 5 toward Sacramento. Take Highway 99 to Fresno. Exit at Highway 41 through Fresno and continue on another forty minutes to Corsical, 7 miles south of the Château. At inn's sign, turn left at the second lane, through the gates on the right.

The Willows
Historic Palm Springs Inn
Palm Springs, California 92262

INNKEEPERS: Tracy Conrad and Paul Marut

ADDRESS/TELEPHONE: 412 West Tarquitz Canyon Way; (760) 320–0771; fax (760) 320–0780

ROOMS: 8, all with private bath, telephone, cable television, individual room climate control; some have fireplace, private balcony, garden patio, separate entrance and/or view of the waterfall. Limited handicap access. No smoking inn.

RATES: $175 to $375 summer (June through September); $250 to $550 Season (October 1 through June 1). Afternoon wine and hors d'oeuvres, full breakfast. Multiple-course dinner for two at nearby Le Vallauris or in your room included with two-night stay.

OPEN: All year.

FACILITIES AND ACTIVITIES: Swimming pool, gardens and patios; available for weddings, special gatherings. Nearby: four-star French restaurant across the street; walk to Desert Museum, downtown shops, theaters, restaurants, boutiques, antiques shops.

There was a time when the claim "George Washington slept here" gave a certain cachet to a lodging. More recently, a celebrity can provide a bit of rub-off glamour and attract attention to a place. But I've just scored a much bigger plum. How about Albert Einstein's bedroom for a really classy sleepover?

Einstein, with his wife, Elsa, was a frequent guest at this Mediterranean villa, built in 1927 as a winter home for a former Secretary of the Treasury. And if one can judge from a photograph that was in our room of the two standing on the front stairs, they were having a happy (and one hopes romantic) visit. The house has been splendidly renovated as a small luxury inn with striking architecture and subdued elegance. And, of all places, it sits only a block from the main thoroughfare of downtown Palm Springs, but it's light-years away from the glitz usually associated with that desert town.

The Willows is the triumphant achievement of a young couple who are emergency-room physicians. After buying the neglected villa, they were faced with an extended renovation project. Their goal was no less than restoring eight bedrooms and large common areas to the intimacy of an elegant private home. They also wanted to capture the spirit of the early thirties and the glamour of the movie stars who visited and to provide guests with an unrivaled sense of luxury.

The details of their accomplishment are wonderful to see: vaulted ceilings, crown moldings, and a mahogany-beamed ceiling in the living room; a veranda and dining room with frescoed ceilings. Cindy found photographs taken in 1938 that showed the living room then and selected elaborately carved European antique reproductions then in vogue. A  wall of French doors lead to a pair of verandas overlooking the pool. Everything seems massive: a grand piano in one corner, dozens of roses in a huge bouquet, sofas and fat chairs around a large fireplace.

The dining room is stunning. Enormous sliding doors along one wall open to a patio and a 50-foot waterfall. A stone floor, a massive armoire against one wall and a tiled fireplace at the other, and four or five tables set with white linen and Wedgwood china were background for a leisurely paced breakfast.

Each of the eight bedrooms is unique. They have in common the finest linens, comfortable upholstered furniture, and elegant appointments. We slept in Einstein's Garden Room, where Einstein and his wife were guests many times. Their photograph, taken on the front steps of this house, is in the room. All the bedrooms have gorgeous bathrooms; this one has a travertine stone floor, claw-foot tub and separate shower, and a pewter chandelier. French doors open to a private garden beside the waterfall.

Two other rooms stand out: The Library—in mahogany, with fireplace and private garden patio—is where Clark Gable and Carole Lombard stayed. The Marion Davies Room is a romantic fantasy with antique furnishings, an elaborately carved bed, and a bathroom suitable for a screen queen.

A beautifully landscaped hillside garden above the waterfall is a quiet spot that gives you a sweeping view of the entire Coachella Valley. Try it early in the morning.

The rates here may strike you as a tad pricey, but in my opinion you get full value. Surroundings, service, and ambience are top quality. Guests who stay two nights receive a certificate good for dinner at La Vallauris, a highly rated French restaurant across the street.

HOW TO GET THERE: Approaching Palm Springs on Highway 10 from Los Angeles, exit on 111 business route. Proceed through the town to Tahquitz Canyon Way and turn right. The inn is on your right at the end of the street.

Casa Madrona Hotel
Sausalito, California 94965

INNKEEPER: John Mays

ADDRESS/TELEPHONE: 801 Bridgeway; (415) 332–0502 or (800) 288–0502

ROOMS: 34; all with private bath; some with fireplace, private deck, water view.

RATES: $138 to $260, double occupancy; cottages, $205 to $260; 3-room suite, $448; continental breakfast and wine-and-cheese social hour.

OPEN: All year.

FACILITIES AND ACTIVITIES: Dinner, wine and beer bar nightly; lunch Monday through Friday; Sunday brunch. Outdoor Jacuzzi. Elegant wedding and special events facilities. Nearby: Sausalito's shops and galleries, ferryboat rides across the bay, fine dining, hiking, bicycling.

RECOMMENDED COUNTRY INNS® TRAVELERS' CLUB BENEFIT: Stay two nights, get third night free, Monday to Thursday, November to May, subject to availability.

*J*ohn Mays is an innkeeper who knows how to create an atmosphere. He's turned this luxurious old mansion perched on a hill above Sausalito into one of the most romantic inns you'll find. Of course, he has a lot going for him with a town almost too winning for words and spectacular views of the yacht harbor.

Casa Madrona is more than a century old. Time had taken its toll on the former residence, hotel, bordello, and boardinghouse when John Mays rescued it in 1978. It nearly slid off the hill during the rains of '82, but renovations already begun saved it from gliding away.

Since then Mays has added an elegant tumble of cottages that cascade down the hill to Sausalito's main street. Each one is different, with dormers, gables, peaked roofs, and hidden decks. Amazingly, the whole gray-blue jumble lives perfectly with the old mansion.

You've seen "individually decorated" rooms before, but these beat all. Mays gave each one of his hillside cottages over to a different Bay Area decorator. The range of their individual styles resulted in rooms with themes from nautical to equestrian (The Ascot Suite) to a Parisian artist's loft. Most have private decks and superb views. And since it *is* fabled, sybaritic Marin, there are luxurious tubs for two (sometimes elevated and open to the room), refrigerators stocked with fruit juice and mineral water, and fresh flowers. (But no peacock feathers.)

If you're indifferent to unique rooms surrounded by lush gardens, exotic bougainvillea and trumpet vine spilling over decks and walkways, perhaps elegant food will ring your bell. A beautiful wine bar and uncluttered dining room in the old house on top of the hill are lighted and decorated to enchant. Only white linen on round tables and fresh flowers compete with the view from the deck of the bay and Sausalito Yacht Harbor . . . that is, until the food is served.

We began with what I thought was a California standard but which has become a part of American cuisine: radicchio and Belgian endive salad with baked chèvre (goat cheese). Perfection. Our waiter was agreeable when I ordered another first course (Asian crab cakes and lobster mayonnaise) instead of an entree. (I love places that encourage you to order by *your* appetite instead of *their* rules.) Others at our table raved about a grilled rare Ahi tuna and a guava-and-macadamia-crusted rack of lamb. The meal could not have been lovelier.

If this inn can't rekindle a dying ember, no place can.

HOW TO GET THERE: Cross the Golden Gate Bridge; take Alexander Street exit to center of town. San Francisco Airport pickup available. Ferry service from San Francisco.

Timberhill Ranch
Timbercove, California 95421

INNKEEPERS: Barbara Farrell, Frank Watson, Tarran McDaid,
Michael Riordan

ADDRESS/TELEPHONE: 35755 Hauser Bridge Road, Cazadero 95421;
(707) 847–3258

ROOMS: 15 secluded cottages; all with private bath, fireplace, minibar.
Handicap access. Smoking restricted to designated areas.

RATES: $415, double occupancy, Friday, Saturday, Sunday; $395, double
occupancy, weekdays; breakfast and six-course dinner included.

OPEN: All year.

FACILITIES AND ACTIVITIES: Lunch. World-class tennis courts, swimming pool, outdoor Jacuzzi, hiking. Nearby: 4 miles to ocean beach;
Salt Point State Park, Fort Ross, The Sea Ranch public golf course.

When your stress level hits an octave above high C and you can't bear
making one more earth-shaking decision . . . when you want to
seclude yourself with nature (and a close, close friend) for some
spiritual renewal . . . when you demand the best in fine food, service, and
amenities . . . then head for Timberhill Ranch.

This classy resort on a very intimate scale is off the beaten track, perched
high in the hills above the Sonoma Coast. Once you've checked in at the reception and dining area, you're shuttled to your cottage in a golf cart, and not a
telephone or a discouraging word will ruffle your brow until you grudgingly
conclude it's time to go home.

That Sonoma has fabulous climate, rugged beauty, unspoiled high meadows, and redwoods is undisputed. What *is* surprising is to find an inn with such luxury blending into these surroundings. All credit must be given to the two innkeeping couples who planned and built 80 percent of the resort themselves. Their vision accounts for keeping the ranch an underdeveloped oasis of tranquility for only ten cottages, despite eighty acres of land; for building their world-class tennis courts far from the swimming pool, because "when you're lounging quietly by the water you don't want to hear tennis chatter."

The spacious, cedar-scented cottages are situated for maximum privacy. Each has a stocked minibar, a fire laid, a well-appointed tile bath, a handmade quilt on the queen-sized bed, comfortable chairs, good lights, and a radio. In the morning breakfast is delivered to your door to enjoy on your private deck as you look out at a stunning view.

What more? Superb food served beautifully in an intimate dining room with windows overlooking hills and forest—but without reservations, hurry, hassle, or check to interrupt. (Breakfast and dinner are included in the rate.) The six-course dinners (now open to the public by reservation) are what you might expect in one of San Francisco's finest restaurants. Here's a sample of one recent night: chilled artichoke with lemon mayonnaise, beef barley soup, salad with hearts of palm, raspberry sorbet, loin of lamb with red-pepper butter (among five other entree choices), and a dessert selection including puff pastry blackberry torte.

The four owners are hands-on innkeepers, always giving a level of personal attention far removed from a slick resort atmosphere. One told me, "We really like taking care of people and giving them the kind of service and privacy *we* looked for when *we* used to get away." As I watched the reluctant farewell of one couple, the hugs and promises to be back soon, I decided that Timberhill has all the right stuff, including a warm heart.

HOW TO GET THERE: From Highway One north of Fort Ross, turn east on Timber Cove Road. Follow to Sea View Ridge Road. Turn left; follow to Hauser Bridge Road and inn sign on the right.

Mt. Ashland Inn
Ashland, Oregon 97520

INNKEEPERS: Chuck and Laurel Biegert

ADDRESS/TELEPHONE: 550 Mt. Ashland Road; (503) 482–8707 or (800) 830–8707

ROOMS: 5, including 1 suite with Jacuzzi for two, and 1 with gas fireplace; all with private bath, queen- or king-sized bed, and individual thermostat; VCR available. No smoking inn.

RATES: $85 to $130, double occupancy; full breakfast and beverages. Special rates November through April, excluding holidays and weekends.

OPEN: All year.

FACILITIES AND ACTIVITIES: New high-tech, lightweight snowshoes for guests' use; hiking, sledding, cross-country and downhill skiing. Nearby: river rafting, Ashland Shakespeare Festival February through October, Britt Music Festival June to September in Jacksonville.

A late April snow was falling the first time I drove up the road to Mt. Ashland, making the passing scenery all the more breathtaking. At 5,500 feet, just 3 miles from the summit, the beautiful Mt. Ashland Inn sits nestled in the Siskiyou Mountains 16 miles south of Ashland, a snug romantic haven of outstanding craftsmanship and hospitality.

The cedar log structure was handcrafted from lumber cut and milled on the surrounding property. But don't picture a woodsy cottage improvised by a couple with some land and a chain saw. Remarkable design and woodworking skills are apparent everywhere your eyes rest—in hand-carved mountain scenes on the doors, the decorative deck railing, log archways, stained-glass windows, and a unique log-slab circular staircase. Most amazing to me were the six handmade Windsor chairs, each one a smooth, perfect piece of art.

The peeled log walls of a common room draw you in with the warmth of cushy furniture, brilliant Oriental rugs, mellowed antiques, and a stone fireplace. Can you imagine how a fire, music playing softly, and wine or hot spiced cider will hit you on a cold afternoon? Right. It means sleepy time in the mountains.

Each of the guest rooms upstairs has a view toward Mt. Shasta or Mt. McLoughlin, or into the beautiful forest. The Sky Lakes Suite comprises the entire top floor and offers the ultimate in mountain magic. Surrounded by a window and a skylight overhead, its large jetted tub for two is filled by a river-rock waterfall. The king sleigh bed surveys a splendid view of Mt. Shasta. A river-rock gas fireplace, a wet bar, a small refrigerator, and a microwave complete this coziest of hideaways.

When I looked out the window in the morning, the fir trees were thickly frosted with snow, and I felt like Heidi in Oregon. But pretending I was roughing it in the wilderness just wouldn't fly in the face of all the comforts nearby: big chairs with reading lights by the windows, a comfortable bed topped with a handmade quilt, and the woodsy aroma of cedar filling the air.

Breakfast in the dining room was fresh juice and fruit and a tasty entree of puffy orange French toast. Daffodils on the table were picked that morning as they popped through the snow.

If you must stir from this comforting cocoon, these innkeepers are prepared to make it easy for you to enjoy the outdoors. They have excellent ski equipment, mountain bikes, snowshoes, and bobsleds for guests. They'll arrange lessons and guided tours. A cross-country skiing trail that ties into old logging roads is just out the back door. Just 3 miles up the road, Mt. Ashland offers fairly demanding downhill skiing. For hikers, the Pacific Crest Trail passes right through the property. The Dog Sled Express is a big hit with guests. Snow permitting, you can leave the inn and be whisked over the mountain.

For many visitors the premier attractions of Ashland remain its theaters, about a thirty-minute drive from the inn. But staying in and enjoying this cozy mountain snuggery is not a bad idea at all. Slip on one of the thick robes in your room, slide your tootsies into the fluffy slippers provided, and stride out to the large jetted outdoor spa. After a visit to the adjacent cedar sauna and shower, you'll float back to your room.

HOW TO GET THERE: North on I–5, take Mt. Ashland exit 6; turn right under the highway. At stop sign turn left; parallel highway ½ mile. Turn right on Mt. Ashland Road to ski area. Inn is 6 miles from the highway.

Tu Tú Tun Lodge
Gold Beach, Oregon 97444

INNKEEPERS: Dirk and Laurie Van Zante

ADDRESS/TELEPHONE: 96550 North Bank Rogue; (503) 247–6664 or (800) 864–6357

E-MAIL: tututun@harborside.com

WEB SITE: www.tututun.com

ROOMS: 16, river-view rooms, 2 suites, 2 houses; all with private bath. Wheelchair access.

RATES: $135 to $225 for river-view rooms; $190 to $215 for suites; $325for house; double occupancy; meals extra. $10 each additional person. Daily rate for meals including hors d'oeuvres, dinner and breakfast: $41.50.

OPEN: April 27 to October 27. Two suites with kitchens available all year.

FACILITIES AND ACTIVITIES: Breakfast, lunch, dinner for guests or by reservation, full bar. Swimming pool, four-hole putting green; jet-boat whitewater Rogue River trips; salmon and steelhead fishing, seasoned guides available. Nearby: scenic flights over Siskiyou Mountains, hiking, beachcombing, scenic drives, gambling in Gold Beach.

*H*ere is a hideout for couples whose romance never glows more brightly than when they're fishing together, but dims when faced with the gritty realities of camping. Consider the motto of Tu Tú Tun Lodge: "Casual elegance in the wilderness on the famous Rogue River."

That's summing it up modestly, for this is a very special blend of sophistication and outdoors-lover's paradise. Top-notch accommodations and superb food are those of a classy resort, but the young owners create a friendly atmosphere that's more like that of a country inn.

Guest rooms are situated in a two-story building adjacent to the lodge. Each has comfortable easy chairs, extra-long beds, a dressing area, and a bath with tub and shower. Special touches that make wilderness life civilized aren't forgotten—fresh flowers, good reading lamps, and up-to-date magazines. Two recently redecorated rooms now have Japanese-style soaking tubs in their outdoor area. The suites can accommodate up to six persons each. No telephone or television intrudes as you watch the changing colors of the Rogue's waters at sunset from your private balcony or patio.

A bell at 6:30 P.M. calls guests to the lodge for cocktails and hors d'oeuvres. The innkeepers and staff are superb in their hosting role—introducing everyone, starting conversations, and putting everyone at ease. By the time they seat you for dinner at round tables set for eight, you'll feel you're at a lovely private party dining with old friends. The set entree dinner they serve is outstanding. It always features regional specialties, frequently grilled over mesquite. Fresh chinook salmon, soup, crisp salad made from locally grown greens, freshly baked bread or rolls, and raspberry sorbet make up a typical dinner.

After dinner, guests usually gather around the two fire pits on the terrace overlooking the river to enjoy a drink, inhale the scent of jasmine, and take in the beauty all around. There's much to talk about as you share ideas for the next day's plans. If those plans call for an early-morning rising for fishing, a river trip, or hiking, breakfast and lunch baskets will be ready for you.

One adventure almost every visitor to the lodge tries is the exciting 104-mile whitewater round trip up (and down) the river. Jet boats stop at the lodge's dock to pick up passengers in the morning.

The inn's name comes from the Tu Tú Tun Indians, who lived in a village on the very site of the Lodge. *Tunne* meant "people"; the *Tu Tú Tunne* were "people close to the river."

HOW TO GET THERE: Driving north on Highway 101, pass through Gold Beach, cross bridge, and watch for signs on right to Rogue River Tavern. Turn right and drive 4 miles to tavern; follow signs another 3 miles to lodge on the right.

Heron Haus
Portland, Oregon 97210

INNKEEPER: Julie Keppeler

ADDRESS/TELEPHONE: 2545 N.W. Westover Road; (503) 274-1846; fax (503) 248-4055

WEB SITE: www.europa.com/~hhaus

ROOMS: 6; all with private bath, telephone, alarm/radio, air-conditioning, and sitting area; 1 with spa; television available. No smoking inn.

RATES: $135 to $350, double occupancy; generous continental breakfast; $65 additional person; $95 single corporate rate.

OPEN: All year.

FACILITIES AND ACTIVITIES: Swimming pool, panoramic views of city and mountains. Nearby: just above Portland's Nob Hill shops, boutiques, restaurants.

*I*f an exciting city figures into your plans for a romantic tryst, Portland is a wonderful choice. But instead of an impersonal downtown hotel, consider a very civilized nesting spot like Heron House.

This is a gorgeous house! Its impact comes not from flashy, ostentatious appointments but from the combined impression of its gleaming wood floors, fine furniture, beautiful art and rugs, and hillside setting with stunning views of Mt. Rainier, Mt. St. Helens, and Mt. Hood.

Owner/innkeeper Julie Keppeler has drawn from her former life in Hawaii, her knowledge of Northwest Indians, and her innate good taste in transforming this 1904 Tudor house into a perfect urban inn. The labor of all those many months of work getting back to the original parquet floors, varnishing woodwork, and stripping wallpaper is invisible today. The house has such a solid, tastefully mellow feeling that you can perceive it as always having looked this way.

An abundance of common rooms are here for guests to enjoy: an enclosed east-view sunroom overlooking the pool, the morning room, a mahogany library and study, and a television room. Guests are encouraged to make themselves at home and roam through the house.

Guest rooms—all with Hawaiian names—are on the second and third floors and are especially spacious. Decorated in blues, lavender, and rose, they feel light and airy. All the rooms have queen- or king-sized beds, and all have generous sitting and work space. A beautiful suite on the third floor occupies

the entire east end of the house. Called Mahina, meaning moonlight, it looks out toward Mt. Hood and Mt. St. Helens.

It is ironic that the casual elegance of this house, with its atmosphere of gracious living, is every bit as convenient for the business traveler as a downtown hotel, and it's certainly more pleasant. Its close proximity to the heart of Portland, the beautiful library, good lights, and telephone and desk in your room provide no excuse for avoiding your work while you're in Portland. But you're here for romance—so put down that phone!

Julie's dining room is another light-filled, handsome room. She does a sit-down breakfast service here between 8:00 and 10:00 A.M. In addition to fresh fruit, coffee, and teas, she offers cinnamon, raisin, and pumpkin pastries, date nut and orange rolls.

Heron Haus sits in the hills of northwest Portland in a neighborhood of some of Portland's oldest and finest homes. Directly below the house, an orange grove bordered by laurel, holly, and mature rhododendrons provides privacy.

It's an interesting area to walk in. Julie said that some of the best eating places in Portland as well as a lively mixture of small businesses are close by. Marvelous views of downtown Portland (and what a spectacular city it is) and its bridges over the Willamette River are just part of the perks that come with staying at this classy inn.

HOW TO GET THERE: From Highway 405 through Portland, take Everett Street exit to Glisan, a one-way street. Turn right at Twenty-fourth Street, go 3 blocks to Johnson Street, and bear right onto Westover Road. At top of ½-block incline, you are facing the inn's driveway; proceed all the way up to parking area.

Gilbert Inn
Seaside, Oregon 97138

INNKEEPERS: Dick and Carole Rees

ADDRESS/TELEPHONE: 341 Beach Drive; (503) 738–9770 or
(800) 410–9770; fax (503) 717–1070

WEB SITE: www.clatsop

ROOMS: 10, including 2 suites; all with private bath and TV.
No smoking inn.

RATES: $89 to $105, April through September; $79 to $95, October
through March; double occupancy; full breakfast. Garden units $95,
double occupancy, $114 for four, breakfast not included.

OPEN: All year except January.

FACILITIES AND ACTIVITIES: Nearby: 1 block to the beach, 1 block to
main street shops, restaurants, other attractions; Quatat Marine Park,
Seaside Museum, Tillamook Head Trail, Fort Stevens State Park,
Cannon Beach.

Poets and dreamers are always struggling to express the magic of
Oregon's exquisite coast; lovers are only required to enjoy it. That
you'll be inspired is almost a guarantee. One special place to experience it is at an exceptionally attractive coastal lodging called Gilbert Inn.

This Queen Anne Victorian was built by Alexander Gilbert in 1892. It must
have been the most beautiful house in town then, but today, after the lavish
attentions of innkeepers Carole and Dick Rees, it is the very picture of a seaside inn—a yellow-and-white stunner with turret, porches, flagpole, gardens,
and white picket fence. The parlor you enter signals the refreshing style of

these innkeepers. They have a century-old house but have opted for traditional comfort and contemporary good taste rather than quaint clutter. The big fireplace in the center of the room and the natural fir tongue-and-groove ceilings and walls throughout the house contribute a cozy warmth and appealing period charm. But the dazzling green rug and fresh floral coverings on sofas and chairs are fashionable and lively.

Each of the eight guest rooms and two suites is distinct and decorated so engagingly that I couldn't choose one over another. The thick carpeting, down comforters, linens, and pillows are all of fine quality. Again, Carole has decorated captivating, pretty rooms but without clutter. The Turret Room is popular with its tall four-poster bed, old fir ceilings and walls, and the turret window. The Garret constitutes the entire third floor and has a queen and two twin beds, a sitting area and an ocean peek through a dormer window.

Four new accommodations in the garden offer unusual privacy and flexibility. Each one has a full kitchen, two bedrooms (one with a queen-size bed, the other with two twins), full bathroom, living and dining rooms. Each has its own outside entrance and private patios and gardens. These garden units are a real bargain when you're traveling with children or another couple.

Breakfast is served on a restored side porch that looks out on a flower garden. Pink walls, white iron tables and chairs, pink-and-white Oriental rugs, and lots of green plants make the setting one of the prettiest places you'll ever linger over breakfast. I wonder how the Reeses ever get their guests to move on. Breakfast menus include a wide variety of Rees specialties, but one recipe is an especially big hit—French toast with a filling of cream cheese and walnuts, baked and served with an apricot sauce.

But Seaside is a popular and historic town and there are things to see. Many of the town's attractions are within walking distance of the inn. The Turnaround, at the end of Broadway (the main street), is the official end of the Lewis and Clark Trail. This is a spot to watch the sun set over the Pacific.

The standards of quality and comfort to be enjoyed at Gilbert Inn make it one of the best bargains to be found on the Oregon Coast.

HOW TO GET THERE: Driving north, exit Highway 101 at the City Center on Holiday Drive. Continue to a flashing red light, Avenue A; turn left and proceed to the beach. Inn is on the left corner at A and Beach. Driving south, exit 101 at North Broadway. Proceed 2 blocks past Broadway to Avenue B. Turn right to the ocean. Inn is on the left.

Run of the River
Leavenworth, Washington 98826

INNKEEPERS: Monty and Karen Turner

ADDRESS/TELEPHONE: 9308 East Leavenworth Road (mailing address:
P. O. Box 285); (509) 548–7171 or (800) 288–6491

ROOMS: 6, including 2 suites; all with private bath, spacious deck, and
cable TV; 3 with Jacuzzi tub; some with loft. No smoking inside inn or
on grounds.

RATES: $100 to $155, double occupancy, full breakfast and afternoon
refreshments. Two-night minimum stay on weekends and holidays.

OPEN: All year.

FACILITIES AND ACTIVITIES: Hot tub, mountain bikes available March
through November; magnificent views of river and wildlife from decks;
will arrange horse-drawn sleigh rides, horseback rides, cross-country ski
lessons, rafting, day hikes. Nearby: bird refuge; hiking or cycling along
river; cross-country and downhill skiing; snowshoeing; Bavarian Village
with Leavenworth's restaurants, unique shops.

T's safe to say that before you leave Run of the River you'll be planning
a return visit. Situated on two acres in an alpine meadow in the Cascade Mountains, this log inn is a hidden jewel. For a romantic hideaway, for nature lovers, for the world-weary, this is a beautiful, safe haven with
all the comforts you could desire.

The six bedrooms are uniquely private and quiet. While each is distinct, all
the rooms have the warmth of log walls, tall cathedral-pine ceilings, hand-
hewn log furniture, luxurious baths, and private decks.

They differ in their appointments of colorful Northwest Indian objects,
excellent-quality bed linens, and handsome furniture pieces. Three rooms have
lofts, snug places to take a snooze or read away a quiet afternoon. But it's the
private deck that is each room's most important appointment; it puts you in
a front-row seat for one of nature's "tens" on the gorgeous scale.

The inn sits in a meadow sliced through by the Icicle River and surrounded
by the magnificent Cascade Mountains. A small island in the river is a wildlife
refuge, and if you sit quietly, you'll see the movement and hear the subtle
sound of nature all around you—a host of migrating waterfowl, Canada geese,
bald eagles, osprey, and the kingfisher, fluttering above the water to dive in
and nab a fish. In summer at twilight, deer drink from the river, and there is
even an occasional black bear.

Every season has its special rewards here, but innkeepers Monty and Karen say they look forward most to winter. Covered with fresh white snow, meadow and river frozen, Cascades white-tipped, the inn and the entire valley are a spectacular sight. This is when young, enthusiastic innkeepers (like M. and K.) go into action. They know a dozen great cross-country ski trails, which ones are worth buying a pass for, which are free. They'll book you on an old-fashioned sleigh ride or a snowmobile safari. They'll provide the carrots and charcoal if you want to build a snowman in the meadow, and they'll have a fire, the hot tub, and hot coffee ready when you come inside.

A large common room with an attractive kitchen in one corner is the heart of the inn. A big, full breakfast is served here at a long pine table. Windows across the front of the room look out at the meadow and river. You could very cozily spend the day right here.

I haven't told you the delights of spring, summer, and fall at the inn or detailed the Bavarian Village of Leavenworth's attractions, but here's the main lesson: Run of the River is quite special, with two especially caring—and fun—innkeepers.

Slow down . . . listen . . . watch . . . breathe in and out . . . feel the air. This just might be heaven on earth.

HOW TO GET THERE: Traveling south on Highway 2 through Stevens Pass or driving north from Wenatchee, exit at East Leavenworth Road. Drive exactly 1 mile, and turn down gravel driveway to the inn.

Edenwild Inn
Lopez Island, Washington 98261

INNKEEPERS: Jamie and Lauren Stephens

ADDRESS/TELEPHONE: Lopez Road (mailing address: P. O. Box 271); (360) 468–3238; fax (360) 468–4080

ROOMS: 8; all with private bath; some with fireplace, garden and water views. Handicapped facilities. No smoking inn.

RATES: $100 to $155, double occupancy, full breakfast and afternoon aperitif. Winter rates November through March: All rooms $75.

OPEN: All year.

FACILITIES AND ACTIVITIES: Nearby: Lopez Village shops, hiking, bicycling. Ferry landing, seaplane, or airport pickup available.

When your request from a reservation is answered with a map of an island, a ferry schedule, and the assurance that ferry landing, seaplane, and airport pickup are available, I say you're on your way to an adventure. The Edenwild Inn on Lopez Island is such a place. Just getting there is a romantic adventure.

The island slopes gently up from the ferry landing to reveal rural nature at its most picturesque. Pasture, fields, and farms are interspersed with dense woodland, and the shoreline is notched with bays and coves.

The contemporary inn is about 4½ miles from the ferry landing and sits on two landscaped acres of green lawn and gardens. A broad porch dotted with chairs wraps around three sides of the large house, giving it an inviting, traditional look. Inside is a spacious, casually elegant country house with pale oak floors and fresh bouquets. In the common sitting room, comfortable sofas and chairs are grouped before the fireplace. Walls and fabrics are mostly serene misty greens, grays, and heather. An old upright piano sits here, and attractive art is displayed here and all through the inn. Breakfast is served in the adjoining dining room.

Each one of the seven bedrooms appeals to me. It could be because they are new and fresh, or perhaps it is the comfortable built-in beds, or the good-looking black-and-white tile bathrooms, or the views: Fisherman's Bay, the garden, or San Juan Channel. From Room 5 we thought our view of the main garden and the channel the best in the house . . . until we watched a magnificent sunset from the porch outside Room 1 that beat them both.

Breakfast at Edenwild wins high marks for me. First, the coffee is brewed and set out early for those morning grouchy types to help themselves, stroll around or rock on the front porch and gradually edge into the morning. Second, everything—and this includes the innkeepers—looks superfresh and inviting; crisp cotton on the servers (no stained aprons here), attractive linens and fresh bouquets on the tables.

Jamie usually cooks breakfast, often starting you off with his prize-winning raspberry coffee cake in addition to fresh juice and granola. At my visit, this was followed by orange French toast with real maple syrup, bacon, and a generous fresh-fruit salad on the side.

If you're young and have more energy than money, you should consider buying a "walk-on" ferry ticket (much cheaper than taking a car). Bring your bicycle and backpack, or you can arrange for an inn pickup. This is a wonderful island for bicycling.

A point of information about that preferred arrival pickup: The innkeepers keep a white 1973 Checker limo—23-feet long, four doors on each side, plus luggage space and seating for twelve—for just such service. Take them up on the offer. Quiet Lopez Island sits up and takes notice when, Jamie at the wheel, this hilarious vehicle makes its appearance at the ferry landing. Talk about a grand entrance!

HOW TO GET THERE: From the Lopez Island Ferry Landing, proceed 4½ miles to Lopez Village Road. Turn right.

Freestone Inn
Mazama, Washington 98833

INNKEEPER: John Coney, general manager

ADDRESS/TELEPHONE: 17798 Highway 20, Wilson Ranch; (800) 639–3809, Jack's Hut (509) 996–2752

ROOMS: 12 inn rooms, 2 Lakeside Lodges, and 6 cabins; all with private bath, fireplace, refrigerator, coffeepot, television, private deck. Cabins have fully equipped kitchen, fireplace, 1 and 2 bedrooms. Smoke-free environment.

RATES: $95 to $195 inn rooms, spring and fall; $130 to $225 summer and winter; generous continental breakfast; cabins $85 for studio to $195 for 2-bedroom.

OPEN: All year.

FACILITIES AND ACTIVITIES: Restaurant, library, common areas inside and out. Accommodates small weddings, gatherings, reunions. Nearby: Nordic and cross-country skiing, ski instruction, sleigh rides, ice skating, mountain biking, hiking, backpacking, horseback riding, river rafting, fly-fishing, swimming, boating, rock climbing; equipment rentals.

*I*f you think a romantic idyll requires only the simple pleasure and civilized comforts of a lodging in the great outdoors, wait till you see Freestone. To be blunt, it knocked my socks off.

In a mountain setting of year-round beauty, only twelve spacious rooms, a first-rate restaurant, and a Great Room common area share the luxury of the long, handsome main lodge. Close by in the trees are six very private cabins (the Early Winters Cabins) with woodsy charm, decks, and surprising comforts and two luxurious Lakefront Lodges an easy walking distance from the inn.

At the heart of the inn is the Great Room with vaulted ceiling, a small paneled library at one end, and a stunning 30-foot—maybe more—river-rock fireplace that separates the room from the dining room. Windows and glass doors open to the broad deck. Those who know the grand lodge at Yosemite Park will understand why I named it the "Little Awanee."

You can't help but notice a sensitivity to the environment here that makes the construction and decoration of the inn all the more impressive. Against a background of rock, pinewood, and natural grandeur, appointments in the Great Room are few and chosen for maximum effect: an antique saddle, ironwork around the fireplace by local craftsmen, local black-and-white photography. The most riveting of the latter is a study in silhouette of local rancher Jack Wilson on his horse, probably at sunset, that hangs on the rock fireplace.

The inn and the Early Winters Cabins both trace their beginnings to Jack Wilson and his 75-acre Wilson Ranch. In the 1940s he was known for the hunting, fishing and backcountry tours he led. He and his wife, Elsie, built the original four cabins that have now been restored and copied with two new ones. Additional windows to let in the views, secluded decks, window seats, fresh decor, and updated kitchens and baths provide the ultimate in mountain comfort.

When I was taken to my room, I walked quickly past the fireplace (already lit and welcoming), the inviting chairs with good reading lights, the minibar, and the elegant bathroom with spa tub, and headed straight for my own

deck, suitably furnished with log chairs and a vista of lake, woods, and mountains. Right on cue, an osprey soared across the scene.

Jack's Hut is the inn's one-stop center for helping guests access all the recreational activities available. These hills and valleys have the second-largest trail system in the United States. Ski passes, lessons and clinics, sleigh rides, skating, and equipment rentals are arranged here. Heli-skiing, offering one- to three-day packages of alpine and nordic programs; rock climbing; and mountaineering guides also operate out of the inn.

Surrounded by North Cascades grandeur and fresh air, you might expect plain, hearty fare in the restaurant, and you would be, oh, so wrong. Sophisticated menus skillfully executed and pleasantly served are the rule. Some of the choices for starters during my visit were grilled shrimp and seared risotto cakes, caramelized onion tart, and potato-and-blue-cheese gnocchi. Main course choices included Pinot Noir–braised lamb shank and Pacific salmon with horseradish crust and gratin of polenta.

It doesn't get much better than this. Even if your sporting activities go no further than lifting your binoculars, Freestone is a unique experience you won't soon forget.

HOW TO GET THERE: On the Cascade Loop, take Highway 20 north through Twisp and 15 miles west of Winthrop. Pass the sign to Mazama, continue 1.5 miles west. Follow signs to Early Winters and then Freestone Inn. When Highway 20 is closed, take either Stevens Pass (U.S. 2) or Snoqualmie Pass (I–90).

Turtleback Farm
Orcas Island, Washington 98245

INNKEEPERS: Bill and Susan Fletcher

ADDRESS/TELEPHONE: Crow Valley Road (mailing address: Route 1, Box 650, Eastsound); (360) 376–4914 or (800) 376–4914

ROOMS: 7; all with private bath and individual heat control; 4 rooms in separate Orchard House with gas fireplace, private deck. Wheelchair access. No smoking inn.

RATES: $80 to $110, winter; $80 to $160, April 1 to November 1; double occupancy; full breakfast and afternoon beverage.

OPEN: All year.

FACILITIES AND ACTIVITIES: Farm animals, pond. Nearby: hiking trails in Moran State Park; bicycle and moped rentals; swim, picnic at Lake Cascade; fishing, kayaking, sailing; good restaurants.

hen an escape from the fast track is high on your list of romantic priorities, a picturesque inn on one of the San Juan Islands is an ideal choice.

Set back from a country road, Turtleback Farm looks like an attractive, well-kept old farmhouse, a big green two-story clapboard building. But it's been featured in numerous articles, and, despite a remote location, it is usually booked months in advance. This may well be the gem lodging of Orcas Island.

The reasons are clear once you settle in. This is a first-rate, impeccably maintained inn. It delivers the quiet country charm that so captivates inngoers but with all the comforts you could ask for.

The inn was once an abandoned farmhouse being used to store hay, now restored from the ground up. There are seven guest rooms, a parlor, a dining room, and a tree-shaded deck that runs the length of the house. This is a wonderful place to sit on a warm day and look out at 80 acres of meadow, a rim of thick forest and the silhouette of mountain peaks beyond. We're talking idyllic, tranquil setting.

The decor is tasteful and nonfussy, with muted colors and mellow wood trim and floors, and open-beam ceilings. Each guest room has a modern bath appointed with antique fixtures, claw-footed tub, pull-chain toilet, and wall shower. The pedestal sinks came from the Empress Hotel in Victoria. A separate building set in the apple orchard looking east to Mt. Wollard is the Orchard House, new in 1997. The four rooms here, two up and two down, are especially spacious and have gas fireplaces, sitting areas, and private decks. A full breakfast is delivered to your door in a basket to enjoy in your room or on your deck. An out-standing breakfast is served in the dining room of the main house, course by course at individual tables on bone china. The menus change, but a typical morning would see juices, local berries, gra-

nola, an omelette with ham, and English muffin. Seconds are always offered. Breakfast is served between 8:00 and 9:00 A.M., but the innkeepers are always ready to accommodate an early ferry schedule.

What do you do on an eighty-acre farm if you're fresh from the city? If you're smart, you settle yourself on the deck with a blade of grass between your teeth, a big hat tipped down over your nose, and think things over—very, very slowly. Then there are the exhausting demands of critter watchin'. There are ducks and blue heron, sheep, chickens, a rambunctious brown ram named Oscar, and visiting Canada geese. If you're a picnic fan, the paths leading to private little spots will be irresistible.

Even if the weather turns dismal, the comforts of this house will keep you charmed. There's a cozy parlor where you can curl up and read before a fire. (The custom here is, "If you find a book you can't put down, take it with you and return it when you finish.") The Fletchers make every effort to acquaint you with all that the island offers. They'll make arrangements for you to charter a boat, fish at the nearby park, rent a moped, play golf, or whatever sounds good to you.

HOW TO GET THERE: From Orcas Island ferry landing, proceed straight ahead on Horseshoe Highway to first left turn; follow to Crow Valley Road. Turn right and continue to the inn, 6 miles from ferry landing. Fly-in: Eastsound Airport.

Indexes

Alphabetical Index to Inns

Inns on or near Lakes or Rivers

Inns at or near the Seashore

Ansonborough Inn (SC), 134

Applewood Inn and Restaurant (CA), 285

Beach House Bed and Breakfast, The
(AL), 98

Bee and Thistle Inn (CT), 7

Blue Lantern Inn (CA), 277

Bradley Inn at Pemaquid Point, The
(ME), 17

Casa Madrona Hotel (CA), 297

Charlotte Inn, The (MA), 20

Edenwild Inn (WA), 311

Father Ryan House Bed & Breakfast Inn,
The (MS), 122

Gilbert Inn (OR), 307

Gilded Thistle (TX), 215

Greyfield Inn (GA), 108

Harbor House (CA), 279

Hotel Carter (CA), 281

J. Harper Poor Cottage (NY), 60

Little Palm Island (FL), 105

Mainstay, The (NJ), 54

Mayfair House Hotel (FL), 104

Saybrook Point Inn (CT), 9

Timberhill Ranch (CA), 299

Turtleback Farm (WA), 315,

Tu Tú Tun Lodge (OR), 303

Ventana Inn (CA), 276

Wequassett Inn (MA) , 19

White Barn Inn (ME), 14

Inns with, or with Access to, a Swimming Pool

American Club, The (WI), 177

Antrim 1844 Country Inn (MD), 52

Applewood Inn and Restaurant (CA), 285

Blackberry Farm (TN), 141

Estate by the Elderberries, The (CA), 293

Father Ryan House Bed & Breakfast Inn,
The (MS), 122

Gaige House Inn (CA), 283

Glendorn, A Lodge in the Country
(PA), 72

Glens Country Estate, The (WV), 88

Grand Hotel (MI), 159

Heron House (OR), 305

Inn at Thorn Hill, The (NH), 29

Inn on Winter's Hill, The (ME), 16

Kimberly Country Estate (MI), 157

Little Palm Island (FL), 105

Lovelander Bed & Breakfast Inn, The
(CO), 241

Madrona Manor (CA), 287

Melhana, The Grand Plantation Resort
(GA), 112

Sardy House (CO), 232

Saybrook Point Inn (CT), 9

Suncatcher, The (AZ), 195

Sunset Heights Inn (TX), 210

Timberhill Ranch (CA), 299

Tu Tú Tun Lodge (OR), 303

Ventana Inn (CA), 276

Village County Inn, The (VT), 39

Whitewing Farm Bed & Breakfast
(PA), 74

Inns with Downhill or Cross-Country
Skiing Nearby

Inns with, or with Access to, Golf or Tennis Facilities

Inns with a Sauna, Whirlpool, or Hot Tub

Inns with a Full-Service Dining Room or Dinners Available by Special Arrangement

American Club, The (WI), 177

Antrim 1844 (MD), 52

Applewood Inn and Restaurant (CA), 285

Bird & Bottle Inn, The (NY)

Blackberry Farm (TN), 141

Casa de Patron (NM), 201

Casa Madrona Hotel (CA), 297

Castle Marne (CO), 233

Clifton: The Country Inn (VA), 76

Delta Queen (LA), 118

Edenwild Inn (WA), 311

Estate by the Elderberries, The (CA), 293

Glendorn, A Lodge in the Country (PA), 72

Glens Country Estate, The (WV), 88

Gold Hill Hotel (NV), 256

Grand Hotel (MI), 159

Greyfield Inn (GA), 108

Greystone Inn (NC), 129

Harbor House (CA), 279

Hillbrook Inn (WV), 90

Hotel Carter (CA), 281

Imperial Hotel (CA), 274

Inn above Onion Creek, The (TX), 225

Inn at Chagrin Falls (OH), 168

Inn at Little Washington, The (VA), 85

Inn at Montchanin Village, The (DE), 46

Inn at the Citadel (AZ) 190

Inn at Vauclause Spring, The (VA), 83

Izaak Walton Inn (MT), 253

Lake Placid Lodge (NY), 64

Lovelander Bed & Breakfast Inn, The (CO), 241

Madrona Manor (CA), 287

Meadow Creek Bed & Breakfast Inn (CO), 244

Melhana, The Grand Plantation Resort (GA), 112

Old Chatham Sheepherding Company Inn (NY), 68

Old Drovers Inn (NY), 58

Red Castle Inn, The (CA), 291

Richmont Inn (TN), 139

River Song Inn (CO), 239

Rockledge Country Inn (CO), 242

Rose Inn (NY), 62

Sardy House (CO), 232

Swag, The (NC), 131

Timberhill Ranch (CA), 299

Tu Tú Tun Lodge (OR), 303

Ventana Inn (CA), 276

Woodlands Resort and Inn (SC), 137

Inns with Bicycles, Canoes, or Other Sports Equipment

Inns Offering Travelers' Club Benefits